D1494010

GLOBAL
SPORTS
POLICY

WITHDRAWN

LIVERPOOL JMU LIBRARY

3   1111   01440   6928

SAGE has been part of the global academic community since 1965, supporting high quality research and learning that transforms society and our understanding of individuals, groups and cultures. SAGE is the independent, innovative, natural home for authors, editors and societies who share our commitment and passion for the social sciences.

Find out more at: **www.sagepublications.com**

GLOBAL
SPORTS
POLICY

CATHERINE PALMER

Los Angeles | London | New Delhi
Singapore | Washington DC

Los Angeles | London | New Delhi
Singapore | Washington DC

SAGE Publications Ltd
1 Oliver's Yard
55 City Road
London EC1Y 1SP

SAGE Publications Inc.
2455 Teller Road
Thousand Oaks, California 91320

SAGE Publications India Pvt Ltd
B 1/I 1 Mohan Cooperative Industrial Area
Mathura Road
New Delhi 110 044

SAGE Publications Asia-Pacific Pte Ltd
3 Church Street
#10-04 Samsung Hub
Singapore 049483

Editor: Chris Rojek
Editorial assistant: Martine Jonsrud
Production editor: Katherine Haw
Copyeditor: Sarah Bury
Proofreader: Mary Dalton
Indexer: Charmian Parkin
Marketing manager: Michael Ainsley
Cover design: Lisa Harper
Typeset by: C&M Digitals (P) Ltd, Chennai, India
Printed by: MPG Books Group, Bodmin, Cornwall

MIX
Paper from
responsible sources
FSC
www.fsc.org   FSC® C018575

© Catherine Palmer 2013

First published 2013

Apart from any fair dealing for the purposes of research or
private study, or criticism or review, as permitted under the
Copyright, Designs and Patents Act, 1988, this publication
may be reproduced, stored or transmitted in any form,
or by any means, only with the prior permission in writing
of the publishers, or in the case of reprographic reproductio
in accordance with the terms of licences issued by the
Copyright Licensing Agency. Enquiries concerning
reproduction outside those terms should be sent to the
publishers.

Library of Congress Control Number: 2012935401

British Library Cataloguing in Publication data

A catalogue record for this book is available from
the British Library

ISBN 978-1-84920-517-7
ISBN 978-1-84920-518-4 (pbk)

CONTENTS

ABBREVIATIONS AND ACRONYMS

ACF: Advocacy Coalition Framework

AFL: Australian Football League

AIGCP: Association International des Groups Cyclistes Professionels

AIS: Australian Institute of Sport

ATHCOS: Athens Olympic Games Organizing Committee

BOCOG: Beijing Organizing Committee of the Olympic Games

BRIC: Brazil, Russia, India and China

CPSU: Child Protection in Sport Unit

CSO: civil society organizations

CSR: corporate social responsibility

DCMS: Department of Culture, Media & Sport

EMAS: Eco-Management and Audit Scheme

ETA: Euzkadi Ta Askatasuna

EU: European Union

FARE: Football Against Racism in Europe

FFC: Fédération Française de Cyclisme

FIFA: Fédération International de Football Association

FLEC: Front for the Liberation of the Enclave of Cabinda

GEO: Grupo Especial de Operaciones

GRAPO: Grupo de Resistencia Antifascista Primo

HECTOR: HEritage Climate TOrino

IAAF: International Association of Athletics Federation

ICC: International Cricket Council (originally the Imperial Cricket Council)

IOC: International Olympic Committee

LOCOG: London Organizing Committee of the Olympic Games

MCG: Melbourne Cricket Ground

NADO: National Anti-Doping Organization

NEC: Norwegian Environmental Organization

NGB: national governing bodies

NGO: non-government organization

NOC: National Olympic Committee

NSB: National Sporting Body

NSO: national sports organization

NSPCC: National Society for the Prevention of Cruelty to Children

OCIEP: Office of Critical Infrastructure and Emergency Preparedness (Canada)

OCOG: Organizing Committee of the Olympic Games

OECD: Organization for Economic Cooperation and Development

PLO: Palestine Liberation Organization

PPG 17: Planning Policy and Guidance – Open Space, Sport and Recreation

SSC: Swedish Sports Confederation

TOROC: Torino Organizing Committee for the 2006 Olympic Winter Games

UCI: Union Cyclistes International

UNESCO: United Nations Education, Scientific and Cultural Organization

UN: United Nations

UNEP: UN Environmental Programme

VANOC: Vancouver Organizing Committee for the 2010 Olympic Winter Games

WADA: World Anti-Doping Agency

WTO: World Trade Organization

ABOUT THE AUTHOR

 Catherine Palmer is Associate Professor in Sociology at Deakin University, having previously held posts at Durham University, Flinders University and the University of Adelaide. Her research principally explores the relationships between sport and social policy, where her focus is on sport-related social interactions, the consequences that might follow from those interactions, and their implications for policy and practice.

Catherine serves on the editorial boards for the *International Review for the Sociology of Sport*, the *Sociology of Sport Journal* and *Qualitative Health Research*, and is a frequent reviewer for a number of international social science and health journals. Catherine has served as a member of the College of Fellows, Economic & Social Research Council (UK), the Executive Committee, Social Policy Association, UK, the Social Exclusion Board, South Australia, and has acted as a reviewer for the Austrian Science Fund, the Israel Science Foundation, the Economic & Social Research Council (UK), the Australian National Health & Medical Research Council (Population Health Grants), the Human Services Research Initiatives (Large Projects) South Australia and the South Australian Department of Health's Strategic Health Research Priority.

ACKNOWLEDGEMENTS

The writing of this book has benefited from two periods of research leave from Durham University, and from an International Visiting Research Fellowship at the University of Sydney. I thank Raewyn Connell for her intellectual generosity during this time. Durham colleagues along the way have provided invaluable moral and oral support and I am grateful to Sarah Banks, Sue Bock, Shane Collins, Simon Hackett, Sam Hillyard, Jim McKay, Martin Roderick and Nicole Westmarland. More recent colleagues at Deakin University experienced my final flurry of activity.

I also have David to thank for his willingness to go the distance – literally at times. I am grateful for so much.

Finally, thanks to Chris Rojek, Jai Seaman and Martine Jonsrud at SAGE for their guidance along the way.

INTRODUCTION

The idea for this book was prompted by what I saw to be a gap in how we think about sports policy. Despite cross-border travel, communication and consumption being key parts of our everyday lives, and despite sport itself being an increasingly global phenomenon, there has been no real attempt to locate the study of sports policy within a broader consideration of global processes, practices and consequences. It is this gap that this book takes as its point of departure.

The central argument developed is that in the last two decades in particular, several key events and societal shifts have occurred which now play important roles in the development, implementation and analysis of sports policy. The events on September 11, 2001, for example, have profoundly shaped the policy and practice aspects of ensuring safety and security at sporting mega-events. The emergence of a 'risk society' has influenced the nature of sports policy as it relates to child protection, public liability, risk management and the welfare of athletes. The movement of particular population groups across the globe has seen policy responses develop in relation to athletic migration at the elite level, while those fleeing persecution and abuses of their human rights have created a need for more inclusive, culturally aware, sports policy and provision for refugees, asylum seekers and other displaced persons. Following the Beijing Olympic Games in 2008, and the emergence of BRIC (Brazil, Russia, India, China) countries on the global mega-events circuit, there has been a growing questioning of the notion of sport in the context of social justice and human rights. Equally, growing environmental concerns have prompted the 'greening' of sport in relation to the hosting of sporting mega-events such as the winter Olympics and the growing popularity of outdoor sports, leisure and recreation worldwide. An examination of this interplay between sport and globalization at the policy level is the focus of the next ten chapters.

The book is also, although less so, concerned with the shifting nature of the relationship between research and policy. Although the potential for sport to contribute to social interventions such as crime reduction, community cohesion and urban regeneration is widely (although not uncritically) acknowledged, the increasing public scrutiny of government investment in sport demands robust evidence to ensure the delivery of a government's policy goals. Despite this, there remains a critical lack of research evidence through which to inform policy and practice. The aspirational claims that the London 2012 Olympic Games will leave a tangible, sustainable legacy for current and future generations provides an obvious example of the need for an improved evidence base in the field of sports policy. In the context of increasing spending cuts, a global economic downturn, and public scrutiny and accountability for the deliverables of sports policy, the issues for evidence-based and evidence-informed policy-making are particularly important.

The role of new technologies in the development and dissemination of sports policy is something I address. New forms of communication enable the rapid dissemination of research findings, and the wide availability of policy documents and data from all continents enables the comparative study of sports policy on an unprecedented scale. Equally, consumers of policy decisions, as they relate to sport or anything else, have adopted new technologies, which enable the global sharing of resistant and subversive critiques of – most notably – the human rights and environmental track records of cities and nations in relation to the hosting of sporting mega-events. The place of public resistance and new technologies in policy critique is also discussed in the ensuing chapters.

STRUCTURE AND ORGANIZATION

Given the kinds of issues the book engages with, I haven't written a book about comparative sports policy. That is, I am not concerned to compare and contrast particular domestic policy issues (e.g. elite sport or sport for all) across different countries. Rather, my focus is on the effects of globalization on the policy land-scape, and the possibilities that a study of sports policy open up for us to engage with broader debates about globalization. My interest, fundamentally, is in tak-ing the debates about the impacts of globalization on social life that are prevalent in the social sciences more broadly and applying these to analyses of public policy as they relate to global sport. That is, I am concerned to foreground the *social* aspects of globalization in the context of sports policy. Adopting a 'production of consumption' approach, the book is informed by debates about the political economy of sport and the socially constitutive and constructed nature of both sport and sports policy.

With this as background, the book is organized into two sections. The chap-ters in the first section – Key Debates in Globalization and Sports Policy – explore the theoretical and conceptual issues that relate to the nature, structure and governance of sports policy in a global context. The chapters variously introduce the key terms and definitions encountered in the rest of the book and offer an overview of the main organizations and institutions responsible for the delivery and governance of sports policy at supranational, national and sub-national levels. The chapters in this section also explore the tensions between 'the local' and 'the global' – a key debate in studies of globalization – and their effects on the ways in which sport, and policy, is understood and interpreted. In addition, this section examines our changing relationship to policy, particularly the ways in which opposition to and critiques of policy have opened up through the emergence of anti-globalization and related social movements and the use of new, mediated mechanisms through which to harness and express dissent.

The last chapter in this first section argues for a greater, more globally inclu-sive, use of social theory to interpret the effects of globalization on the develop-ment and implementation of sports policy. Although the study of sports policy borrows from the political sciences and related policy analysis literature to generate understanding of the policy process, it remains relatively bereft in its use of *social* theory to inform understandings of policy outputs and outcomes. To address this limitation, I introduce some of the theoretical perspectives from the social sciences that can be used to interrogate the impact of globalization on sports policy. I explore as well the challenges of 'doing' theory and policy in a globally inclusive way.

The second section – Globalization and Sporting Mega-events: Policy Implications – examines the policy implications of hosting sporting mega-events; undoubtedly the major global feature of sport and sports policy in the twenty-first century. Drawing on empirical case studies (the Tour de France and the Olympic Games and Paralympics, among others), the chapters in this section variously explore the sporting mega-event as a key site at which global concerns such as abuses of human rights, the impacts of environmental policy, and terrorism, surveillance and security can be played out. These chapters are principally concerned with the ways in which the movement of people across the world has pricked a global conscience that has then been incorporated into some of the key social and policy discourses that surround the staging of global sporting mega-events.

The book refers to sports policy in the plural. This is deliberate. There is no single sport that I focus on and there is no single approach to policy that I favour. That said, I cannot hope in the following pages to cover all sports, all policies or all policy issues that are implicated in the conditions of globalization. Equally, I cannot hope to cover all countries, cities or continents. Most of the chapters offer an extended case study of a particular policy issue – doping, race relations and multiculturalism, children at risk, human rights, safety and security, among others – or focus on a particular sporting event; the Tour de France and the 2012 Olympic Games being cases in point here. These case studies are offered as exemplars by which key debates can be extrapolated to other policy contexts and I direct the reader towards some of the conceptual linkages here. A further qualification is needed. Sport, and sports policy, moves fast, and there will inevitably be events that will 'break' which I cannot describe in any real detail. Where possible, I've acknowledged this and suggested further research to accommodate these emerging policy agendas.

Thus, the material covered is a deliberately diverse and eclectic selection that reflects my previous, current or emerging research interests in relation to globalization, sport and sports policy. Although a book on sports policy, it is informed by my background as a social anthropologist and I hope something of this comes through in what I've written. Because of this, I adopt a critical interpretivist approach to the analysis of sports policy and its location within a broader global social context. Following Sugden and Tomlinson, my approach is characterized by 'a healthy disrespect for disciplinary boundaries, an adventurous cross-cultural curiosity and a commitment to critical social scientific scholarship not beholden to patrons, agencies or sponsors' (2011: xiii). I have long and unashamedly admired the work and writing of Clifford Geertz and Ulf Hannerz, and I hope this influence is apparent in what follows.

PART ONE

KEY DEBATES IN GLOBALIZATION AND SPORTS POLICY

1

GLOBALIZATION, SPORT AND POLICY

THIS CHAPTER

- provides an overview of globalization and sets the context for the rest of the book;
- reviews the influence of globalization on sports policy;
- examines the relationships between sports policy, social policy and public policy.

INTRODUCTION

> Each year in the spring, the countries of Europe meet in a televised song contest, a media event watched by hundreds of millions of people. [In Sweden] a controversy erupted. ... The winning tune was a Calypso tune with the refrain 'Four Buggs and a Coca Cola'. (Hannerz, 1992: 217)

Almost twenty years ago, the Swedish anthropologist Ulf Hannerz sketched the above scenario of a mosaic of languages, music and nationalities coming together in the Eurovision Song Contest. Along with Eurovision, a number of public events have emerged that provide important sites through which to examine the global movement of people, values, goods and experiences or what we might refer to as 'globalization'. Of concern for this book, sport provides an important and enduring backdrop against which to consider the global connections that have been created by world capitalism and then mediated by contemporary and emerging communication technologies; again, what we might also call globalization. As Giulianotti and Robertson note 'sport is an increasingly significant subject for global studies, in its dual role as a long-term motor and metric of transnational change' (2007a: 1).

While sporting events like the Olympic Games and Paralympics, football's World Cup, Formula One Grand Prix or the Tour de France, among others, provide opportunities through which to consider the production and consumption of globally circulating cultural, political, financial and human capital (still another way of describing globalization), the concerns of this book lie elsewhere. My main concern is to locate debates about globalization within a critical analysis of its effects on the development, implementation and analysis of sports policy in various contexts around the globe.

Events such as the Olympic Games or football's World Cup are, of course, fully implicated in any discussion about globalization and sport, however we cannot separate the *consumption* of these kinds of 'sports spectaculars' (Cheska, 1979) from a consideration of their *production*. As I note elsewhere:

> Too often, studies of 'the spectacular' have focused on the razzle dazzle, the pomp and the ceremony, whilst ignoring the processes of human intervention and accomplishment whereby spectacles are *made* to possess these qualities. In other words, it is not sufficient to assume that public spectacles are just part and parcel of the fall out of popular culture. As sports analysts, we need to address the role of human agency in the mounting of the mega-event. (Palmer, 2000: 366, emphasis in original)

Similarly, Carter maintains that

> Even when our critical, analytical gaze turns towards these spectacles, the emphasis is on the media imagery of said spectacles and the consumption of said vistas in particular. The tendency has been to focus on the most visible, the biggest and the best, without probing the hidden, interwoven local and global politics within the production of such events. (2011a: 132)

It is here that policy and policy-making play key roles in what sport (and sports events) looks like in this increasingly global order. A key theme developed is that sports policy is the product of considerable cultural work on the part of a whole range of individuals and organizations, and this has significant implications for the management, administration and governance of sport and sports policy. Policy and policy-making, in other words, are key to what the landscape of contemporary sport looks like in terms of tensions between exogenous and domestic sport as well as the events that are staged, sponsored and mediated on a global scale. Shifting policy agendas and competing tensions around the funding of sport also raise a number of debates about taste, culture, values and political priorities, which further makes an understanding of the 'work' of policy-making an integral part of any discussion about sports policy in the twenty-first century.

At the same time, a number of trends, developments and events have occurred that are significantly 'global' in their impact to have had a major influence on sports policy along with social, political and economic life more broadly. Issues of risk management and public liability, for example, which are now what seem to be unavoidable consequences of the global 'risk society', have had a significant impact on the staging of sporting competitions, particularly those that rely on a volunteer base. Equally, the terrorist events on September 11, 2001, and then again in Madrid in 2004, London in 2005 and Mumbai in 2009, have profoundly shaped the policy and practice aspects of ensuring safety and security at sporting events worldwide, and a whole raft of policies have been developed in an attempt to mitigate the potential threat to human life that the spectre of terrorism now poses for events like the Olympic Games and Paralympics, football's World Cup or the Commonwealth Games. The consequences of these happenings, which are felt worldwide, also need to be considered in any critical discussion of sports policy.

It is this two-way tension between the policy dimensions that underpin the *production* of global sporting events and the *effects* or, to use Houlihan's (1994) terms, the 'reach' and 'response' that globally occurring social forces and events have on the development, implementation and analysis of sports policy more locally with which this book is centrally concerned.

This movement between a consideration of both production and effects requires some careful points of clarification, and the rest of this chapter unfolds in the following way: I provide, first, an overview of globalization and the key definitions and debates that have emerged over the past thirty years or so. I then consider the scope of global policy, and global sports policy. What do we mean when we refer to 'global' policy? Is this the same as international policy? Or transnational policy? What are the similarities and differences? While there is certainly some overlap, there are nonetheless some important distinctions in terminology as well.

To help frame these – and other – questions, I focus in the next sections on the concepts, definitions and debates that set the stage for understanding sports policy in the context of globalization. Given the complexity of the 'globalization debate', I do not adopt any particular theoretical or conceptual framework, but recognize a number of ways through which we might understand globalization as being a diffuse cultural phenomenon; an exogenous set of values and institutions that mediates or acts as a conduit for all kinds of social relationships. Thus, I draw (at times eclectically) upon these different conceptualizations to frame an analysis of both the *production* of global sports policy and the *effects* of globally occurring social forces, trends and events on the development, implementation and analysis of sports policy.

GLOBALIZATION

The concept of globalization is by no means new. The Ancient Greeks had the idea of 'an ecumene' or *oikoumene* (Hannerz, 1992); an inhabited earth that stretched from Atlantic Europe to the Far East. Equally, the notion of an interconnected world has been with Western Europeans since at least the discovery voyages of Columbus and da Gama. It is the sense of urgency and speed, however, with which we now connect with one another that is perhaps the hallmark of this global, interconnected world. As I note elsewhere, 'the defining feature of the twenty-first century is that public culture is transmitted for global consumption at extraordinary speeds indeed. In the time it takes to log on, open a magazine or book a plane ticket, one can experience the constituents of popular culture across truly diverse registers of interpretation' (Palmer, 1998a: 34). Similarly, Janssen et al. write: 'globalization ... is a prolonged process that has increased greatly in speed, scope, and impact in the latter half of the twentieth century' (2008: 72), while Giulianotti and Robertson (2007a) and McGarry (2010) note that globalization represents an acceleration of the intensity of forms of cross-cultural change and interactions due to the introduction and intensification of various agents of change such as communication technologies.

While we have long had a sense that we are part of a bigger, interconnected 'whole', it took until the twentieth century for us to define and debate it. The term 'globalization' first appeared in the 1980s to supplement terms like 'transnationalism' and 'internationalism' and to characterize what was then perceived to be an ever-shrinking social world where time, borders, local identities and cultural distinctiveness had all but collapsed. As Robertson rather apocalyptically put it, 'globalization is the rapidly increasing compression of the entire world into a single, global field' (1992: 174).

Globalization became a shorthand for 'cultural homogeneity', with many commentators arguing that the global circulation and consumption of goods and commodities would see those produced by culturally, politically and economically dominant nation-states (read: the United States) being introduced to local markets at the expense of 'home grown' goods, commodities, labour and services (Hardt & Negri, 2001; Ohmae, 1995; Ritzer, 2000, 2004). Alongside these arguments, debates about local resistance began to counter such fears about the homogenizing effects of globalization, with empirical research exploring concepts such as hybridization and creolization (Dirlik, 1996; García Canclini, 1995; Morley, 1992; Morley & Robins, 1995). As a counter to these arguments about perceived cultural imperialism, the activities of anti-globalization and new social movements offer highly politicized and very public critiques of the dominance of the European and Northern American metropoles on the global arena and the inequalities that are embedded within (Connell, 2007; Held & McGrew, 2007; Leite, 2005).

In an early piece, Houlihan (1994) outlines the variety of conceptualizations of globalization in the context of sport. He concludes that a fundamental dichotomy exists between a view of globalization as an extension of cultural imperialism and a more participative understanding of globalization where local culture is not merely a passive recipient but an active agent in its reception and interpretation. In short, debates about structure and agency coexist in concert, and I will return to them at several points in the book. Maguire, borrowing from Elias, also acknowledges these tensions, conceptualizing sport as existing in the 'interlocking process of "diminishing contrasts" and "increasing varieties"' (1994: 395). For Maguire, 'global flows' are a profound feature of late-twentieth-century sport.

In light of these various ways of thinking about the transnational movement of people, objects and ideas, it is perhaps not surprising that there is little consensus as to how to define and interpret 'globalization'. Guillén notes that 'globalization has become a key concept in the social sciences, even though its meaning is contested and its systematic study has proved difficult' (2001: 235). Similarly, in his introduction to the then new journal *Global Social Policy*, Deacon notes the contested nature of globalization as well as its undeniable intersection with and impact upon policy-making:

> The scope and impact of the globalization process has yet to be subject to sufficient empirical investigation. The extent of globalization and the form it takes is open to normative evaluation and political struggle. Despite these areas of disagreement about the meaning, impact and desirability of globalization few would argue with the proposition that globalization, either as an economic reality or as a political project, is impacting on the making of social policy and the process of social development at national, regional and global level. (2001: 5)

As such, in the following chapter, I explore some of the debates – still largely unresolved – that have argued for a redefinition of the basic concepts that can help comprehend the complexities of the cultural, political and social effects of globalization, particularly as they relate to 'the local' and 'the global' in sports policy.

Although no one single grand theory of globalization exists, considerable thinking has emerged over the past three decades within disciplines such as anthropology, sociology, politics, economics and international relations.[1] In crude terms, approaches to globalization tend to stem from either a world system theory, in which globalization is fundamentally seen as the product of the spread of capitalism; that is, globalization is seen in terms of *economic* determinants and consequences, or from a way of thinking that conceptualizes globalization as being fundamentally the spread of cultural relationships and exchanges; that is, as a key determinant of *social* experiences. Clearly, both approaches frame the tension between the production and consumption of global sporting events and sports policy, in different, but equally applicable, ways and I engage with each in the ensuing chapters.

World System Theory and Globalization

First conceived by the American sociologist Immanuel Wallerstein (1974) to explain development and world inequalities (Robinson, 2011: 724), World System Theory seeks to explain the dynamics of the capitalist world economy in terms of what he called a total social system. Inspired by the work of C. Wright Mills, Wallerstein had an abiding interest in understanding 'macro-structures'; what he conceived as 'world systems'. For Wallerstein, a world system is:

> A social system, one that has boundaries, structures, member groups, rules of legitimation, and coherence. Its life is made up of the conflicting forces which hold it together by tension and tear it apart as each group seeks eternally to remould it to its advantage. It has the characteristics of an organism, in that it has a lifespan over which its characteristics change in some respects and remain stable in others. ... Life within it is largely self-contained, and the dynamics of its development are largely internal. (1974: 347)

Taking this notion of a self-sufficient organic entity that is held together by competing tensions, Wallerstein went on to further conceptualize a world system as being, in essence, a 'world economy' that is fully integrated by virtue of two or more regions being dependent on one another for food, fuel or protection, as well as by competition between two or more countries for domination without any one single political or economic centre emerging as superior (Wallerstein, 2000; see also Goldfrank, 2000). For Wallerstein, the world was essentially divided into four sectors: the core (North West Europe, North America, Japan), the semi-periphery (Southern Europe and the Mediterranean region), the periphery (Eastern Europe, North Africa, parts of Asia) and the external area (most of Africa, parts of Asia, the Indian sub-continent). A country's position within this world system was determined by a combination of colonial history and economic power. More recent thinking, however, has expanded this notion of interdependence and competition into one that links many countries and regions in particular forms of supra and sub-national economic, social and political relations.

Such a focus on globalization as an economic activity has clear resonance when thinking about sport and sports policy, and World System Theory has been used to understand athletic labour migration in sport (Magee & Sugden, 2002), the global sporting goods industry (Sage, 1994, 1999) and the playing success of countries relative to their position in the world system (Darby, 2000a). More broadly, the global economics of sport are big business. The revenue generated by events like the Olympic Games, football's World Cup or the Indian Premier League, in terms of ticket prices, tourism spin-offs and media rights, among other things, means that the global circulation of capital and commodities can scarcely be avoided in any discussion of contemporary sport. The Beijing Olympics had a projected revenue of US$3 billion (*Forbes*, 31 January 2007). The men's 2010 football World Cup in South Africa raised a total of US$3.3 billion (£2.1 billion) through television coverage and sponsorship of the event. The Fédération International de Football Association (FIFA) contributed US$1.1 billion (£800 million), alongside the US$5 billion (£3.5 billion) investment from the South African government that went towards providing the necessary infrastructure – stadia, roads, transport links etc. – for the event (Bond, 2010). At current estimate in 2011, the London 2012 Olympic Games is expected to cost £11.3 billion (City of London, 2011), but the purported bene-fits of hosting this and other mega-events far outweigh their costs. Despite a global economic recession and its crippling effects, sponsors continue to come on board for reasons rather optimistically summarized by Joel Seymour-Hide, director of the sports marketing consultancy group Octagon: 'sport tends to be relatively recession proof. … It's an irrational love which creates more loyalty and resilience' (quoted in Black, 2009: 40).

This, of course, has implication for the development of particular forms of policy that relate to the economic regulation of sporting activity, media acquisi-tion of sporting content and the global transfer of players and athletes. Each of these issues is developed further in subsequent chapters.

Cultural Approaches to Globalization

While world system approaches to globalization cast transnational movement very much in terms of the circulation of goods, capital, labour and commodities (that is, the stuff of a world economy), such approaches have been criticized for failing to acknowledge the cultural or social dimensions of cross-border travel, communication and consumption (Bauman, 1998; Cohen & Kennedy, 2007; Eriksen, 2003, 2007; Featherstone, 1990, 1995; Featherstone & Venn, 2006; Held & Kay, 2007; Held & McGrew, 2007; Robertson, 1992; Robertson & Scholte, 2007; Tomlinson, 1999). As Hannerz writes, 'the world has become one network of social relationships, and between its regions there is a flowing of *meaning* as well as goods' (1990: 237, emphasis in original).

Rather than focusing on the economic nature and effects of the movement of capital and commodities, the approach espoused by Hannerz and others concep-tualizes such movement as being first and foremost a cultural activity whereby people, values, attitudes and beliefs move between and across borders. As Tomlinson notes: 'globalization lies at the heart of modern culture; cultural practices lie at the heart of globalization' (1999: 1). Such an approach argues that events that occur between and beyond national borders shape the collective life of those nations, as well as the individual lives and outlooks of their citizens (Tomlinson, 1999). Thus, globalization cannot be conceived in purely economic terms; understandings of globalization must also consider the impacts of cross-border movement on the *social* lives and interactions between and within nations, states and regions.

Such sentiments resonate with the work of the sociologist Roland Robertson, who has argued for the development of a 'global consciousness'. For Robertson, globalization represents 'the compression of the world and the intensification of consciousness of the world as a whole' (1992: 8). This notion of a global con-sciousness understands globalization as an inherently social, reflexive process, in which there is an intensified awareness of the world at large. Robertson argues that, as individuals living in a world in which we are connected to others at an accelerated pace, we are in a unique, historical position from which to gauge the impact of global change upon our individual and collective lives. That is, as Robertson suggests, we must identify our own social position in relation to wider global processes (1992, 1995; Giulianotti & Robertson 2007b). Such sentiments echo those of C. Wright Mills and his formulation of a 'sociological imagination' that can 'grasp history and biography and the relations between the two in society' ([1959] 2000: 20). Indeed, Robertson's formulation of the global consciousness seeks to develop a global sociological imagination that understands the historical and social contexts in which practices and experiences are located, and the impact of global events, processes and consequences on these.

It is perhaps not surprising that such cultural approaches to globalization find their ontological and epistemological origins in disciplines such as social anthropology. Over the past three decades, the Swedish anthropologist Ulf Hannerz has been particularly influential in terms of pursuing an intellectual programme that examines the cultural dimensions of globalization, a programme developed more recently by his compatriot, Thomas Hyland Eriksen (2003, 2007), who has equally been influential in 'shifting world anthropology's focus to the global dimensions of local processes' (Giulianotti & Robertson, 2007a: 2) that is elaborated further in the following chapter.

Describing his approach to globalization as a study of 'the world system of culture where the varied currents of cultural flow come together and mingle' (Hannerz, 1992: 22), Hannerz has developed a research agenda that focuses on the use of ethnographic inquiry in the comparative study of global modernities and local modernities (Eriksen, 1997; Hannerz, 2003). Central to Hannerz's (1989) interpretation of globalization is his concept of the 'global ecumeme' or 'a network of networks'. As he writes: 'now more than ever, there is a global ecumene. The entities we routinely call cultures are becoming more like subcultures within this wider entity, with all that this suggests in terms of fuzzy boundaries and more or less arbitrary delimitation of analytic units' (Hannerz, 1992: 217).

In much the same way, the terrain of sports policy can be thought of as a network of networks; as an interconnected, inhabited world. The governance of many aspects of sports policy is made up of a range of interconnected organizations and agencies – the case of the worldwide fight against doping in sport is a prime example of this. While this is a theme I develop in Chapter 3, the point here is that in attempting to develop coordinated responses to anti-doping across countries, regions and jurisdictions, policy has become uniform and fragmented in equal parts. It is unilaterally governed by the World Anti-Doping Agency yet regulated by local and national agencies, reflecting an extension on the debate about the dichotomous relationship between the global and the local elaborated in the next chapter.

Although I have posited a fairly crude distinction between globalization as being the product of the spread of capitalism or the product of the spread of cultural relationships and exchanges, this is done for reasons of analytical simplicity.

In practice, this separation is far too blunt. Globalization is, in fact, a far more complex process whereby the organization of the global economy has far-reaching social consequences, and the market cannot be separated from the cultural. Saskia Sassen makes this point in *Global Networks, Linked Cities*, where she takes the control needs of global business as her point of departure, examines the growth of new service markets and elite workforces, and then studies the consequences of these for urban inequalities in major metropoles; what she refers to as 'global cities' (2002).

Tropes of 'scapes' are thus used to conceptualize globalization as being a number of interconnections that bring together its material, cultural and political dimensions in ways that recognize the importance of human agency in imagining a global order that flows across boundaries and borders.

SPORTING SCAPES

This notion of 'scapes' finds resonance in the ideas of the anthropologist Arjun Appadurai (1991, 1996). In his seminal work, *Modernity at Large: Cultural Dimensions of Globalization*, Appadurai proposes that the global cultural economy is constituted of five scapes. Extending Benedict Anderson's (1986) notion of the 'imagined community', Appadurai (1996: 32) argues that these scapes are the building blocks of an imagined world.

For Appadurai, these scapes consist of:

1 Ethnoscapes: 'landscape of persons who constitute the shifting world in which people live'. This shifting landscape of people includes tourists, immigrants, guest workers and other moving groups.
2 Mediascapes: the 'distribution of the capabilities to produce and disseminate information and the large complex repertoire of images and narratives generated by these capabilities'. Mediascapes, in other words, are both the images of the mass media and the processes of the production and dissemination of these images.
3 Technoscapes: 'the global configuration of technologies moving at high speeds across previously impermeable borders'. That is, technoscapes capture the global flow of technology across borders and boundaries.
4 Financescapes: 'the global grid of currency speculation and capital transfer' or the transfer patterns of global capital.
5 Ideoscapes: 'ideologies of states and counter-ideologies of movements, around which nation-states have organized their political cultures'. Ideoscapes refer to the images, discourse and beliefs that are invested with political and ideological meaning.

Although I have treated these scapes relatively discretely, they are in fact a system of interconnected 'flows', after the fashion of Hannerz (1996). Importantly, as Robertson (1992) notes, such flows are not unidirectional, but are dynamic, interlocking and multidirectional. For Appadurai, the relationship between these scapes is 'deeply disjunctive and profoundly unpredictable because each of these landscapes is subject to its own constraints and incentives, [...] at the same time as each acts as a constraint and a parameter for movement in the others' (1996: 35).

Importantly for this book, Appadurai's conceptualization of 'scapes' offers a useful way of framing global sports policy. **Ethnoscapes** can take the form of athletic migration across international borders (Bale & Maguire, 1994) or the geographic relocation of professional sports workers, such as professional foot- ballers (Giulianotti & Robertson, 2006, 2007b) and the effects of this on their partners and families (Roderick, 2006). They can also take the form of new policy responses for culturally appropriate and inclusive sporting provision for refugees, asylum seekers and those crossing borders to flee abuses of human rights (Amara, 2008; Benn et al., 2010; Kay, 2008; Palmer, 2008, 2009).

Technoscapes are most obviously reflected in the speed with which informa- tion and images, particularly those from globally broadcast sporting mega- events, can be transmitted to audiences worldwide. They can also take the form of new and emergent technologies through which resistant or counter-hegemonic critiques of the politics of sporting mega-events, and their governance, can be communicated. The 2008 Beijing Olympic Games, in which China's alleged poor record on human rights was globally condemned by Amnesty International, or the activist work of the Olympics Resistance Network, which critiqued the 2010 Winter Olympic Games in Vancouver on environmental concerns, its cost and its representation of First Nation Canadians, both provide examples of this.

Financescapes are most easily thought of in terms of the global economy of sport. As argued by Horne and Manzenreiter, 'sport has become inextricably linked to agents, structures and processes of global capitalism' (2002: 5). The sheer capacity of sport to generate revenue of stratospheric proportions outlined in earlier comments on the World Cup and the Olympic Games involves the global circulation of financial resources from investors and sponsors from around the world (Miller et al., 2001).

Sport has long been conceptualized as a **mediascape**; a site for the production and consumption of a number of well-chosen images and narratives of local, regional and national identity (Rowe, 2004; Tomlinson & Young, 2006). Jackson, for example, describes the concept of a 'mediascape' as 'the process by which corporations (both local and global) use "the nation", national symbols, images and memories as part of their corporate advertising and marketing strat- egy' (2004: 20). In my own work on the Tour de France (Palmer, 2002a, 2010), I show how particular images of France and 'Frenchness' are selected and then progressively elaborated to a global media audience by the key cultural interme- diaries who are responsible for the image management of the race.

Finally, there is no shortage of literature on how **ideoscapes** are borne out in sport (see Bairner, 2001). As Bale and Maguire point out, 'at the level of ide- oscapes, global sports festivals such as football's World Cup, the Olympics and the Asian Games have come to serve as vehicles for the expression of ideologies that are trans-national in character' (1994: 5). There is far less literature, however, about how counter or resistant ideologies are produced. Jackson, Batty and Scherer (2001), in their analysis of the global sporting goods company Adidas and its 1999 sponsorship deal with the All Blacks (the men's national rugby union team of New Zealand), illustrate how Adidas faced resistance for its (mis) representation of Māori culture by using the All Blacks' infamous pre-game challenge, the *haka*, in their advertising (see also Jackson & Hokowhitu, 2002). As I have documented elsewhere (Palmer, 2001, 2010; Polo, 2003), the Tour de France provides an important, annual opportunity for the expression of both dominant and resistant ideologies that draw on particular political images and symbols that provide a way of organizing the political culture(s) in France.

GLOBAL SPORTS POLICY

I mentioned earlier that the notion of globalization or, at least, an interconnected, inhabited world, is by no means new; people and goods have travelled and communicated across borders (with varying degrees of speed and distance) for thousands of years. What *is* new, however, is the notion of global studies of policy or the development of a global policy that transcends borders and boundaries. This relatively under-explored area is, in part, the motivation for writing this book. Moreover, sport, unlike other areas of policy, such as social welfare, health or the environment, remains, as Houlihan puts it, 'on the margins' despite the 'capacity of policy analysis to provide fertile territory for conceptual innovation, model building, and analytical and normative theorizing' (2005: 163).

Just as sports policy sits within a broader field of social or public policy, global *sports* policy, I argue, has developed out of a broader field of global social policy. Sports policy, like public policy and social policy, is made in the public realm in terms of certain public issues, and in terms of particular social concerns, so some discussion of the key questions and debates that emerge is warranted.

The emergence of global social policy, as an identifiable field of research, commonly dates back to the work of Deacon, who defines global social policy as 'a practice of supranational actors [which] embodies global social redistribution, global social regulation, and global social provision and/or empowerment, and ... the ways in which supranational organizations shape national social policy' (1997: 195). Borrowing from Deacon (1997), it is this coming together of actors, regulation, provision and empowerment in a context of supranational and national interrelationships that I adopt as my (loose) definition of 'global sports policy'.

Certainly, the notion of a global social policy has invited considerable debate. Critics have argued that the development of global policy – policies adopted across different countries – has resulted in a regulatory, normative order or a form of social control in which countries are expected to adhere to unilaterally imposed international treaties and conventions (Deacon, 2007). While there are some positives to this (a commitment to policy initiatives to ameliorate poverty or to reduce carbon emissions, for example), there are nonetheless some important questions that an examination of global policy can both pose and address (Yeates & Holden, 2009).

The particular constellations of power and privilege, and the configurations of wealth and resources that are inevitable outcomes of the global movement of people, commodities and capital raise questions such as: how are social rights, social redistribution and social regulation being shaped at the global and regional levels through various types of international policies and institutions? What is the impact of global and regional social policy orders on national social policy? Are global, regional and national policy regimes working synergistically in the same direction, or are they being designed and implemented in a fragmented and incoherent manner (Yeates & Holden, 2009)?

While framed, very much, within a discourse of social policy, such questions are still useful for thinking about global *sports* policy. We see the issue – and the difficulties – of a unilaterally enforced policy, most obviously, in the World Anti-Doping Agency's policy on performance-enhancing drugs in sport. We see questions of social rights and social redistribution raised in the advocacy and activism work of campaign groups rallying against human rights abuses, environmental degradation and the social dislocation of vulnerable population groups in relation to sporting mega-events, and we see questions of the movement of policy between local, regional, national and global as a constant tension in relation to all kinds of policy initiatives, particularly in priorities for funding different sports, sporting organizations and domestic policy agendas.

Given that global sports policy fits within the broader class of global social or global public policy, it can ask and answer the same kinds of questions that are asked and answered by these more traditional forms of policy. Issues of rights and responsibility, issues of equity and access, and issues of inequities between developed and developing nations all manifest themselves in different ways (and through different policies, and policy responses) across sport policy, social policy and public policy. These central debates are developed further in subsequent chapters.

Sports Policy, Social Policy, Public Policy

Broadly speaking, social policy can be conceptualized as policy that is concerned with securing the welfare and well-being of citizens. That is, it has a fundamental concern with social justice at its core. There are two broad approaches to these notions of welfare and well-being. The first is that the focus of social policy is primarily on the activities of governments, which modify the free play of market forces to shape social redistribution, social regulation and social rights at national, regional and global levels (Deacon, 2007). The second is that social policy should be conceptualized as those public, market and informal mechanisms that enable individuals and communities to face social risks, such as the risk of loss of livelihood either by prevention or mitigation or through coping strategies (Yeates & Holden, 2009). Conceived as *global* social policy, these competing conceptualizations are 'promulgated by international actors, mani-festing themselves in different, and at times similar ways, depending on the country and context in which they occur' (Yeates & Holden, 2009: 31).

In terms of sports policy, it is the first understanding of social policy that I adopt as the focus of the book. Aspects of sports policy have an explicit inten-tion of securing the welfare and well-being of citizens. That is, sports policy can have a fundamental concern with social justice, social redistribution, social regulation and social rights. This position distinguishes my approach to sports policy from that of others. A more common way of thinking about sports policy is to conceptualize it as being the work of sports *development* in which the pro-motion of sport is part of a broader government agenda whereby sport is used to achieve a range of non-sport-related objectives such as crime reduction, desistance from substance misuse, curbing anti-social behaviour, and the like (Bergsgard et al., 2007; Coalter, 2007). As Bergsgard et al. note, the particular character of sport allows it to be 'a distinctive public service and, in many coun-tries, an important aspect of overall welfare provision, but is also an important element of the economy in terms of job creation, capital investment and balance of payments' (2007: 3–4). Rather than seeing sport as a tool for the advance-ment of social policy and social development, as has been argued elsewhere (Bailey, 2005; Sherry, 2010; Spaaji, 2009; Walseth & Fasting, 2004), I argue that sports policy *is*, in fact, a form of social policy (see Box 1.1 below).

BOX 1.1   SPORTS POLICY AS SOCIAL POLICY: SUMMARY OF KEY CHARACTERISTICS

Social policy, sports policy and global sports policy are concerned with:

- social rights, social redistribution and social regulation
- impacts of global and regional social policy orders on national social policy
- the uneven relationship between developed and developing nations (i.e. the Global North and the Global South)
- dynamics of power and exploitation that characterize inter- and intra-country relationships in the twenty-first century
- securing the welfare and well-being of citizens

My contention that sports policy is a key constituent in the broader field of social or public policy alerts us to a lacuna in the literature on public policy for sport. While there is considerable recognition by governments worldwide that sport is an increasingly important area of policy, this has not been matched by academic interest in the *analysis* of sports policy (Houlihan, 2005; Houlihan, Bloyce & Smith, 2009), or indeed in the level of government investment that is directed towards other areas of public policy, such as defence, education or health. There is something of a blind spot here: as Houlihan notes, 'a survey of English language journals from January 2001 to September 2003 found that only 3% of the articles utilized the extensive array of concepts, analytical frameworks and theories developed in mainstream policy analysis to aid understanding of sport policy-making and the role of government' (2005: 164).

While Houlihan takes issue with the under-representation of sport in mainstream analyses of public policy, my concern is slightly different. While sport receives its fair share of attention from sociological and related social science theories to generate an understanding of t he phenomenon under investigation, sports *policy* does not. Unlike studies of social policy more broadly, which draw on established concepts and theories across the social and political sciences, the application of social theory to sports policy as social policy is far more limited. As I argue in Chapter 5, studies of sports policy remain relatively bereft in their use of social theory to generate understanding of policy outputs and outcomes, and there is a need for wider engagement with social science concepts to generate a theoretically informed framework for understanding the processes of sports policy-making, and its constructed and contested nature.

CONCLUSION

The concern of this chapter has been to sketch out some of the key concepts and debates in globalization, particularly how they inform the analytical framework of this book, namely the two-way movement between thinking about the production of global sports policy and the effects of globally occurring social forces on the development, implementation and analysis of sports policy. This provides the overarching dynamic within which to consider the material developed in the rest of the book. That said, this framework is best thought of as just that – a framework. A more nuanced elaboration of the key concepts and debates introduced here is needed to consider sport and sports policy in a global context. With that in mind, the following chapter addresses perhaps the axial theme of studies of globalization – the tensions produced by the relationship between 'the local' and 'the global'.

BOX 1.2   QUESTIONS FOR DISCUSSION

- What are the key ways in which globalization can be conceptualized?

- What are the five 'scapes' that underpin Appadurai's programme of work?

- What are the implications of global sports policy for the study of social/public policy?

SUGGESTED FURTHER READINGS

Appadurai, A. (1996) *Modernity at large: Cultural dimensions of globalization.* Minneapolis, MN: University of Minnesota Press.

Eriksen, T.H. (2007) *Globalization.* Oxford: Berg.

Giulianotti, R. & Robertson, R. (2007) *Globalization and sport.* Oxford: Blackwell.

Miller, T., Lawrence, G., McKay, J. & Rowe, D. (2001) *Globalization and sport: Playing the world.* London: Sage.

Scherer, J. & Jackson, S. (2010) *Globalization, sport and corporate nationalism: The new cultural economy of the New Zealand All Blacks.* Oxford: Peter Lang.

Note

1 *Sociological Abstracts*, for example, currently lists more than 7,000 texts with 'globalization' as a descriptor (Connell, 2007: 52).

2

THE LOCAL AND THE GLOBAL IN SPORTS POLICY

THIS CHAPTER

- introduces key debates and concepts concerning 'the local' and 'the global';
- provides a framework of flows and frames for understanding global sports policy;
- describes the limits and inequalities of globalization;
- offers multicultural policy in relation to London 2012 and Australian Rules football as a case study.

INTRODUCTION

Tensions between the 'local' and the 'global' have long been features of debates about globalization and sport. As Miller et al. note, 'sport is both intensely local – we support "our team", and we go to the local gym, and very distanced; we watch that local side on a TV network owned by a foreign company' (2001: 1). The nexus where the global meets the local remains the subject of persistent scholarly interest and, in various forms, it continues to influence both research and debate (Donnelly, 1996; Featherstone, 1995; Hannerz, 1996; Robertson, 1992, 1995; Rowe, 2003; Sassen, 2002; Schuerkens, 2003a, 2003b; Swynedouw, 2004; Therborn, 2000).

The relationship between the local and the global is far from fixed or static and as academic interest in the effects of globalization on social, political and economic landscapes has grown, so too has the sophistication with which we understand local–global relations. From an early, fairly blunt, distinction between a submissive 'local' and an imposing, homogenizing 'global', the social relations embedded within the local and the global have been conceptualized as increasingly fluid, embracing heterogeneity and hybridity in concepts like creolization, the grobal and the glocal.

For sports policy, such concepts are both inviting and problematic. On the one hand, they open up interpretative possibilities for analyses of fine-grained studies of public policy in sport, in particular the production values that underpin the making of policy decisions that resonate in different contexts (and sports) around the globe. On the other, such concepts draw attention to the imbalances of social, political and economic power implicit in policy-making (and, indeed, sport) and they highlight questions of scope, scale, structure and agency that all processes of policy-making must contend with.

With this as background, this chapter explores three debates that have emerged from academic interest in local–global relations: (i) the reification of the local; (ii) conceptualizations of the local; and (iii) hybridities of relations *within* the local, or the global *within* the local. Each of these debates respond to the 'the problematic of polarity' (Robertson, 1995: 29) between the global and the local and attempt to transcend these oppositional categories. Throughout the chapter, I am concerned to elaborate the impacts that the relationships between the global and the local – and the bits in between – have had on the development and delivery of sports policy. To illustrate this, I draw on the Australian Football League's Anti-Racial and Religious Vilification policy, which is located within a context of supranational colonialism, as well as multicultural policy as it relates to 'the Games of Diversity', as the London 2012 Olympics have been dubbed.

GLOBALIZATION AS HOMOGENIZATION

Throughout the 1980s and 1990s, the dominant paradigm in studies of globalization was one of 'cultural imperialism'. As people, goods and commodities began to circulate at an accelerated pace, critics argued that globalization represented a form of dominance of the global over the local, of universalism over particularity – we all face the same risks, we all follow the same best practice, we all use the same technology, and so on.[1] As Guillén (2001) notes, this emphasis reflects 'homogeneity's' origins in business and management literature, where the project of linking national markets was driven by an attempt to create standardized business environments. This discourse of imperialism was captured in terms like 'Disneyfication', 'Coca-colonization' and 'Westoxification' (Tomlinson, 1991: 140), where it conveyed the notion that cultural power is not evenly distributed, but is held by 'the West', the United States in particular. Conceived as such, globalization was, as Hannerz observed, the 'take over by giant cultural commodity merchants, who make sure that Coca-Cola can be sipped, Dallas watched, and Barbie dolls played with everywhere in the ex-Second World and Third World as well as in the First World where they originated' (1996: 24). While the exercise and distribution of cultural power is a point to which I will return, it is important to note here that in these early formulations, the processes and the consequences of globalization were seen as 'a worldwide standardisation of lifestyles' (Latouche, in Tomlinson, 1999: 89) that was to be lamented.

Although referring primarily to leisure, consumption and lifestyle, these early notions of globalization as homogenization resonate with global sports policy. I mentioned in the previous chapter that critics of global social policy have argued that the growth of global policy (that is, policies adopted across different countries) has resulted in a regulatory, normative order in which countries are expected to adhere to unilaterally imposed international treaties and conventions (Deacon, 2007). This top-down approach to enforcing legislative behaviour is not that dissimilar to the purported homogenizing effects of globalization on social life. Much of the institutional organization of sports policy bears these same characteristics.

The homogenizing effects of globalization on policy-making are evidenced in the emergence of supranational sporting organizations, the standardization of rules and regulations relating to international competition and the expectation that national and sub-national governing bodies will operate within a single regulatory framework. This is especially true of anti-doping policy where the International Olympic Committee (IOC) has 'tried to impose the same definition of prohibited substances and the same penalties on all sports' (Foster, 2005: 68). While the global governance of sport and the international harmonization of anti-doping policy are dealt with in the following chapter, the analytical point here is that the institutional regulation and standardization of sport, and sporting organizations, is by no means new.

The universalization of sporting governance took hold during the late nineteenth and early twentieth centuries, and this worldwide organizational infrastructure has facilitated the management of sport in ways that are relatively standardized. The establishment of the International Olympic Committee in 1896, for example, the Fédération International de Football Association (FIFA) in 1904, the International Cricket Council (ICC, originally the Imperial Cricket Council) in 1909, or the International Association of Athletics Federation (IAAF) in 1912, among others, created an institutional architecture to which national sporting bodies were compelled to adhere if they wanted to be included in international sporting competition (Andrews & Ritzer, 2007: 32).

This organizational infrastructure, while standardizing policy with regard to rules and regulations, membership requirements or technical compliance (for sports like cycling or triathlon) has also been instrumental in standardizing the normative values of sport. Competition, performance and achievement are now universally valued in global sport, unsurprisingly, as Andrews and Ritzer point out, for they 'simultaneously underpin the liberal democratic, urban industrialist and market capitalist societies from whence modern sport emerged' (2007: 32). Equally, allusions to fair play, ethics, teamwork and commitment are part of this universal discourse. The World Anti-Doping Agency (WADA) makes the following plea to shared values in their justification for stringent regulations against performance-enhancing substances:

> The spirit of sport is the celebration of the human spirit, body and mind. ... [It is characterized by] ethics, fair play and honesty; health; excellence in performance; character and education; fun and joy; team-work; dedication and commitment; respect for rules and laws; respect for self and other participants; community and solidarity. (Beamish & Ritchie, 2006: 111)

This global codification of the normative values in global sport returns us to one of the central themes of this book: the constructed nature of policy-making. The promotion of a commonly shared set of normative values that are then carried through a universal structure of policy and practice highlights the role of human agency, and the beliefs, values and assumptions that are brought to bear on the policy-making process.

From Homogeneity to Hybridity

The argument that globalization equates with homogenization was soon regarded as being overly simplistic. In particular, critics claimed that the dichot-omy produced reductionist binaries – evidenced in Barber's (1995) oppositional category of McWorld vs Jihad, for example – that were unsatisfactory for inter-preting social relationships in the global order. As Grossberg notes:

> Thinking about globalization is too often structured by an assumed opposition between the local and the global, where the local is offered as the intellectual and political corrective of the global. This is captured in the popular demand to 'think globally and act locally'. (1997: 8)

Since this early dichotomy, globalization research has become more fully engaged in an intellectual shift that has recast the local and the global as being far more interlocking than these early ideas of discord and polarity suggests.

The next wave of theorizing the local and the global adopted the themes of cultural mixing, mosaic and hybridity (Nederveen Pietese, 2004; Tomlinson, 1999), linked 'homogenization and heterogenization, universalism and particu-larism, sameness and difference' (Andrews & Ritzer, 2007: 29), and led to expressions like 'creolization', 'hybridization', 'the grobal', 'the glocal' and 'glo-calization' entering cultural parlance. Each of these terms attempted to dissolve the binaries between the local and the global. Glocalization, for example, was translated from Japanese business jargon *dochakuka*, meaning 'global localiza-tion' or 'localized globalization' (Robertson, 1995) to refer to the distinctive local marketing strategies of transnational advertisers, or 'the complexity of local–global or universal–particular relations in the context of intensified global compression and transnational change' (Giulianotti & Robertson, 2007b: 60).

These word hybrids attempted to tease out the idea that cultural practices, such as policy-making, operate in a constant tension between the global and the local, yet this tension is made manifest in various ways, depending on the emphasis placed on the perceived dominance of the global over the local, the declining or ascending importance of the local, and the capacity of social actors and institutions to resist or redefine the relationship between the local and the global. In other words, there has been a shift in emphasis from analyses that examine the effects of globalization *on* the local to analyses of relationships *between* and *within* the local and the global in which writers are more attentive to the complexities of the *intra*-relationship(s) between the two. As Ong observes, 'the problem [for me] is not one of finding the global in the local, but apprehending the global through its articulation with the particular, and how this interplay creates new conditions of ethical living and problem solving' (2009: 90).

These attempts to recast the oppositional categories of the local and the global, however, brought with them a new set of conceptual problems. Critics such as Connell argue that word amalgams like 'glocalization' simply restate the opposition between the local and the global in a different way; they do not transcend it.[2] 'To speak of "glocalization" is to resolve nothing. It is to assert both terms of a static polarity at once' (Connell, 2007: 57). Similarly, Rowe asserts that 'the analytical utility of the concept of globalization is compromised when it is used, mechanically and teleologically, to describe all manner of developments from growing homogenization to fragmentation' (2003: 282). Elsewhere, Sassen notes that the 'national is one of the terrains for the global and ... [requires an analysis] of the endogenizing or localizing of global dynamics inside the national' (2010: 1).

Three main positions have emerged from these unresolved conceptual debates *vis-à-vis* local–global relations, and which have direct relevance to global sports policy. These are: (i) the reification of the local; (ii) conceptualizations of the local and 'localization'; and (iii) hybridities of relations within the local, that is, the global within the local.

THE REIFICATION OF THE LOCAL

One of the themes to emerge from earlier studies of local–global relations was a celebration of 'the local' as a 'site of agency and resistance' (Grossberg, 1997: 8). Throughout the 1990s, studies of globalization focused on the ways in which local and, more particularly, non-Western, cultures were able to challenge, resist and negotiate the forces of the global.[3] Certainly, we witnessed a surge of academic interest in anti-globalization resistance movements for precisely this reason (Appelbaum & Robinson, 2005; Eckstein, 2002; Mann, 2001). In such formulations, however, 'the local' was often conceptualized in wholly romantic terms, as a space in which acts of subversion and opposition could be played out. As Andrews and Ritzer note, 'scholars have privileged localized identities as forms of resistance and heroism in the face of globalization' (2007: 42). In such conceptualizations, the global is, to paraphrase Hannerz, shallow, the local deep (1996: 28).

There are, of course, texts that resist such romanticizing of the local. Chan Kwok-bun, Walls and Hayward (2007), for example, show how 'East–West' identities are constructed and contested within several Asian countries as part of the fabric of everyday life. Drawing on case studies ranging from representations of David Beckham in Japan during the 2002 World Cup leading, they claim, to a 'sweeping cult of Beckham hairstyles', through to the ways in which Cantonese-English code-switching takes place among young people in Hong Kong, they evidence the complexity of globalization as a particular cultural project in which social agents deliberately and selectively use elements made available through globalization in their own local practices. Here, the local and the global meet and mingle with neither assuming ascendency over the other.

However, such treatments in sports policy are rare, where reifications of the local are especially evident and are often the dominant discourse where they operate as essentially a reification of *culture* as well. To illustrate this, I turn now to the case study of the Anti-Racial and Religious Vilification Law implemented by the Australian Football League (AFL).

The Anti-Racial and Religious Vilification Law

In 1995, the AFL introduced a new rule that specifically prohibited actions or speech that threatened, vilified or insulted another person on the basis of that person's race, religion, colour, descent or national or ethnic origin (Australian Football League, 1995). The new rule was substantially directed at the on-field behaviour of the players, but also included the conduct of coaches, officials and other staff, and it applies to every Australian Rules football competition at junior, senior, local, state and national levels. The Anti-Racial and Religious Vilification Law was the first such policy to be drafted by a major sporting code, and in recognition of this, the AFL was awarded a peace prize by the United Nations (UN) in October 1995 (Gardiner, 1997: 3). There are, of course, anti-racism campaigns such as 'Let's Kick Racism Out' or 'Show Racism the Red Card', which centre on racism in British football; FARE (Football Against Racism in Europe) and 'Hit Racism for a Six' in British cricket, while the 1991 Football Offences Act in the UK prohibited racial abuse of fans, umpires or players. The Anti-Racial and Religious Vilification Law, however, was the first policy with legislative consequences, hence my focus on it here.[4]

As Houlihan (2011) notes in another context, policy often emerges out of 'crisis'. The catalyst for the implementation of the 'race abuse code', as it is more popularly known, occurred in 1993 when St Kilda played Collingwood. The St Kilda player Nicky Winmar had been racially abused by sections of the Collingwood crowd throughout the game, and towards its end, Winmar lifted his jumper, and pointed to the colour of his skin. His actions were captured in the press and television coverage of the game and broadcast around the world. The 'profound and effective image generated a renewed debate on racial abuse in football, while at the same time, signalling that Aboriginal players were

adopting a new stance; one that would confront the issue of racism in football'
(Gardiner, 1997: 3).

Since implementing the Anti-Racial and Religious Vilification Law, the AFL
now boasts that more than 10% of its players are Indigenous, proportionally
more than the 2% of Indigenous people who make up the larger Australian
population (Australian Bureau of Statistics, 2006; Australian Football League,
2010; Cunningham & Beneforti, 2005). While the rise in numbers of Indigenous
players cannot be directly linked to the introduction of the policy, the AFL has
nonetheless taken an assertive stance on redressing the under-representation of
Indigenous players in the sport, and is a 'strong public voice for reconciliation
through events such as the annual Dreamtime at the G match, and the recognition of an Indigenous Team of the Century' (Judd, 2010: 3).[5]

Against this policy backdrop, the growing presence of Indigenous footballers
raises some important questions for the unresolved conceptual debates that this
chapter is centrally concerned with. Winmar's provocative act, along with other
forms of political protest, such as the famous 'Black Power' salute at the 1968
Mexico Olympics, highlight sport as a site for the 'expression of resistance to
racial oppression and socio-political marginalisation before national or international audiences' (Warren & Tsaousis, 1997: 27). In this sense, we have an interaction between the global, as politically charged actions and statements are
broadcast to audiences worldwide, and the local; the intimate, micro-politics of
groups who are oppressed, in this case, through race. I may be taking some licence
with my interpretation of 'the local', but the consensus in other ways of conceptualizing it is that 'the local' consists of a subgroup or a minority group who must
mediate and accommodate national and supranational forces – colonialism,
displacement, dispossession, and the like. In this regard, the particular relationships between Indigenous and settler Australians, which led to the development of the first policy to address racism in sport by a professional code,
provides a unique point of entry into the politics of resistance that are embedded in local–global relationships.

CONCEPTUALIZING THE LOCAL

I suggested earlier that reifications of the local as 'heroism in the face of globalization', to use Andrews and Ritzer's (2007) phrase, are also reifications of culture,
and this is certainly the case with the treatments of Indigenous footballers in
Australia. The regulatory response to racial vilification (that is, the development
of the Anti-Racial and Religious Vilification Law) cannot be separated from the
broader social forces that operate within the particular colonial history of
Australia. In this regard, the AFL provisions are important because they represent
a significant *non-governmental* attempt to address racism which coincided with
the political dominance of the conservative Howard government (1996–2007)
and its hardline stance on race relations in Australia.[6] As MacNamara maintains,

'Australian football is a cultural practice imbued with the history of the nation's race relations. Racist slurs against Indigenous players embody the national history of dispossession and violence; they are not mere taunts by attacks on a person's being, a (re)statement of Aboriginal non-humanity' (2000: 5).

While there has been a steady growth in the number of Indigenous players competing in Australian Rules, this has been accompanied by a discourse that reifies the skills of the players in ways that perpetuate stereotypes of Indigenous athletes. The 'freakish' talents of Indigenous players – 'lightning reflexes of hand and foot, super fast acceleration, and a different sense of time and space are racial and cultural attributes that make Indigenous players a highly sought after commodity in contemporary Australian football' (Judd, 2010: 4). Constructing the skills of Indigenous players as 'innate' has become fairly standard in Australian media representations of the game. Descriptions like 'silky', 'magic', 'lightning' and 'twinkle toes' are commonly used for Indigenous players, perpetuating a stereotype of 'Black Magic' that overrides other cultural traits such as the discipline and determination required to be a professional athlete.[7] In other words, the ascendant discourse continues to reify the culture of Indigenous Australians as being 'Other', and this provides an uneasy counterpoint to anti-racism policy in sport. As Henry (2007) points out, such reifications of culture and 'Othering' are a problem for sports policy more broadly, and stem from the Western-centred nature of much social analysis and policy-making.

The development and implementation of anti-discrimination and other policies of inclusion, I suggest, has created a particular dynamic that reifies (and indeed stereotypes) 'the local', in this case, young Aboriginal players from predominantly remote parts of Australia. The reification of the local, and *culture*, sits within a context of 'enlightened racism' (Jhally & Lewis, 1992) that has enabled particular policies to develop that progress the process of reconciliation and address racism in sport while obscuring the history and continuing practices of colonial domination in Australia. As Hallinan, Bruce and Burke (2005: 68) note, the growing representation and media visibility of Indigenous men in the AFL has led administrators, commentators, scholars and fans of Australian football to idealize race relations in Australia. The imprint of colonialism on community relations in Australia is hugely significant, and we cannot understand that country's contemporary cultural politics without making references to its colonial past. The reification of the local in the context of policy-making and particular representations of race obscure this history and fails to deal with institutional racism in football.

THE PROBLEM OF THE LOCAL

The politics of race, the uneven distribution of power, responses to supranational processes and the colonial history that underpin policy-making in relation to racial vilification in Australian Rules football also raise some questions as to how we conceptualize 'the local'. While much intellectual energy has been spent on thinking about what globalization is, far less has been devoted to conceptualizing what 'the local' and localization may be. Is the local simply a smaller site – a town, a village or a city – that interacts with macro-processes of transnational movement and exchange? Is the local, as I've suggested here, a site of micro-politics and cultural and political struggle that may or may not be bound to a particular 'place'? Or is the local, as Robins maintains, 'a fluid and relational space, constituted only in and through its relation to the global' (1991: 35)?

While these ways of framing 'the local' variously understand localization in either spatial or interactionist terms, each alerts us to the hybridities within locally enacted relationships, or to the global within the local, and suggests a need to rethink relations of difference and imbalance that may occur within cities, towns, regions or nations; typically the spaces cast in opposition to the global.

London 2012 and 'Diversity' in Sports Policy

The London 2012 Olympic Games provides several examples of the need not to name sharply bounded categories such as the local or the global, but rather to emphasize the relations and hybridities within. Debates about the centre and periphery, ongoing tensions between London and the regions over legacies, an extended global economic downturn, a change of national government in the United Kingdom (from Labour to a Conservative-Liberal coalition) and accompanying savage funding cuts across the public sector, all add to the scepticism surrounding the perceived capacity of the London Olympics to truly be a 'Games for All' of the United Kingdom; a rhetorical promise in the city's successful bid. Equally, the cultural politics and racial diversity within London's East End (where most of the Games will be staged) alert us to the global within the local, and an analysis of this perhaps comes some way to addressing Connell's concern that word-plays like 'glocalization' simply restate rather than transcend the binary between the local and the global, and miss relations of difference within.

In addition to the ambitious legacy promise of using the Games to inspire the United Kingdom to become more physically active by promoting and developing sporting participation across the country (DCMS, 2007), the successful case that was advanced when securing the 2012 Games emphasized 'diversity [as] a key reason why London, one of the most multicultural cities in the world, was chosen to host the Games in the bidding process' (LOCOG, 2008; London 2012 Olympic and Paralympic Games, 2010). London is certainly not the first Olympic Games, nor is it likely to be last, to focus on multicultural diversity in its promotional rhetoric. Both the 2000 Sydney Summer Games and the 2010 Vancouver Winter Games appropriated 'ethnic' imagery in their opening and closing ceremonies, while at the same time marginalizing and displacing minority ethnic and/or Indigenous peoples (Lenskyj, 2002; O'Bonsawin, 2010). Few other organizing committees, however, have made 'diversity' such a significant and enduring part of their promotional rhetoric. In contrast to the inclusion of imagery relating to specific Indigenous groups such as Aboriginal and Torres Strait Islander Australians or First Nation groups in Canada, the London bid focused more generally on the notion of 'diversity' as an overarching concept.

In a broader sports policy context, 'diversity' and 'multiculturalism' have much currency. As Henry, Amara and Aquilina note, 'claims about the use of sport as a vehicle for promoting social integration of socially excluded groups in general, and specifically ethnic minority groups, are not new, although they have been increasingly evident in recent years' (2007: 115). That said, nomenclature is both problematic and crucial. Although it is more common to speak of 'multiculturalism', Henry, Amara and Aquilina (2007) suggest that 'interculturalism' may be more appropriate, as policy is less concerned with protecting cultural difference and more with integration and assimilation (Amara, 2008; Amara et al., 2005). Citing the Catalan Generaliat (the regional autonomous government for Catalonia in Spain), Henry et al. note that immigration and integration have been incorporated into sports policy within the government's jurisdiction:

> Sport is probably one of the most effective means of integration. When we take part in sport we are all equal, and so, cultural ethnic and racial differences disappear. Thanks to sport, we are able to create links with immigrants that can be maintained in day-to-day life. (cited in Henry et al., 2007: 128)

Given such rhetorical claims of the capacity of sport to bridge difference, it is perhaps not surprising that there is a plethora of policy initiatives and services aimed at inclusivity and ethnic minorities. In the United Kingdom, for example, initiatives such as *Sporting Equals* (a joint project between the Commission for Racial Equality and Sport England, 2001) or the *Equality and Diversity Strategy* of UK Sport (2004) would be cases in point here, while in the Netherlands, sports policy has moved towards a 'target group' approach to accommodate the needs of the significant immigrant population in cities like Rotterdam from the former Dutch colonies (Surinam and Indonesia) as well as from Morocco and Turkey (Rijpma & Meiburg, 1989).

To return once more to London 2012, Burdsey's (2011) mediation on the 'Technicolor Games' and issues of race and representation within London's East End more broadly provide a compelling illustration of the 'hybridities within' that the movement and migration of people across and within borders has accelerated, highlighting what Sinha labels 'the changing local racialized politics of East London' (2008: para. 1.4). Burdsey notes that:

> The once thriving docks in the area, plus large post-war immigration from the New Commonwealth, means that African, Caribbean and South Asian groups combine to comprise a substantial minority ethnic presence. The 'white' population contains 'established' Greeks, Irish, Maltese, Polish, Turkish and Greek Cypriot, and Jewish communities, as well as more recent migrants from EU accession countries. Since the

1980s development of the docklands and the construction of Canary Wharf, certain districts have also undergone rapid gentrification and become home to white, middle-class professionals. (2011: 69)

As such comments suggest, the East End undoubtedly has a racial and ethnic complexity that sits nicely with the rhetoric of the 'Games of Diversity' espoused during the bidding process. However, as Burdsey continues, the East End of London has a 'darker history ... which goes far beyond the characterisations often espoused by popular cultural representation and the sanitised consumption of ethnic "Otherness" that occurs within the area's rapidly increasing gentrified districts' (Burdsey, 2011: 69). As has been argued elsewhere (Banerjea, 2000; Wemyss, 2006), there are, within London's East End, relations of difference that are often conflictual and give the lie to broader cultural assumptions of multicultural harmony that the representation of London 2012 rests on, and that Henry et al. (2007) render problematic in a more general policy context. As Farrar points out, 'conflict and contestation also characterise the broader historical sociology of the area' (2008: para 1.2) in ways that are highly contradictory. Wemyss (2006) extends this argument, contending that although a discourse of tolerance has traditionally existed among residents of the East End, in practice it has operated co-temperaneously alongside incidents of race-based violence and electoral support for Far Right political parties. Burdsey continues:

East London is enshrined as both a site of (neo)fascism and anti-racism, having witnessed the Battle of Cable Street, British Asians defending Brick Lane from the National Front, and the Rock Against Racism carnival in Hackney's Victoria Park. ... Furthermore, it was in Tower Hamlets that Derek Beackon of the British National Party (BNP) became the nation's first fascist councillor in 1993. (2011: 70)[8.]

In this context, and in the context of the reconciliatory emphasis of the Anti-Racial and Religious Vilification Law outlined previously, it will be interesting to see how, if at all, these politics of race will map onto social and sports policy directed at discrimination and inclusion at London 2012. Will the Games really be the 'Games of Diversity' or will they simply take place in a diverse city? What might this mean for broader issues of social integration of and between cultural and ethnic groups in London or for race-related policy more broadly? While the celebration of cultural difference remains central to the London bid and to the London Organizing Committee of the Olympic Games' (LOCOG) public statements, the language of policy is not unproblematic. Vertovec and Wessendorf (2010: 18) note that 'while "multicultural" has mostly disappeared from political rhetoric and the concept of "integration" has appeared instead (evidenced in the policy examples from the Netherlands and Catalonia), support for immigrant and minority cultural difference is highlighted in the growing use of notions of "diversity" in policy language'.

Accordingly, this latter term has become the term of choice in the promotional literature and discourse around the 2012 Games. In LOCOG's diversity and inclusion strategy, for example, the word 'multicultural' is used just once, while 'diverse' and 'diversity' are mentioned nearly 200 times (LOCOG, 2008; see also Burdsey, 2011). This move enables, as Burdsey (2011) notes, a politically expedient and sufficiently nebulous focus on the multitude of communities in London, without having to engage with a contentious and increasingly redundant political concept; that is, without having to engage with the *realpolitik* of race relations – the hybridities within – in the host city. As Bloyce and Smith contend:

> While London is, indeed, an extremely ethnically diverse city, it is difficult to see how hosting the Olympic Games, like many other sporting events and programmes, will help promote community integration by bringing people from a variety of socio-economic and ethnic backgrounds 'together' in anything other than an ephemeral way. (2010: 175)

The politics of 'race within' – in both Australia and London – I suggest, help to emphasize the relations within as well as those between that characterize debates about local–global interactions. In both cases, there are relations of authority, exclusion, inclusion, hegemony, partnership, sponsorship and appropriation that are enormously problematic for policy-making and compliance, and it is imperative that the uneven relations of power *within* the local are considered in any implementation of public and sports policy.[9]

FLOWS AND FRAMES: THE LOCAL AND THE GLOBAL IN SPORTS POLICY

I have covered some fairly eclectic terrain in this chapter. To bring together the various debates about local–global relations that developed throughout the latter part of the twentieth century, I return to the ideas of Hannerz (1996), and his notion of 'cultural flow'. The concept of 'flow' can provide a useful model for generating understanding of questions of scale and scope that are implicit in the relationships between the local and the global as they are played out in the context of sport and public policy.

Using the notion of 'cultural flows', Hannerz identifies four organizational frames through which to approach the complexity of cultural process, taken here to be the policy process (see Table 2.1 below). Anchoring Hannerz's framework is an understanding of the role that human agency and intervention plays in the production and circulation of culture. As Hannerz notes, 'my point of departure is that cultures are not themselves living beings; they are shaped and carried by people in varying social constellations, pursuing different aims'

(1996: 69). Moreover, Hannerz's typology is useful for conceptualizing the socio-spatial relations that are embedded in notions of the local and the global, for there is at least an implied sense of directionality – of moving either up or down – in the notion of flow.

The first of Hannerz's frames is what he refers to as 'the form of life' (1996: 69); the 'habitual perspectives and dispositions' (1990: 114) that define everyday life. The **form of life** is, for Hannerz, those flows that individuals encounter by going about their ordinary, everyday lives. It is the circulation of meaning within homes, workplaces and neighbourhoods. It is the framework of greatest intimacy, or the most 'local' frame in terms of its impact on those social relations that take place at the micro-level.

In terms of policy, we experience the form of life in the minutiae of everyday life. It is fair to say that we live in a policy-saturated world in which almost every aspect of our lives is defined and governed by policy – from the amount of tax we pay, to whether we can smoke or drink alcohol in public places, to an insistence on wearing helmets and other forms of protection when playing particular sports, to requirements for women to play sport (or not) in ways that respect cultural and religious beliefs, and so on. In the context of globalization, the centrality of policy takes a particular shape. The form of life, I suggest, captured in the banal, routinized policies that we accept, relatively unquestioned, maps onto the conceptual category of 'the local'. As Hannerz puts it: 'much of what we describe as the local is what happens every day' (1996: 26). The repetitive flow of policy into our domestic activities is precisely the micro-level at which the local operates.

Operating at an increasingly larger scale, the second frame Hannerz alerts us to is that of '**the State**'; the 'flow of meaning between the state apparatus and the people defined as subjects/citizens' (Hannerz, 1996: 69). Explicitly located within the political sphere, this frame is centred on the institutional apparatus and actions of the State as an organizational form, but also on the management of particular meanings that are carried from the State to its citizens.

Such a frame clearly resonates with the notions of policy-making that are central to my interpretation of public policy as it relates to global sport. The State acts as an intermediary between the local, micro-effects of the frame of life and the more global or macro-flows of the market and movement that are centrally concerned with the mobility of people, products and policy across boundaries and borders. While the institutions of policy-making and the relationship between supra, national and sub-national governing bodies is the subject of the following chapter (in particular, the IOC, the World Anti-Doping Agency and their roles in governing anti-doping policy in sport), the point here is that the State is particularly adept at controlling the policy apparatus in a form of cultural institutionalism whereby values, beliefs and attitudes feed into the policy-making process.

Hannerz's third frame of '**the market**' conceptualizes the cultural processes that encompass global commodity culture. As its name suggests, the market is concerned with the meanings that are carried by the goods that circulate or flow within the marketplace and pass from buyer to seller and include sports gear, fashion wear, popular music and televised sport. As is the case with the State, the market operates as a form of cultural management: '[in the market], cultural production and distribution seem to be mostly deliberate and asymmetrically organized' (Hannerz, 1996: 69).

For studies of policy in a global context, the market cannot be ignored. As we have seen with the London 2012 Olympics, the movement of finance, capital and cultural products has significant implications for the development of policy that relate to the economic regulation of sporting activity, the media acquisition of sporting content, the bidding process and the branding and imaging of the Games. The most recent example at the time of writing was that of the passing of the London 2012 Act by the British parliament, which designated the 'exceptional status' of the Olympic brand and associated commodities as well as rights of immanent domain over land public space and transport in order to facilitate the production of the Olympic Games (OPSI, 2006).

Finally, Hannerz's fourth frame is the flow of **movement**. Movement is ultimately the crux of globalization. As Hannerz puts it:

> Flux, mobility, recombination and emergence have become favored themes as globalization and transnationality frequently offer the contexts for our thinking about culture ... boundaries do not really contain, but are more often interestingly crossed. Borderlands are often where the action is, and hybridity and collage are among our preferred words for characterizing qualities in people and their products. (n.d.)

Conceived as such, globalization involves the mobility and the movement of people, finance, capital and ideas; of things not staying in their places.

Importantly for this chapter, each of these flows and frames provide a different way of understanding centre–periphery relationship, or local–global relations and the social interactions embedded within. This framework emphasizes the persistent polarity between system and singularity that characterizes the relationship between the local and the global within a model of a 'global society' in ways that recognize both scale and interrelationships. In his use of flow, Hannerz is careful to emphasize that globalization is not tantamount to homogenization, and that globalization does not imply that people acquire a global identity; rather that cultural diversity is organized in new ways in an age of near-universal modernity (Eriksen, 1997). Each of these frames or flows, then, raise questions about the relative significance of particular cultural elements and the implications that these have for the engagement of local cultures with aspects of global culture, in this case the policy dimensions of global sport.

Importantly for the intellectual project at the heart of this book – to insert the social into analyses of public policy as they relate to sport – these flows, flavoured by social anthropology, offer a useful framework for conceptualizing the various social relationships embedded within and between the local and the global that are played out in sports policy. Each captures a different sense of scale, scope,

Table 2.1   *Flows and frames of sports policy (adapted from Hannerz, 1996)*

Flow	Policy level	Example
Forms of life	• 'Everyday life' • Local	• Enforcement of helmets in professional cycling
The state	• State influence on citizens • Mediates relationship between local and national/ supranational	• Regulation of compliance with anti-doping policy (monitoring and testing of athletes' compliance with WADA Code)
The market	• Meanings carried by goods and commodities • National and supranational	• London 2012 (media acquisition, bidding and branding of Games)
Movement	• Circulation of culture • The global	• Regulation of the production and distribution of sportswear (and sports stars)

Source: Adapted from Hannerz (1996)

structure and agency that all processes of policy-making must contend with, and each maps onto the tensions between the local and the global or the centre and the periphery described in this chapter.

CONCLUSION

This chapter has been concerned to apply the central concepts and debates in studies of globalization to some preliminary thinking about social and public policy as it relates to sport in a global context. Following Sassen, I have wanted to explore the sub-national constitution of global processes, rather than just the 'transnational and self-evident constituting of global processes' (2009: 110). A consideration of local–global relations is fundamental to studies of globalization, and studies of sports policy are particularly good at disrupting the pervasive local–global dichotomy by asking us to reflect on the hybridities within as well as between nations and regions. As Henry et al. note, 'global structures are the product as well as the context of human agency, and, in any given locale or policy area, the influence of global phenomena may (consciously or unconsciously) be embraced, adapted or rejected' (2007: 21).

The examples of race relations in Australia and cultural and racial diversity in London's East End are useful correctives to formulations of local–global relations as being simply an imbalance of power between Western and non-Western, or between developed and developing nations – a dominant narrative on globalization discourse. As both examples show, there are considerable imbalances within developed nations, and these internal hybridities of the global within the local need to be considered in analyses of social relations that are globally constitutive. The example of race makes the point that power isn't spread evenly within countries, and the argument could equally be applied to gender, sexuality, disability and other forms of social inequality to which public policy responds.

In the context of globalization and policy, considerably more work needs to be done to extend our understandings of power and exploitation, and how they translate to policy, by examining relationships of imbalance within countries as well as between the polarities of the West and the non-West.

Following on from this, I have attempted to map a framework for conceptualizing the questions of scope, scale, structure and agency in policy-making. Despite some analytical limitations, Hannerz's (1996) framework of cultural flows is helpful for unpacking 'the social' in analyses of globalization as they relate to public policy in sport. Notions of flow capture the different levels of scale that policy operates at – from the micro, domestic sphere of forms of life, through to the macro flows of the market and movement. Such a framework helps to locate shifting configurations of socio-spatial relations as they map onto policy-making and policy compliance. Local–global debates are essentially those of scale, and these frames capture a movement from intimate micro-politics to mid-range interactions between citizens and the state to the macro- or supranational level influence of the market. Building on these questions of scale, and relations between the supra and the sub-national, or the local and the global, the following chapter extends these concepts to an analysis of the organization, administration and global governance of sports policy.

BOX 2.1   QUESTIONS FOR DISCUSSION

- What is the 'problem of polarity'?

- How have concepts like 'creolization', 'hybridization', 'the glocal', 'the grobal' and 'glocalization' changed how we understand globalization?

- What are the key global processes, flows and networks described in this chapter?

- In what ways are local experiences influenced and shaped by globally extensive systems (e.g. production and consumption)?

- In what ways does globalization create a specific experience of time and space? Or does it?

SUGGESTED FURTHER READINGS

Donnelly, P. (1996) The local and the global: Globalization in the sociology of sport. *Journal of Sport and Social Issues*, 20: 239–57.

Giulianotti, R. & Robertson, R. (2007) Forms of glocalization: Globalization and the migration strategies of Scottish football fans in North America. *Sociology*, 41: 133–42.

Hannerz, U. (1996) *Transnational connections*. London: Routledge.

Sassen, S. (2007a) *A sociology of globalization*. New York: W.W. Norton.

Sassen, S. (ed.) (2007b) *Deciphering the global: Its spaces, scales and subjects*. New York and London: Routledge.

Notes

1 According to this perspective, the Western dominance of the economy, politics, technology and culture has permeated analyses of the global economy and capitalism (see, for example, Hardt & Negri, 2001; Ohmae, 1995), global media networks (e.g. Castells, 1996; McLuhan, 1964), and the global standardization of products and services (e.g. Levitt, 1983; Ritzer, 2000).

2 In a similar vein, Robinson notes that the debate is 'old wine poured into a new bottle' (2011: 724).

3 David Howe's edited collection *Cross-Cultural Consumption: Global Markets, Local Realities*, for example, documents a series of encounters through which indigenous communities in North and South America have responded to the 'commodification of their cultural identities' (1996: 13). The central premise developed throughout this collection, as it is in others (Abaza, 2001; Falk, 1999), is that local people, particularly those in low-income countries in the Global South, demonstrate extraordinary resilience and agency to both resist and accommodate global expansion in ways that resonate with their own life worlds.

4 I draw a distinction between specific sport-related policies and the broader 'multinational sport policy' that was introduced in South Africa following the country's expulsion from the Olympic Movement in 1970. This new policy enabled 'Europeans' and 'non-Europeans' to compete in open competition but not in racially integrated South African national teams (Ndlovu, 2010: 144).

5 The 'G' is a colloquial way of referring to the Melbourne Cricket Ground or MCG, where many Australian Rules games are contested.

6 The Howard Government introduced a number of interventionist measures such as the partial suspension of welfare payments and bans on alcohol within Aboriginal communities that were seen as paternalistic and divided public opinion.

7 The counter-narrative for Aboriginal athletes is one of a 'success story', such as when the Aboriginal runner Cathy Freeman won gold in the 400 metres at the Sydney Olympics in 2000, celebrating her victory lap wrapped in both the Aboriginal and Australian flags. As Lenskyj (2002) and Bruce and Hallinan (2001) note, Freeman's world-beating run, and her symbolic prominence during the Opening Ceremony, constructed Australia as a 'new nation' where the legacy of an institutionally racist past had been symbolically erased.

8 The area has also seen a number of high-profile racist murders, most notably that of Stephen Lawrence in Eltham in 1993.

9 In a related vein, Alegi asks, perhaps rhetorically, 'who benefits from world football? Who does not?' (2001: 1).

3

GLOBALIZATION AND THE GOVERNANCE OF SPORTS POLICY

THIS CHAPTER

- provides an overview of governance and global sports policy;
- assesses the key sporting organizations which operate at supra, national and sub-national levels;
- discusses the role of cultural brokers and policy entrepreneurs in the making and governance of sports policy.

INTRODUCTION

The global diffusion of modern sport from the late nineteenth century onwards has seen the emergence of an ever-increasing range of organizations and institutions with competing claims to authority over the production and consumption of sport. From the harmonization of rules and regulations, to the enforcement of policy, to the control of media and broadcasting rights, global governance is, as Murphy (2000) notes, an arena in which struggles over wealth, power and knowledge are taking place.

In the context of globalization, these organizations variously operate as supranational organizations such as the International Olympic Committee (IOC) or the Fédération International de Football Association (FIFA), transnational organizations that span continents – the Supreme Council for Sport in Africa or the Confederación Sud American de Fútbol, for example – national organizations and governing bodies such as the National Rugby League or Sport England, both in the United Kingdom, and sub-national organizations such as the Ministry for Youth Sport in Namibia or Norway that are charged primarily with overseeing and implementing domestic or endogenous policy concerns.

This institutional architecture underscores a particular model of governance that pertains to the analysis of policy in general and to sports policy more particularly (Henry & Lee, 2004).[1] At its heart, this model of 'systemic' govern-ance attempts to understand the relationships and interactions between various stakeholders that are brought to bear on the policy process. As Henry points out:

> Systemic governance, which concerns the way that sport is governed, not directly by national and international sports bodies (such as FIFA or the IOC) but rather through the interaction between such bodies and other major stakeholders [media companies, governmental organ-izations, sponsors, athletes' associations and transnational bodies such as the European Union [EU]] in a network of actors involved in com-petition, cooperation, negotiation and mutual adjustment. (2007: 8)

Moreover, this institutional architecture of sport brings into play a number of tensions that directly affect the governance of global sports policy. Questions of sovereignty and authority, issues of uniform compliance with regulations across nations and jurisdictions, and the increasing pressure on national governments to develop policy that is set within a supranational agenda determined by transna-tional corporations and international non-government bodies are among the concerns for sports policy here. As Woods has argued, 'global governance is increasingly being undertaken by a variety of networks, coalitions and informal arrangements which lie a little further beyond the public gaze and the direct con-trol of governments' (2002: 42). As I develop in this chapter, it is increasingly rare (and difficult) for governments to take governing decisions without including the corporate and voluntary sectors in the process. Forming a 'policy network' of actors aligned by mutual interest and resource dependence, it is the processes through which this takes place that this chapter is largely concerned with.

Building on some of the debates outlined previously, in particular, questions of scale and the socially constitutive interactions between the global, the national and the local, this chapter focuses on the governance of sports policy in the global order, paying particular attention to the tensions that operate within an institu-tional architecture that consists of organizations, bodies and agencies who oper-ate at supra, national and sub-national levels. My concern is not so much with the stages of policy-making (after Hogwood & Gunn, 1984, for example), or the policy cycle (Bridgman & Davis, 2004; Colebatch, 2002), or with how issues reach the policy agenda of governments (Houlihan, 1990, 1991, 1997; Houlihan & Green, 2008), rather it is with the role of human intervention in determining the 'reach' and 'response' (Houlihan, 1994) of sports policy through the mediat-ing process of policy brokerage. That is, my interest is with an institutional analysis of governance that foregrounds socio-cultural and political structures in shaping a policy agenda within a global regulatory framework (Colebatch, 2006a). Policy is essentially a 'thing' that is created by some and implemented by others, and it is imperative that we understand who is involved, how, where, when and why, in the governance of sports policy.

To ground this analysis, I focus on the threat that will not go away; the spec-tre of doping that hangs over global sport, and the relationships between the supranational organizations with responsibility for anti-doping policy – the International Olympic Committee and the World Anti-Doping Agency (WADA) – and the national and sub-national sports organizations and govern-ing bodies who are equally implicated in policy compliance in their efforts to ensure adherence to testing regimes and punishment by and of their athletes within their sports and jurisdictions. Anti-doping provides an instructive case study of some of the issues and debates which underpin global governance and supranational policy-making that transcend sub-national policy interests; a key development of public policy in the context of globalization. As Hanstad, Skille and Loland contend, 'anti-doping has undergone a transformation from a situ-ation in which just a handful of so-called active or activist countries have engaged in anti-doping work to a global affair' (2010: 418).

To provide some preliminary context: many of the changes in the wider sport-ing environment that the processes of globalization have accelerated have also had a direct impact on anti-doping policy. Athletic migration and mobility, inter-national competition and increased travel to training camps in the southern hemisphere mean that many athletes may spend little time in their home country or within the jurisdiction of their own sporting federation. This, coupled with the introduction of out-of-competition drug testing in 2003, now requires a high level of transnational cooperation (and resources) by governments and federa-tions, and it has highlighted some of the inconsistencies between domestic dop-ing regulations and those of the international federation, WADA.

In the context of governance and accountability, changes to the wider political environment have also impacted on the global governance of anti-doping policy. The state-orchestrated and sanctioned doping that occurred in several Central and Eastern European countries ended with the collapse of communism in 1989, and the Council of Europe has been instrumental in ensuring anti-doping policy remains a priority among its forty-seven member states since the signing of the Anti-Doping Convention in the same year (Council of Europe, 1989). Both developments provide an important geo-political backdrop to the progress of anti-doping policy that has struggled to keep pace with new doping practices and substances. As I will return to, this constellation of the global movement of athletes, changes in political structures and difficulties in coordinating policy transnationally form a backdrop to the global governance of anti-doping policy that emerged in 1999 with the establishment of the World Anti-Doping Code by the World Anti-Doping Agency.

TOWARDS GLOBAL GOVERNANCE: SOVEREIGNTY AND SUPRANATIONAL AUTHORITY IN SPORTS POLICY

As Held and McGrew have suggested, the globalization debate projects into a new context the 'cardinal questions of political life concerning power and rule: who rules, in whose interests, by what means and for what ends' (2007: 137). In this century alone, we have seen a 'thickening web of multilateral agreements, global and regional institutions and regimes, transgovernmental policy networks that regulate and intervene in virtually all aspects of transnational activity or world affairs from global finance to the other WTO – the World Toilet Organization ("improving toilets and public sanitation globally")' (Held & McGrew, 2007: 138). Far from being a seamless web, this system of governance is one that comprises supra-state bodies, regional organizations, and transnational policy networks embracing government officials, technocrats, corporate representatives, pressure groups and non-governmental organizations alike. Yeates has highlighted the complexity of these relationships and their impact on global policy, in her case, global social policy, noting that:

> 'National' and 'supra-national' are better thought of as different elements of a multi-faceted governance structure whose different levels or 'tiers' are mutually constitutive and through which influence 'travels' multi-directionally. It is therefore appropriate to ask questions about the ways in, and extent to, which actors located in domestic arenas influence the formation of supra-national policy as it is to ask questions about the ways in which supra-national agencies and actors shape the course of national social policy. (2007: 345)

Importantly for the governance of sport, whether that relates to issues of media content, brand management and imaging, the athlete transfer market or, in this case, anti-doping policy, these bodies and organizations map onto particular socio-spatial relations that roughly correspond to the global, the national and the local outlined in the previous chapter. Penetrating the complexities of these relations is imperative to comprehending globalization, and by inference, global sports policy. Sassen (2009), for example, maintains that to understand globalization, we need to take into consideration the complex architecture of the nation state, the nation-state apparatus and the sub-national, evident in her use of archaeological metaphors to describe the process of 'digging inside the national, inside the local, in order to add to our understanding of globalization' (2009: 116). The cultural politics of global sports policy share this complex architecture. Sports policy brings together bodies and organizations which are involved in an intricate interplay of contested, sometimes complementary, interests that are really about emergent forms of sovereignty and governmentality which are now trans-local and cross-national, as well as transnational in their reach and rule.

To elaborate what I mean by this, the exercise of transnational sovereignty is found in the activities of the International Olympic Committee, a supranational organization rivalled only by FIFA in terms of its presumption of total rule over the substance, structure and subjects of the Olympic Games and global sport (MacAloon, 2011).[2] While analyses of global governance have focused mainly on the World Bank, the International Monetary Fund, the

World Trade Organization (Stiglitz, 2003), the United Nations' network of international institutions (Coles, 2004; Merry, 2006) or the European Union's institutional governance via 'parliaments' in Brussels and Strasbourg (MacDonald, 1996; Shore, 2000), the IOC's network of global governance has only recently been fully considered in this light despite the Olympics being a global institution that has significant social, political and economic relationships with other transnational and national institutions and organizations.

Carter (2011b) provides a fresh analysis of the nature of global sovereignty with regard to the IOC and their presumption of an assertion of total sovereignty over sport and the Olympics. Drawing on the ideas of Foucault (1977) and Agamben (1998, 2005, 2009), Carter contends that the IOC has developed an extraordinary capacity for self-authority that is rarely challenged.[3] As Carter maintains, 'the crucial question, then, is not on the internal political wrangling characteristic of the IOC, but on the worldwide governance of sport and, in particular, the IOC assertions that it alone determines how global sport shall be organized, experienced, and ruled' (2011b: 54). As a self-proclaimed 'international non-governmental not-for-profit organization, of unlimited duration, in the form of an association with the status of a legal person, recognized by the Swiss Federal Council in accordance with an agreement entered into on 1 November 2000' (IOC, 2010: 29, 57), the IOC has unilateral authority over all things Olympic and these claims to sovereignty are increasingly being tested in relation to the World Anti-Doping Agency, which has slowly usurped the policy leadership of the IOC in terms of drugs in sport.

This notion of transnational sovereignty is also evidenced in what Held and McGrew (2007) refer to as 'cosmocracy'; a transnational elite class dominated by the corporate sector. Again, we need look no further than the Olympic Games, where governments and sponsors jostle to host 'the world's longest commercial' (Payne, 2005: 169). This is a point to which I will return, for notions of cosmocracy and corporate elites reflect the increasingly important role of cultural intermediaries and policy brokers in the making – and management – of policy decisions, particularly in relation to those associated with the staging of global sporting mega-events such as the Olympic Games or football's World Cup.

National and Sub-National Modes of Governance

Alongside those organizations, like the IOC or FIFA, which exercise extraordinary rule over the global governance of sport, various national bodies also assert authority over the policy process at a domestic level. Numerato, for example, provides a detailed analysis of what he describes as 'the multifaceted world of Czech sports governance' (2008: 21), focusing on the role of social capital in facilitating governance and civic engagement. The Czech example is by no means unique. Government departments and agencies around the world have seized on sport as a 'high-visibility, low-cost and extremely malleable resource which can be adapted to achieve, or at least give the impression to the public/electorate of achieving, a wide variety of domestic and international goals' (Houlihan & Green, 2008: 3). Sovereignty at a national level is essentially 'meso', and government involvement in sports policy is both varied and extensive, covering everything from the 'licensing of coaches, control of doping, state regulatory activity of broadcasting rights for sporting events, certification of stadium safety, and the licensing of sports clubs' (Houlihan, 2005: 164).

Of the range of domestic policy concerns with which governments engage, it is elite sport that occupies the most persistent presence on the policy hierarchy (Green & Houlihan, 2006; Houlihan & Green, 2008), with elite sports development consistently receiving government funding through 'state-sponsored' programmes (Bloyce & Smith, 2010: 134). This is not surprising. It is a commonly held assumption that elite international sporting success generates domestic benefits that range from the nebulous 'feel good factor' (De Bosscher et al., 2008; Newman, 2007) to more concrete social and economic benefits associated with hosting elite sporting events (Gratton & Henry, 2001; Mules & Faulkner, 1996).[4] The economic benefits of hosting major sports events are increasingly significant in post-industrial countries where 'the sports-related service sector is an important engine for growth and employment' (Gratton & Taylor, 2000). With the lure of such benefits beckoning, it is little wonder that Russia is hosting the Winter Olympics at Sochi in 2014 and the men's football World Cup in 2018. This is not to suggest that elite sport dominates the policy hierarchy or the political agenda at the exclusion of all other policy items. The legacy impacts of the 2012 Olympic Games and those that will follow it are implicated in a policy discourse of increasing participation and promoting 'sport for all' across the lifespan, although this is not without its problems or critics.

Flowing through (to use Hannerz's metaphor) from national governments and their political priorities, there are, of course, a range of sub-national organizations charged with implementing policy at local and regional levels. This interplay between the micro (the sub-national), the meso (the national) and the macro (the supranational) returns us to Sassen's (2009) observation that to understand globalization, we need to take into consideration the nation-state apparatus and the sub-national as well. At the very least, debates within globalization require an analysis that is sensitive to the increasing significance of the role that supranational organizations play in influencing domestic policy and vice versa. As Carter notes, 'the production of global sport involves a myriad of international institutions entangled in an obvious political economic hierarchy of power' (2011b: 132). Figure 3.1 illustrates the various levels and intersections of policy governance.

In terms of public policy as it relates to sport or anything else, these different levels of sovereignty bring into play a tension between 'top-down' and 'bottom-up' policy-making, or between transnational and local interests and authority. Before supranational organizations entered the sports policy arena (a moment marked by the 1984 Olympic Games when Los Angeles allowed a degree of corporate involvement not previously seen), which shifted the dynamics of power

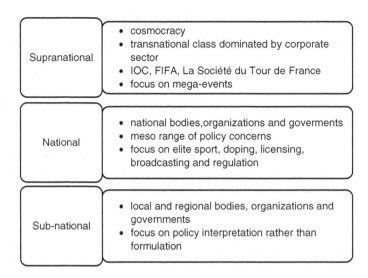

All levels influence each other; tension between top-down and bottom-up policy-making.

Figure 3.1   *Governance of global sport*

in the policy-making process, for the 'existing patterns of global governance have proved incapable of resisting the pressures of commercial interests' (Foster, 2005: 68), the making of sports policy was essentially the preserve of 'street level bureaucrats' (Lipsky, 1980) 'such as teachers, coaches or sports development officers [who made] policy in the everyday context within which they operated' (Houlihan, 2005: 166). That is, policy was made at the level of 'the form of life', to return to Hannerz's earlier formulation. Certainly, there have always been networks of relationships in the process of policy-making that have consisted of, among others, sports development officers, government ministers and a range of other actors, which both enable and constrain the actions and decisions that can be taken. As Dopson and Waddington note, the policy process involves 'many people at different levels within and outside the organization, and the extent to which different groups are committed to or opposed to the prevailing policy, and the strategies which they adopt in relation to that policy, play an important part in determining its outcome' (1996: 546). In other words, 'rule making and rule interpretation in global governance have become pluralized. Rules are no longer a matter simply for states or intergovernmental organizations' (Keohane, 2002: 214).

As the discussion of supranational and national organizations suggests, the organizational architecture of sports policy is now a web of interlocking interests in which sub-national and government departments operate within a 'cosmocratic' supranational agenda that implies a diffusion of power along neo-pluralist lines; that is, in which corporate powers are increasingly exerting political influence over the policy process. Sassen notes that 'transformations are happening in the most complex and accomplished organisational architectures we have constructed' (2009: 117), and in which authority and rights are assembled and disassembled into specific configurations by and within these organizations.

The development and enforcement of anti-doping policy in sport brings together these questions of sovereignty and authority across national, subnational and supranational organizations and jurisdictions. The central theme of this book is that sports policy has been profoundly affected by globalization, both in terms of supranational processes such as colonialism, as well as the development of international policies that cut across nations, borders, regions and jurisdictions. A case study of anti-doping provides a useful point of departure for a more extended analysis of the issues and debates that underpin global governance and forms of supranational policy-making.

THE THREAT THAT WON'T GO AWAY: DOPING IN SPORT

Doping to enhance performance in sport remains a pernicious policy problem that has a long history. In the Tour de France, for example, an event that is no stranger to drug scandals (teams have been expelled for doping practices, winners have been stripped of their yellow jersey for testing positive to prohibited substances and suspicion hangs over the 'natural' abilities of some of the event's most decorated competitors), drug taking has been documented as far back as 1924, when the newspaper *Le Petit Parisien* ran an interview with the Pelissier brothers – Henri and Francis – who were competing in the race of that year.[5], [6] In the article 'Les Forçats de la Route' (the Convicts of the Road), the Pelissier brothers described their experiences of riding the Tour de France as follows:

> We suffer on the road, but do you want to see how we keep going? [Francis takes a vial from his bag]. That's cocaine for our eyes and chloroform for our gums. And pills? You want to see the pills? [They get out three boxes each]. In short, we run on dynamite.

My mention of the Tour de France is not to suggest it is the only event in which doping occurs or cycling the only sport in which athletes cheat. Brissonneau and Ohl (2010) trace a longer, more nuanced history of doping and doping policy in athletics and other sports (as well as cycling) and, without question, the Olympic Games and athletics have form here as well. Marion Jones, the women's Olympic sprint champion at the Sydney Games in 2000, who persistently denied allegations before being jailed in 2007 for lying to a US Federal Agent about her doping practices, or Florence Griffith-Joyner, who died in 1998, aged just 38, a decade after setting new world records in the women's 100 metres and 200 metres finals at the Seoul Olympic Games, are just two examples here. Griffith-Joyner's rivals had long accused her of using steroids and human growth hormones; it was the latter that many suggested had killed her. It was the Seoul Games as well at which Ben Johnson was stripped of a gold medal in the men's 100 metres final after failing a drug test. In the same year as Flo-Jo's death, the Irish swimmer Michelle de Bruin (née Smith) was banned from competition for four years after she was found to have manipulated a drug test by spiking her urine sample with alcohol. De Bruin, of course, rose from obscurity at the 1996 Olympics in Atlanta to claim three gold medals, despite there being no 50-metre Olympic-length pool in her native Ireland, and despite being coached by her husband, who allegedly could not swim.

The point to note from such examples is that doping in sport remains a constant concern for policy makers. It is a 'wicked' policy problem that cuts across sports, agencies, governments and authorities. It is an ongoing policy problem for sporting organizations, departments and agencies worldwide, and in attempting to develop coordinated responses to anti-doping across countries and regions, policy has become increasingly global (and problematic) in its nature. Moreover, the persistence of doping as a policy problem speaks to a global ethics in sport that athletes, coaches and administrators are expected to uphold. Here, we are back to the notion of a universal codification of the normative values in sport discussed in the previous chapter. Of concern here, however, is the organizational infrastructure of governance in relation to the implementation of anti-doping policy that has been instrumental in attempting to enforce standardized normative values in sport as they relate to cheating and fair play.

Towards Global Anti-Doping Policy: The World Anti-Doping Agency

Houlihan (2011) notes elsewhere that government agendas are often set by exogenous events, and the history of anti-doping policy development is one in which significant policy change has been prompted by crisis. The death of the Danish cyclist, Knud Jensen, at the Rome Olympic Games in 1960, led the IOC to establish a Medical Commission. The death of Tom Simpson in the 1967 Tour de France was the catalyst for the Council of Europe to enter the anti-doping policy arena, and the positive drug test of Ben Johnson at the Seoul Olympics resulted in a major policy change towards doping by the Canadian government and by the IOC (Dubin, 1990). Here, the Canadian government established the Commission of Inquiry into the use of drugs and banned practices intended to increase athletic performance. The inquiry was overseen by Chief Justice Dubin, who, through the course of the inquiry, overheard a litany of testimony about the use of performance-enhancing drugs in sport. On the back of his highly critical report, the Canadian government established, in 1991, the Canadian Anti-Doping Organization. However, it was the widespread and systematic practice of doping that was uncovered in *L'Affaire Festina* at the 1998 Tour de France that 'cut through the policy inertia in the late 1990s and eventually led to the establishment of the World Anti-Doping Agency (WADA) in 1999' (Houlihan, 2011: 211).[7]

In terms of governance, sovereignty and authority, WADA is accountable to the IOC as well as to national Olympic federations and to national governments. Initially funded entirely by the IOC, WADA now receives half of its budget from the IOC, with the two hundred-odd governments around the world who have signed up to the Agency contributing the rest. Alongside developmental research into new methods of detection and new forms of doping, WADA's key responsibility (and indeed its main challenge) is monitoring and enforcing the World Anti-Doping Code, the uniform, harmonized set of regulations and requirements to which all athletes, governments and representatives from its signatory countries are expected to adhere.

While I won't dwell on the key principles and requirements of the code, there has been a gradual shift in its remit since its inception in 1999 from drug detection to more 'upstream' educational work with athletes (often involving athletes who have been previously suspended or banned from their sport for doping offences), and an increased involvement of governments in this process. That is, there has been, as Mazanov notes, a shift from 'detection-based deterrence to prevention-based deterrence' (2009: 273). This has had some implications for the governance of WADA, for while the IOC ostensibly shares equal authority with national governments, in practice, it is playing an increasingly peripheral role, as anti-doping policy becomes more and more the remit of national public policy (with links to public health and welfare), evidenced in the stance taken by the Council of Europe and the commitment to anti-doping required by its member states (Houlihan, 2011).

Indeed, the formation of WADA ruptured the traditional sovereignty of the IOC and their perceived rule over anti-doping policy. As Houlihan notes:

> Today the IOC's role as the putative leader in the 'fight against doping' has been assumed by the World Anti-Doping Agency (WADA), but for many years the IOC was the acknowledged global lead organisation and much of the current anti-doping framework was initiated by the Committee. (Houlihan, 2011: 101)

This presents some challenges for global policy, and for enforcing a harmonized global code of practice. I mentioned earlier that many of the changes in the sporting environment that globalization has helped facilitate have had a direct impact on anti-doping policy (e.g. athletic mobility, international competition and training outside home jurisdictions). As well as the practical challenges of ensuring a coordinated approach to anti-doping policy (differences in time zones and languages for out-of-competition testing, for example), there is also considerable variation in interpretation – of the policy, of the list of banned substances, of the requirements of out-of-competition testing – between and within countries that speak to some of the debates about the global and the local, universalism and particularism discussed in the previous chapter.

The four 'c's in regulating anti-doping

In many ways, these challenges correspond to Houlihan's 'four issues associated with complexity, capacity, commitment and compliance' (2011: 104). I'll expand on these terms below, using the approach to anti-doping taken in Sweden and other Scandinavian countries to illustrate.

Briefly, **complexity** refers to:

> The tendency for international legal and quasi-legal agreements to become more complex over time as policy-makers seeks to close loop-holes, satisfy legitimate sectional interests/special cases, respond to change in the external environment etc. The best codes and conventions are those that retain the clarity that is the product of parsimony. Complexity confuses implementers and those that the code is designed to protect. (Houlihan, 2011: 104)

The issues of athletic mobility, international competition, differences in languages and time zones mentioned previously would be examples of changes in the external environment that make anti-doping policy more 'complex'.

In the case of Sweden, however, there are several mechanisms in place that serve to reduce the complexity of implementation. The enforcement of codes and regulation is a collaborative responsibility between the Swedish Sports Confederation (SSC) and the other Scandinavian countries. This system has been in place since 1983 (well before the introduction of the first World Anti-Doping Code in 1999). The crux of this uniform, coordinated approach to monitoring anti-doping practice is that all Scandinavian countries sign up to the Scandinavian anti-doping agreement (*Nordiska Antidopingkonventionen*), which is the only multilateral anti-doping agreement in the world that allows the unlimited testing of each country's athletes (Gilberg, Breivik & Loland, 2006; Hanstad & Skille, 2008; Hoberman & Møller, 2004). At the same time, however, Denmark and Norway have established independent anti-doping agencies (Wagner & Hanstad, 2011). What this means is that the degree of complexity added by out-of-country competition and training, athletic mobility and language differences is considerably reduced, with the only caveat being that athletes must be present within a Scandinavian country when required for testing (Hanstad & Loland, 2009). To maintain the pressure on a harmonized approach to drug testing that can offset the issue of complexity, Swedish representatives are members of many of the international sports associations that include anti-doping activities on their agendas, and Sweden is part of the multilateral International Anti-Doping Arrangement (along with Australia, Canada and the Netherlands) which enables the sharing of good practice and serves as a vehicle for lobbying within the wider political and sporting communities.

In other words, there is a concerted effort to maintain anti-doping as a policy priority within Swedish sport. As Andrèn and Holm note, the 'fundamental aim

of the Swedish sports movement's international policy is to influence and support the development of internationally harmonized, high quality anti-doping
programmes, by its example, its international activities and its collaboration'
(2008: 7). In addition, much public health and education work has been undertaken in Sweden, in much the same way that anti-smoking messages have been
adopted in health promotion work in other countries (Chapman, 2010).
Positioned as a 'public health' issue, anti-doping becomes a concern of health and
body care, rather than a debate about ethics or morality; a position that has been
suggested as being crucial in advancing anti-doping in Sweden, more than Norway
or Denmark (Hanstad & Waddington, 2009; Wagner & Hanstad, 2011).

To turn now to the issue of '**capacity**', Houlihan notes that 'capacity is a more
significant issue [than complexity], but less so for WADA and more for the
organisations on which it relies for policy implementation, i.e. NADOs, international federations and NOCs' (2011: 104). Mention has already been made of
the sometimes limited capacity and resources of national anti-doping organizations (NADOs) and national Olympic Committees (NOCs) to ensure adherence
to testing regimes and punishment by and of their athletes within their sports
and jurisdictions, given the high level of transnational cooperation (and
resources) required. The Scandinavian system that allows the unlimited testing
of each country's athletes helps both balance and build capacity for the implementation of the 'whereabouts system' by effectively guaranteeing that there is,
at least, a multilateral sharing of the minimum necessary resources (administrative capacity, expertise and financial and legal support). However, critics maintain that the whereabouts system amounts to little more than a 'form of
surveillance, after the fashion of "Big Brother"' (Hanstad & Loland, 2009). The
relationship between the whereabouts system and athletes' civil rights is discussed further in Chapter 8 – Mega-events, sports policy and human rights.

Commitment refers to the potentially difficult task of maintaining momentum
and enthusiasm for anti-doping, not only because there are competing pressures
within governments and federations for anti-doping resources, but also because
demonstrating progress and value for money is extremely difficult, if not simply
impossible, to do. Over the last forty years or so, anti-doping activists have had
to be alert to those 'windows of opportunity' when policy can be advanced.
Most of those opportunities have arisen as a result of scandal and crisis, which
is a fragile basis on which to build and deepen commitment to a policy. After a
period of time what was once considered scandalous is considered routine; that
is, doping practices – and responses – become normalized.

In the case of Sweden, it would seem that this is a greater issue for smaller, less
'joined-up' organizations and federations in their attempts at policy implementation. Mention has already been made of the limited capacity of many organizing
committees and federations to implement one of the fundamental elements of the
Anti-Doping Code – the whereabouts system. Sweden and, by association, her
partner countries have the resources – administrative capacity, expertise, finance
and legal support – to implement this aspect of the code. The challenge remains,
however, to ensure that smaller federations, organizations and committees,

particularly those in developing countries and the Global South, are supported through similar resource opportunities to those offered by UNESCO (United Nations Education, Scientific and Cultural Organization) through the International Convention against Doping in Sport (2005), thus enabling the development of capacity globally.

Building on some of the issues of governance and authority over policy implicit in the Swedish model, Houlihan's (1994) conceptualization of 'reach' and 'response' offers a useful framework to theorize these disjunctive approaches to policy enforcement, as his approach is informed by the need to appreciate the variety within the policy process that is highlighted by the complexity of global anti-doping policy, and its situatedness within the institutional architecture of supranational, national and sub-national governance and sovereignty. For Houlihan, 'reach' refers to the 'depth of penetration by the global culture of the local culture', whereas 'response' refers to the 'reaction of the recipient culture' (1994: 370). Framed as such, policy within individual countries will thus vary due to the differential 'reach' of global influences and the variability in 'response' within countries. In light of this, we can see how the essentially harmonized Anti-Doping Code is then negotiated and applied within countries.

There are, of course, some more general challenges that cut across the reach and response of nations. 'Commitment' and 'compliance' are widespread problems for governments and federations around the world. Given the persistence of doping in sport and the subsequent normalization of particular doping practices and substances, it is very difficult to evidence that real progress has been made in the 'fight against doping'; that is, to the shift towards prevention rather than detection deterrence to which countries are committed. In an already crowded policy space, this inevitably puts a question mark over whether allocating resources (both financial and human) is a sound investment. This is a challenge for all governments and federations as they fight for their share of the policy pie and the resources that then follow.

Equally, demonstrating policy compliance is a difficult task for all. At present, compliance with the WADA Code is monitored by little more than a self-completion questionnaire, widely criticized in other evaluations of organizational compliance (Houlihan, 2011). Certainly, more systematic (and frequent) means of monitoring such as inspection visits would be expensive but, as Houlihan invites, 'the funding of independent monitoring visits by the IOC would be an important way for the Committee to provide a high profile endorsement … and ensure public recognition of its continuing support for anti-doping' (2011: 106). Equally, new forms of communication – such as those described in the following chapter – may offer emergent means of monitoring compliance by national federations.

So far, I have examined doping as a public policy problem that governments respond to, with varying degrees of success, within their national jurisdiction. My argument has been that this is increasingly difficult to do in the context of globalization. As Houlihan and Green note, 'the assumption that the major determinants of public policy are confined within sovereign state boundaries has, in recent years, become progressively less persuasive as an increasing

LIVERPOOL JOHN MOORES UNIVERSITY
LEARNING SERVICES

number of formerly domestic policy issues are now embedded in a series of supranational policy networks' (2008: 9). So significant have supranational actors become in the policy process that commentators such as Andersen and Eliassen (1993) argue that the proper focus for analysis should be on the global or the regional policy arena rather than the sphere of domestic or sub-national policy. In addition to challenging the sovereignty of national governments, the supranational figure of the cultural intermediary or the policy entrepreneur now occupies a key role in influencing the policy agenda and in determining the 'reach' of policy.

CULTURAL INTERMEDIARIES AND POLICY ENTREPRENEURS[8]

The notion of a cultural intermediary already has much currency in analyses of the production of sporting mega-events, and it is possible to extend our concep-tualizing of the nature of brokerage to that of the policy entrepreneur; a power-ful elite or 'cosmocracy', to return to Held and McGrew's notion of corporate actors and players. The policy implications of mounting mega-events, and the centrality of sports mega-events to analyses of global sports policy, are the sub-ject of chapters in the second section of the book. The analytical point here, however, is that the globally mediated nature of these events has given rise to a particularly influential cultural intermediary or policy broker who is increas-ingly involved in setting the policy agenda in the global order.

Cultural Brokers and Intermediaries

There is no doubt that sporting bodies such as the Fédération International de Football Association, the International Olympic Committee or La Société du Tour de France are powerful organizations which enjoy wealth, celebrity, status and global influence on a scale with few rivals. They are what Sudjic calls 'the flying circus of the perpetually jet lagged' (2005: 117). As much media cover-age and anecdotal evidence attests, the major events staged by these sporting bodies – the Olympic Games, football's World Cup and the Tour de France – are run by a coterie of select personnel who exercise an extraordinary degree of institutional power over many aspects of the event itself.

It is here that I introduce the notion of the 'cultural broker', that occupational category which works the boundary between production and consumption, between spectacle and spectator (Negus, 2002). Television and radio producers, journalists, public relations officers, marketing entrepreneurs and advertising agents, to name but a few, these brokers are part of an occupational group who specialize in the production and dissemination of symbolic goods and com-modities – the very stuff of which mega-events are made. Horne, for example, examines the role of architects in the production and design of the material infrastructure of the hugely iconic stadia associated with mega-events (e.g. the Bird's Nest stadium in Beijing), arguing that these men and women form part of the 'transnational capitalist class' (Sklair, 2001). Working to produce (and profit from) the ideologies, images and resources of popular culture, these brokers have become an imperative class in contemporary times. As the anthropologist Ade Peace points out, brokers are both 'middlemen of renown and masters in the politics of cultural dissembling' (1998: 278).

In the cultural broker, we see the dovetailing of several different intellectual legacies. First, 'the broker' evokes Ewen's (1973) earlier conceptualization of 'captains of consciousness', although Ewen reserves his term for brokers of the advertising industry. Second, the idea of the broker resonates with the notion of the 'cultural intermediary' coined by Bourdieu (1987). And third, the new cultural broker has come to assume the role of the 'power elite' first coined by C. Wright Mills ([1959] 2000) more than forty years ago. In a specifically sporting context, the notion of the broker is not incompatible with the idea of the 'sportsnet' popularized by Nixon (1993, 1996).

It is the idea of the 'power elite', however, that has the most mileage as far as the brokerage of [mega-events] is concerned. As Mills sees it, 'the power elite' – groups such as warlords, celebrities and chief executives – as well as 'the big rich' form a tightly knit centre of power that is, at its core, basically irresponsible. Critically, and it is a point I develop later, Mills argues that power elites are not solitary rulers, but rather, it is their interpersonal support and associations that make them so very powerful. In other words, it is by exercising their institutional authority and interpersonal influence that these new power elites or brokers impose their own political imprint upon the cultural landscape of postmodernity.

[As cultural intermediaries], much of the work of the cultural broker can be evidenced in the staging of the sporting mega-event. Journalists, photographers, sports administrators, publicists and sports agents are indisputably key personnel in the staging of the Summer and Winter Olympics, football's World Cup and Formula One Grand Prix, among others. In each instance, the role of the broker is to present a series of creative and well-chosen ideas and images about the event which serve to direct the greater public's understanding of the particular mega-event in question. When orchestrated by these ideological entrepreneurs, mega-events never just happen. They are *made* to happen by the broker, whose work it is to impose definitions and understandings upon the spectacle, which are then apprehended directly (at the event itself) or indirectly through the global media coverage of it. In other words, it is through the work of the cultural broker that we see the undeniable role of human agency in mounting a mega-event.

What is imperative to note, however, is that brokerage often requires processes of disguise, diversion and discursive manipulation. Much of the influence of the broker in the staging of a mega-event comes through in an entrepreneurial discourse which seeks to persuade the mass audience that the fruits of the brokers' labour will be of wide-ranging and long-lasting public benefit. There is an almost implicit belief, for example, that hosting the Olympic Games, the World Cup or the Tour de France will provide a significant boost to regional and national economies, with mega-events now assuming key roles in tourism marketing and promotion strategies, and these claims are interrogated further in Chapter 6. Hoffman (2006), with reference to neoliberal governmentality in China, writes of 'the patriot professional', a nice image to describe the work of brokerage in the context of the practices of image manipulation and cultural management that are central to the work of the cultural broker or intermediary.

Policy brokers and entrepreneurs

In terms of the policy process, these kinds of brokers are increasingly common. The watershed Los Angeles Olympic Games, with its unheralded scale of commercial involvement, gave rise to a 'cosmocracy' of corporate actors and players. After 1984, a veritable cabal of transnational players began to assert influence over the policy workings of sporting events and associated practices (such as uniform requirements). While corporations like McDonalds or Reebok and sponsors and broadcasters had no formal role in the governance of events like the Olympics, they nonetheless still made claims to authority in the process of Olympic governance. In addition to the IOC and FIFA, 'media corporations, transnational sponsors, politicians, members of the bid team and national organizations have been considered as constituent parts of the network of power and influence that produce, mediate and transact sports mega-events' (Horne, 2011: 220). They are, as MacNeil maintains, 'part of the "circuit of cultural production"' (1996: 105).

Indeed, within this cosmocracy, we have seen policy brokers or policy entrepreneurs emerge, which raise questions for the sovereignty of sports governance, and the management of policy decisions that relate to the staging of global sporting mega-events. Entrepreneurs such as Juan Antonio Samaranch, Jacques Rogge or Sepp Blatter exercise extraordinary power and leverage over what mega-events can look like. By implication, this exercise of power must inevitably constrain or enable policy choices and decisions. As Carter notes, 'the reach of governing bodies that run [mega-events] is undeniable in terms of how they shape the practices and organizations of sport' (2011b: 132). Close, Askew and Xin similarly note that there is an 'evolving and strengthening *global power elite*, an elite the power of which is accorded in the advance of the *global political economy* in accordance with the progress of globalization' (2007: 35, emphasis in original). These elites govern, even dictate [mega-events] and, with the help of these events, 'exercise power and control over the rest, the non-elites or the ordinary people' (Close, Askew & Xin, 2007: 35).

The analytical point to emerge from this discussion of the policy broker or entrepreneur is that policy-making is essentially a process of structured interaction between a whole range of actors, with varying degrees of agency and authority. Thus, sports policy-making, and the governance of sport does not operate within a field of coherent global power, but is cut through by competing tensions and interests. In their analysis of the 2010 Commonwealth Games in Delhi,

Majundar and Mehta (2010) describe how political bosses in India took control of national sporting bodies and then stayed there, operating largely as autocrats, which resulted in the Indian Congress moving to restrict the terms for Presidents of Federations and then set an upper age limit of seventy for office holders. In other words, in the governance of global sport, we have what Coleman (1990) describes as 'disjoint constitutions' where one set of actors create arrangements that impose constraints and demands on different sets of actors.

CONCLUSION

This chapter has been concerned with the governance of sports policy in the context of globalization. The interdependence between supra-, national and sub-national organizations means that the iterative process of the development of public policies, such as those which relate to anti-doping in sport, is a complex and multifaceted one that involves the interaction of a range of actors from the transnational 'cosmocracy' to local and regional individuals and interest groups.

While many of the issues of governance and authority I have addressed are issues for social and public policy more broadly, the global diffusion of sport has created a form of governance which raises a number of questions about power, rule, sovereignty and authority. Contested claims to authority are made by supranational organizations like the IOC, along with those made by cultural brokers or policy entrepreneurs, in setting a particular agenda for sports policy that necessarily emphasizes and constrains other policy interests and priorities. Indeed, 'policy' is a complex process involving a range of actors with competing interests, who may be inside or outside government.

Analyses of the interactions between supra-, national and sub-national level organizations and governing bodies also return us to one of the central debates in studies of globalization more broadly; the tension between homogeneity and heterogeneity or between universality and particularity. Sports policy, in the context of globalization, is increasingly sensitive to the politics of universalism, and we see this most clearly in the adoption of an internationally harmonized code on doping in sport. The World Anti-Doping Agency's worldwide policy on performance-enhancing drugs raises questions as to whether such global policies represent a return to the 'cultural homogeneity' of early forms of globalization, or offer a challenge for a more nuanced form of policy-making that can take into account local (and national) variations when considering policy compliance and uptake.

Certainly, the notion of global policy raises the question of whether the adoption of policy across countries will result in a regulatory, normative form of social control, whereby countries are expected to adhere to unilaterally imposed policy directives that are certainly fashioned after global, cultural imperialism. Here, the fundamental question remains whether global, regional and national policy regimes can work synergistically in the same direction, or whether they are designed and implemented in a fragmented and incoherent manner (Yeates &

Holden, 2009). The challenges of implementing anti-doping policy suggest that synergy may take some time to achieve.

Moreover, studies of the global governance of sport, and sports policy, also raise a number of question that are classic issues for political science and sociology, namely issues of 'representation, responsibility, accountability, agency-structure and, above all, power and abuse' (Sugden & Tomlinson, 2005: 26). Extending these ideas of policy-making and policy brokerage, the following chapter examines the role of new forms of technology and the impact that emergent modes of communication have had on the reach of policy and public expectations of autonomy and accountability.

BOX 3.1   QUESTIONS FOR DISCUSSION

- Which level of influence (national, supranational and sub-national) plays the greatest part in shaping the sports policy agenda? Can you differentiate?

- What changes in the external global environment have impacted upon the governance of anti-doping policy?

- What roles do cultural brokers and policy entrepreneurs play in the making and governance of sports policy?

SUGGESTED FURTHER READINGS

Carter, T. (2011) The Olympics as sovereign subject maker. In J. Sugden & A. Tomlinson (eds), *Watching the Olympics: Politics, power and representation*. London: Routledge (pp. 55–68).

Chappelet, J.-L. & Kübler-Mabbot, B. (2008) *The International Olympic Committee and the Olympic system: The governance of world sport*. London: Routledge.

Green, M. & Houlihan, B. (2006) Governmentality, modernisation and the 'disciplining' of national sport policy organizations: Athletics in Australia and the United Kingdom. *Sociology of Sport Journal*, 23(1): 47–71.

Houlihan, B. (2005) Public sector sport policy: Developing a framework for analysis. *International Review for the Sociology of Sport*, 40(2): 163–85.

Sugden, J. & Tomlinson, A. (2005) Not for the good of the game. In L. Allison (ed.), *The global politics of sport: The role of global institutions in sport*. London: Routledge (pp. 26–45).

Notes

1   Henry (2007) notes that there are two other models of governance: corporate or 'good governance' and political governance. These are less relevant to the governance of sport and sports policy, so are only noted here.

2 See Darby (2003) or Sugden and Tomlinson (1998) for analyses of the politics of universalism that surround FIFA. Relatedly, MacAloon (2011) offers an ethno-graphically based analysis of the work of the IOC 2000 Commission, the official body established in the wake of the IOC bribery scandals during the bidding process for the 2002 Salt Lake City Winter Olympics.

3 Exceptions being the work of Jennings (1996), Lloyd, Warren and Hammer (2008), Pound (2004) and Senn (1999), who are highly critical of the inner workings of the IOC.

4 The tangible and intangible benefits and the increasingly contested nature of the perceived social, cultural and economic benefits of hosting mega-events are the subject of chapters in Part Two.

5 Incidentally, Henri Pelissier won the race the previous year.

6 Most notably, in 1967, the British rider Tom Simpson died while climbing the slopes of Mont Ventoux during the thirteenth stage of the race. Wobbling his way up the mountain, Simpson fell twice. Both times he remounted his bicycle, before his heart eventually stopped beating and he died on the side of the road. The post mortem found traces of amphetamines in his body and a stash of the drug were later found among his personal belongings. As Simpson lay dying by the side of the road, he uttered the words that have become the stuff of cycling legend – 'put me back on my bike' – final words that speak of classic stimulant abuse as amphetamines cancel out any warning sign of approaching exhaustion that the body may be trying to send to the brain.

7 On the eve of the Tour's departure from Dublin, the *soigneur* for the Festina team was stopped on the Franco–Belgian border with a haul of drugs in his car. Riders on the Festina squad, along with their *Directeur Sportive*, then admitted to systematic doping within the team and were expelled from the race. The 'affair' highlighted wide-spread doping within the Tour – the hotel room of the TVM team was subsequently searched – leading riders to boycott latter stages of the race, resulting in one stage being annulled.

8 Much of this section has been previously published in Palmer, C. (2000) Spin doctors and sports brokers: Researching elites in contemporary sport – a research note on the Tour de France. *International Review for the Sociology of Sport*, 35(3): 385–98.

4

NETWORK POLICY – NEW TECHNOLOGIES AND GLOBAL SPORTS POLICY

THIS CHAPTER

- explores the changing nature of policy production, dissemination and reception through the emergence of new forms of communication;
- examines the impact of transnational communication on the evidence base in the (comparative) analysis of sports policy;
- explores the role of new media in facilitating 'mediated mobilization' (Lievrouw, 2006) against policy decisions and initiatives.

INTRODUCTION

In his 2009 book, *Communication Power*, Manuel Castells argues that we are living in the midst of a revolution in communication technologies that affects the ways in which we think, feel and behave. Chiming with some of the ideas from the previous chapter – the rise of cosmocracy, the ascendancy of cultural brokers and policy entrepreneurs – Castells suggests that the media (mass and web-based alike) has become the space in which political and business power is played out; power now lies in the hands of those who understand or control communication. This argument has much resonance with the ideas I develop in this chapter about the increasing, and changing, role of the media and communication technologies in shaping and controlling the production, dissemination and reception of sports policy. As with other aspects of the sporting landscape, the effects of new media on global sports policy have been significant. New forms of communication and changing social relationships with technology have had a particular impact on how policy is debated and disseminated by policy makers and policy brokers as well as how it is received, interpreted and challenged by consumers of policy decision and directives.

As such, this chapter explores the changing nature of sports policy against the backdrop of technological communications that are part and parcel of globalization. Drawing on the concept of 'connectivity' (Tomlinson, 1999), I look at three, not unrelated, issues that have emerged out of the 'technoscape' (Appadurai, 1996). First, I explore the changing nature of policy production and policy dissemination afforded by these new technologies. Second, I look at the emergent nature of the analysis of sports policy that the communication of policy across transnational borders and boundaries now enables. Third, I examine the role of new media in facilitating what Lievrouw (2006) calls 'mediated mobilization' against policy decisions and initiatives. This mediated mobilization plays a key role in organizing dissent in ways that reflect the heightened reflexivity that is embedded in the 'disconnect' of globalization (Robertson, 1992: 8). As Leonard notes, 'technological innovations have changed the landscape of sports media and culture ... narratives, identities, and even the representational field of contemporary sports culture is contested through and because of new media' (2009: 2).

Before developing this analysis, some preliminary points on the nature of this changing mediated world as it relates to sport and contemporary life more broadly provide a more general context to the particular dynamics of policy-making, dissemination and reception that sit within it.

Connectivity and Communication

There is no question that new forms of technological communication have developed apace in the twenty-first century. From the early days of the Internet, where communication was largely restricted to military and government activity, there is now a flourishing web (literally) of interconnected computer, telephone and optical networks. These have radically changed our lifestyle and consumption habits, in which, I would argue, policy is assuredly implicated. Online shopping has replaced personal visits to stores and supermarkets, with implications for the ongoing viability of the latter.[1] Medical advice is sought (and diagnoses made) via the Internet and cheap, often illegal, pharmaceuticals are bought and sold online. 'Friends' are made and poked via social networking sites, and snippets of news and gossip are 'tweeted'. Budding musicians can record a song in their bedroom and upload it to *YouTube* within minutes, while in Benghazi, Libya, four friends can establish and broadcast the first ever English-language radio station in open defiance of the Gaddafi regime (Williams, 2011).[2]

Indeed, people now have access to a whole raft of new technologies of communication, and these are increasingly occupying key places among our leisure pursuits. A 2005 'Time Use' survey from the United States, summarized in Rojek, for example, places 'watching television as the leisure activity that occupies most time [for women] although this is being challenged, and may already have been overtaken by internet surfing and mobile phone use' (Rojek, 2010: 241). This is a point to which I will return, for the cultural literacy that many people now have with these kinds of technologies, and their growing centrality to leisure time, affords them an especial role in harnessing dissent and resistance to policy initiatives and directives as well as their use in *communicating* policy initiatives and directives. Certainly, through interactive voting for contestants on reality television programmes – *The X Factor, Eurovision, Dancing with the Stars* – we are already seeing a movement towards the 'electronicization' of public opinion and the democratic process which has the potential to transform our social, cultural and political lives. As Castells notes, 'the shift from traditional mass media to a system of horizontal communication networks organized around the Internet and wireless communication has introduced a multiplicity of communication patterns at the source of a fundamental cultural transformation, as virtuality becomes an essential dimension of our reality' (2010: xviii).

This use of communications technologies describes what the cultural theorist John Tomlinson refers to as 'connectivity'. For Tomlinson,

> Connectivity pretty much defines our use of communications technologies – mobile phones, computers, e-mail, the Internet. In all these ways, it is quite clear that we are living in a much more globally connected world today than even 20 years ago, and in longer historical terms, the level of global interdependence is without precedent. ... If we add to these technological developments innovations in media institutions themselves – for instance 24-hour television, online news services, multimedia delivery systems via domestic broadband provision – there emerges a sense of what we could call the increasing 'immediacy' of modern global culture. (1999: 2)

Such observations are shared elsewhere. Building on the notions of immediacy and interdependence in Tomlinson's comments, Giulianotti and Robertson succinctly note that 'connectivity' registers the 'social electricity' of globalization (2007b: 62). For Tomlinson and Giulianotti and Robertson alike, 'connectivity' captures the 'rapidly developing and ever-densening network of interconnections and interdependences that capture modern life' (Tomlinson, 1999: 2). As Hardt and Negri (2001) and Leung et al. (2005) also contend, our existence in a global era is characterized by increased interconnectivity; by an array of national and supranational organizations operating across different geographical spaces. Finally, such observations strike a chord with those of Sassen, who notes that '...the new networked, computer-centred technologies allow multiple people to participate simultaneously in a digital domain ... [people] are part of an incipient global commons' (2009: 116).

These ideas of interconnectedness, facilitated by the circulation of new media content across new media systems, have resonance with sport more broadly, and a considerable body of literature has examined the changing relationship of the sports fan or audience to the sports/media complex (Davis & Duncan, 2006; Hutchins, 2008; Leonard, 2009; Scherer, 2007). Cleland (2011), for example, argues that the media–fan relationship has changed (and been strengthened) due to the increasing number of 'active' fans; fans who actively use media texts such as radio phone-ins and their self-produced 'fanzines' in opposition to more passive fans; fans who support their club though television and similar forms of media. In my own work on fans of Australian Rules football, I have outlined the ways in which rules, rituals, norms and behaviours are shared virtually via the World Wide Web (Palmer & Thompson, 2007). As Leonard (2009: 3) notes, '...new media technologies have facilitated the transformation of a passive sports fan who once simply received/experienced media texts into an "auteur" increasingly responsible for generating "media sports texts"' (Rowe, 1999: 168)'.

While much work has focused on the ways in which new media enables fans to assert power and agency *vis-à-vis* their experience of their team, often from afar (Ben-Porat, 2000; Farred, 2002), far less has examined the way in which new media has equally changed the relationship of sports policy consumers to the policy-making process. As I argue later in this chapter, in as much as sports fans have done so, policy consumers have equally mobilized new technologies to express dissent, power and agency with regard to particular policy decisions and directives that affect their sporting lives, as well as their experiences of and attitudes towards the broader political milieu within which sports policy (and policy-making) is located.

POLICY AND NEW MEDIA

To provide some broader context here, politics and policy are most assuredly implicated in the connectivity of new media (Baum, 2008; Dahlgren, 2005; Negrine, 2008). In addition to the cultural broker who works the boundary between the production and consumption of the images and narratives carried through this new media, policy makers and political figureheads – those responsible for the public governance of policy – are equally located within the politics of this new media, and the new media of public policy, as it relates, in this case, to global sport.

These new technologies are a matter for policy production, not so much in terms of the decisions that are made about a particular policy direction, but in terms of the production *values* that underpin the policy cycle in which that agenda is then made public. Colebatch (2002, 2006a) outlines an elliptical approach to the development of policy which begins with the identification of key issues, moves through a process of policy analysis and the development and review of policy instruments, before leading into a period of consultation, communication and evaluation (see Figure 4.1 below).

It is in the stages of consultation and communication where these new technologies come into greatest effect; they are now key points in the policy cycle in which policy, policy-making and, indeed, policy *makers* are both broadcast to and then consumed by a global media audience.

The growing use of new technologies in the political arena has prompted burgeoning academic interest. Ward and Lusoli (2005), for example, have examined

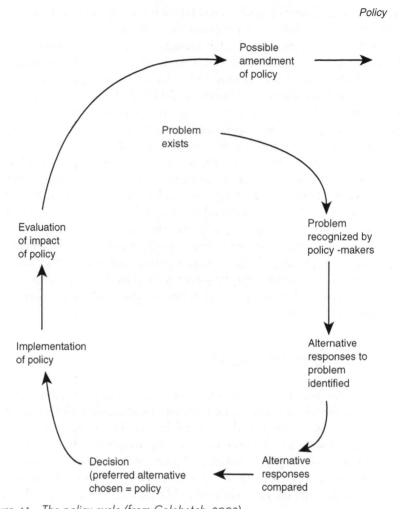

Figure 4.1   *The policy cycle (from Colebatch, 2002)*

Colebatch, Hal, *Policy*, © 2002. Reproduced with the kind permission of Open University Press. All rights reserved.

the use of the Internet by Westminster politicians in Great Britain, arguing that a growing number of politicians are now capitalizing on the Internet as a way of communicating, with a heightened sense of intimacy and immediacy, with the electorate. Elsewhere, Francoli and Ward (2008) have provided a comparative study of 'blogging' by ministers in Canada and the UK. The democratic, 'relatively barrier free' (Wilson, 2007: 458) medium of the Internet has also been adopted by activists operating from within more repressive political regimes (Ignatow, 2011), a point to which I will return when considering the dynamics of social movements in the context of policy resistance and dissent.

So significant is the Internet, and associated platforms, as a medium of communication with regard to public policy (including sports policy) that there is now an entire scholarly journal devoted to the subject. As the Editor in Chief of

Policy & Internet notes: 'the Internet is now the most important international medium of communication and information exchange, embedded in interactions between citizens, firms, governments and NGOs, and bringing with it new practices, norms and structures' (Margetts, 2011). It is Margetts' last observation about the Internet bringing with it new practices, norms and structures that is of particular relevance here. In addition to the change in the nature of policy dissemination – there is an immediacy and availability to policy in a way that we've never seen before – there is now an expectation of public access to and accountability of government decision-making and policy rhetoric.

Importantly for this chapter, these new technologies and ways of communicating and connecting with one another have also changed forms of dissemination and reception (each forms of 'connectivity' in themselves). As I'll turn to now, these have important implications for the reach and response (Houlihan, 1994) of policy – in this case, sports policy.

POLICY DISSEMINATION AND COMMUNICATION IN THE AGE OF CONNECTIVITY

As I've begun to suggest, the growth of these forms of technology and their inherently public, shared dimensions has meant that policy can now be communicated in very different ways. Prior to the advent of new media, the Internet in particular, very few people saw, heard or read policy, other than what was 'brokered' for their consumption via traditional forms of media – the nightly news or the morning newspaper. Policy decisions, transcripts from the sittings of Parliament or accounts from within organizations that described policy directives (annual reports, mission statements, strategy documents, and the like) were more often than not paper-based, housed in archives, and accessible only to those inside the organization. The sharing of public policy (findings, recommendations, new initiatives, political and party priorities, and so on) was largely 'closed' to a limited audience who were privy to reports, or who were present when the policy instruments or recommendations were put forward in Parliament or the boardroom, in the case of policy relating to supranational cosmocracies. As has been documented elsewhere (MacAloon, 2011; Palmer, 2000; Sugden & Tomlinson, 1998, 2005), these organizations are hierarchical, with a closed bureaucracy rarely experienced in other forms of governance. Having hitherto operated as a large private club, effectively outside legal and ethical scrutiny, the closed nature within which policy and other decision-making occurs in these 'cosmocratic' organizations and government departments is now coming under greater public scrutiny, with expectations of accountability and transparency increasingly commonplace.

With an approximated 10% of the world estimated to have access to connected computing, along with desktop publishing and associated software packages, policy dissemination has been pushed into a far greater public arena. The

German sociologist Jürgen Habermas wrote of 'the public sphere' as the 'realm of our social life in which something approaching public opinion could be formed' (1962/1989: 30). Connected communications are increasingly the mechanism through which public opinion is formed and debated, and the policy process is now one, inevitably, of public pressure. The web pages of government departments and agencies are a significant source of information in relation to policy initiatives, directives, recommendations and priorities. In the click of a mouse, it is now possible to download, and send to a friend, the full text of President Obama's announcement of the death of Osama bin Laden (Politico, 2011), capturing a flavour of a particular set of geo-politics in an instant, while television channels like Al-Jazeera can offer an alternative reading of events, thereby opening up the possibilities for contentious politics. Equally, it is now possible to have a list of banned substances under the WADA Anti-Doping Code sent to your smartphone as an 'app' (Ó Conchúir, 2011). Certainly, the Internet–policy interface brings to life Robertson's argument that globalization represents 'the compression of the world and the intensification of consciousness of the world as a whole' (1992: 8) and creates a new dynamic to the public sphere.

The introduction of new technologies into the policy arena has facilitated a particular normative shift with regard to the practices and structures of policy analysis, giving rise, in particular, to a number of changes in the policy process, including the rise of 'evidence-based' policy-making and a more sophisticated (and problematic) comparative study of sports policy. Here, my focus shifts slightly, to that of the relationship between research and policy, in terms of the impacts that the increased transparency of the technological society has had on the policy process; that is, to the impacts of 'connectivity' upon what Colebatch (2006b) refers to as 'the work' of policy.

The Changing Nature of Policy Analysis: Evidence-Based Policy-Making

One of the upshots of the increased availability of mediated 'policy traffic' is the expectation of accountability of policy makers for the policy decisions that they take. In the context of a global economic recession and its crippling effects around the world, and with concomitant spending cuts across many government sectors, an increasing pressure has been placed upon governments and organizations, in this case sporting organizations, to 'prove' that the policy they initiated or the programme they implemented did, in fact, deliver on its objectives or, more precisely, did deliver 'value for money'. Within policy communities, there is an increased pressure to search for knowledge so as to demonstrate 'what works' in order to then justify policy-making and implementation.

Terms like 'evidence' and 'best practice' are now fully incorporated into the discourse of sports policy, extending, as Hulme (2006) maintains, the language of 'new managerialism' in which the work of teachers, health workers and other public service professionals is regulated and codified through the promotion of an 'evidence-based' notion of good practice (Hulme & Hulme, 2008: 61–2). This shift towards 'evidence-based' or 'evidence-informed' policy-making provides some important insights into global sports policy. In evidence-based sports policy, there is a search for appropriate knowledge and expertise that can help justify the decisions that underpin policy-making. In the context of globalization, this becomes a global search for knowledge, ideas, language and practice which policy makers and policy entrepreneurs across the globe can learn from one another. New ways of communicating have accelerated the pace with which this policy knowledge travels, as research reports, academic articles and other forms of knowledge and evidence are circulated from think tanks and research institutes to governments as part of the '"weaponry" to mould and shape policy' (Solesbury, 2001). As I'll come to later, when reflecting on comparative sports policy analysis within this 'emerging knowledge-based society' (OECD, 2001), this is not without its problems or challenges.

For the moment, some context and definitions will suffice. The shift towards evidence-based policy-making developed in the United Kingdom under the New Labour government of Tony Blair. The 1999 White Paper *Modernising Government* (Cabinet Office, 1999) set out this particular agenda of evidence-informed policy, arguing that government departments must:

> Produce policies that really deal with problems, that are forward look-
> ing and shaped by evidence rather than a response to short-term pres-
> sures that tackle causes not symptoms ... this Government expects
> more of policy makers. ... More new ideas, more willingness to ques-
> tion inherited ways of doing things, better use of evidence and research
> in policy-making and better focus on policies that will deliver long-
> term goals. (Cabinet Office, 1999)

In such statements, the 'simple logic of rational decision making that underpins most basic policy transfer models, namely that policy can be better made by seek-ing "scientific" knowledge or evidence from expert organizations' (Hulme & Hulme, 2008: 62) is treated as largely self-evident. I address elsewhere (Palmer, 2008) some of the challenges for research transfer – the process by which 'evi-dence' enters into the policy-making arena – but the crux of my argument is worth repeating here for it illustrates the complexity of the evidence–policy inter-face. Far from being 'simply' a process by which scientific evidence enters the policy cycle, evidence-based policy-making is fraught with broader strategic, highly politicized movements and decisions that are executed, defined and limited by 'policy actors' in the process of policy-making.

In brief, some of my previous research has explored the role of sports-based interventions in facilitating a dialogue around preventative health, particularly sexual health, among young refugee women in South Australia. While I direct readers to Palmer (2008, 2009) for the details, the point here is that when it came to assessing the impacts of the soccer programme in improving sexual health across a number of indicators (such as knowledge of and access to sexual health services), particularly invasive or inappropriate means of gathering 'evidence' (such as skin-fold tests of young women who had suffered physical and psychological trauma or questionnaires administered in English to newly arrived refugees) were requested of me by the government agency who had funded my research, despite these methods not being featured in the original research study they had commissioned. The point I'm making is that assumptions of rationality in the policy-making process rarely hold. Policy-making, policy transfer, policy learnings and policy decision-making are inherently political and the balance of power frequently comes into play when weighing up the merits (and definitions) of 'evidence' (Green, 2007). Following Coalter, there is a need to understand the process; there is a need to understand 'which sports work for which subjects in which conditions' (Coalter, 2007: 29), to which I would add 'which policies work for which subjects in which conditions', rather than unilaterally imposing particular assumptions and definitions as to what constitutes 'evidence'. As Keech notes, 'until practitioners develop a greater strategic awareness of the complex policy context within which they operate, they will not be fully able to realize why policy doesn't always work in practice and therefore lobby more effectively for the resources required to fulfill their responsibilities and do their job' (2003: 211).

In this context, it is even more remarkable that the evidence as to 'what works' in sports policy is rarely questioned or contested, with the efficacy of sport development, in particular, being by and large taken for granted (Donnelly, 2009; Kidd, 2009). Coalter draws attention to what he refers to as the 'mythopoetic nature of sport' (2007: 22), in which sport is perceived to be good without question. As Coalter suggests, 'there is a need to think more clearly, analytically, and less emotionally about "sport" and its potential' (2007: 7).

Evidence of the Legacy?

As we approach the 2012 London Olympic Games and Paralympics, we see the 'mythopoetic' status of sport loom large. Certainly, the Olympics are by no means alone. As has been suggested elsewhere, 'policy makers … hold particular ideological views and assumptions about the supposed worth of sport in conferring upon participants what are regarded as pro-social behaviours and values' (Bloyce & Smith, 2010: 97). That said, it is the purported 'legacy' of London 2012 that raises and for the moment leaves unanswered several questions about the mythopoetic status of sport and the transfer of evidence into future sports policy. As Poynter notes, [the IOC] is 'now firmly focused upon non-sport related outcomes as a source of legitimation for hosting the Games' (2008: 135).

The London 2012 Games has committed to several ambitious legacy promises that were instrumental in the award of the Olympics to the city, and without doubt, the Games has set itself a formidable task of 'proving' legacy with regard to its five core promises. As identified in the UK Labour government's Legacy Action Plan (DCMS, 2008: 6–7), these legacy promises were to:

1 make the UK a world-class sporting nation, in terms of elite success, mass participation and school sport;
2 transform the heart of East London;
3 inspire a new generation of young people to take part in local volunteering, cultural and physical activity;
4 make the Olympic Park a blueprint for sustainable living;
5 demonstrate that the UK is a creative, inclusive and welcoming place to live in, to visit and for business.

Each of these legacy promises will come under scrutiny at different points in the book – in future chapters on the environmental impacts of staging mega-events, for example – given that 'since 1992, "Legacy" has assumed a considerable significance to the IOC – as its evaluation process has incorporated environmental and other social dimensions' (Poynter, 2008: 135).

But when considering the mythopoetic status of sport and the question of evidence, it is the issue of developing and increasing sporting participation across the UK that presents perhaps the biggest challenge in evidencing improvements or achievements against the legacy ambitions of the Games. As Keech notes:

> When considering the challenges facing the Games, developing increased participation and achieving a legacy for young people is an objective more difficult to achieve than the other four commitments combined. ... Using a six-week, time-limited mega-event to inspire young people to participate for a lifetime and ensure that adults return to, or increase, participation in sport and physical activity is an immense undertaking. (2011: 80)

In a broader context of a shifting policy agenda and changes to the political landscape, this is particularly problematic. In 2010, the Conservative–Liberal Coalition government in the UK instituted a programme of drastic public spending cuts which saw the budgets committed to youth and school-based sport axed significantly. In May 2010, the Department of Education announced it was axing the entire £162 million PE and Sports Strategy, which was introduced by the previous Labour administration with the aim of providing five hours of 'high-quality' sport for all five to sixteen year olds. In an interview with a daily newspaper, Ivan Lewis, the shadow Culture, Media and Sports Secretary, claimed that 'at a time when we are preparing to host the Olympics, bidding for the World Cup and fighting an obesity crisis, this dismantling of support for school sport is perverse and short-sighted' (*The Telegraph*, 2010).[3] Elsewhere, the legacy potential of the Games receives strong criticism. Writing in *The Independent*, Vinner notes 'the legacy promise will come in time to be viewed as a highly effective sales pitch that was never fully realized. ... The bar was set impossibly high, setting goals that could never be reached' (2011: 24). Thus, the scrutiny of policy is necessarily analytical and descriptive in various measures, but in the case of sports policy for young people and the associated legacy of London 2012, the scale of its ambition requires careful examination in this broader policy (and political) context.

To return once more to the issue of policy-making in the context of new technologies, not only do they facilitate the global sharing of policy, they also enable the critique of sports policy – the assumptions that are embedded within, or the methodological sloppiness on which 'evaluations' of programmes and interventions are based. In the environment of an economic downturn and the need to effectively argue for resources that may flow from policy decisions, it is imperative that the research–policy interface is transparent, enabling comparisons within and between programmes, as well as initiatives within and between sports, countries and contexts.

THE CHANGING NATURE OF POLICY ANALYSIS: COMPARATIVE SPORTS POLICY

'Global sports policy' is essentially the global movement or the global 'travel' of policy, in Ozga and Jones' (2006) terms, which includes the travel of the values, ideologies and practices as they relate to sport that are embedded within this process. 'Global sports policy' refers to the ways in which policy may be influenced by broader supranational factors and may take a different 'shape' in different countries and in different contexts (different interpretations of 'sport for all', 'participation' or indeed 'sport', for example). This in turn is influenced by a number of factors, including the composition of the policy community; that is, the players or the actors involved in policy-making, the history and culture of countries, as well as particular local circumstances such as the balance of power between national and regional governments, or between supra, national and subnational organizations, as we saw in the previous chapter in relation to the governance of sports policy.

The global travel of policy documents and research evidence, which has been facilitated by new and emergent technologies, has also enabled *comparative* analyses of sports policy. The wide availability of data and policy documents from most continents now enables cross-national studies of sports policy on an unprecedented scale. The growing repertoire of publicly available data and policy documents from different continents and contexts now facilitates a more nuanced study of sports policy from a range of countries, and this enables governments, academics, researchers, policy professionals, and other users of public policy to share the kind of best-practice, policy knowledge and evidence discussed previously.

Comparative analysis has seen a growth in policy studies. Even a cursory scan of the literature suggests that comparative studies are among the favoured methodological, conceptual and theoretical approaches to analyses of sports policy. Elite sport, in particular, is given much mileage in this literature. While not intended to provide an exhaustive bibliography, titles such as Houlihan's (1997) *Sport, Policy and Politics: Comparative Perspectives*, Bergsgard et al.'s (2007)

Sports Policy: A Comparative Analysis of Stability and Change, Houlihan and Green's (2008) *Comparative Elite Sport Development: Systems, Structures and Public Policy*, or the country-to-country comparisons offered by Green and Collins (2008) (Finland and Australia) or Henry and Uchiumi (2001) (Britain and Japan) are nonetheless indicative of this particular trend in policy discourse. In the context of 'evidence-based policy-making', the measures of elite sport (medal success as an outcome of government investment) are particularly easy to measure and compare across countries.

As Henry et al. argue, comparative sports policy analysis can take one of two basic forms: to either look for similarities or to describe differences; to make 'comparisons along the multiple cases of political systems' or to account for 'how and why societies differ' (2007: 23–7).

Building on the ideas of evidence-based policy-making outlined earlier, the first approach tends to gather 'objective', largely statistical, data that is widely available in the public domain described earlier. Numbers of sports clubs in a country, rates of participation, gender (or age) differences in participation, levels of government expenditure or the amount of media coverage of sport and other kinds of information that can routinely be collected through surveys and other forms of data gathering are by and large the focus of this first type of comparative sports policy analysis. However, these large-scale comparisons across multiple cases tend to obscure local-level differences, along with questions and ambiguities as to how and why things may differ (or stay the same) between countries and nation states.

Nonetheless, these large-scale cross-country comparisons have considerable mileage in the policy-making process. As mentioned earlier, measures of elite sport success are frequently subject to this form of comparative analysis. Reduced to a simple 'input–process–output' model (De Bosscher et al., 2010) – (i) money, time and facilities are invested; (ii) schemes, programmes and athletes are funded; (iii) medals are won, participation increases – it is reasonably easy to isolate these various factors so as to compare scales of investment or increases in achievement across or between countries.

The second approach of describing how and why societies differ in terms of the policies they adopt and privilege lends itself to an analysis of 'meaning' rather than a search for general laws. Certainly, history is important in such an approach – how and why did this policy, in this country, emerge at this moment in time to respond to this particular crisis or challenge – is perhaps the axial question underpinning such approaches to this second, more discursive form of policy analysis. Anti-doping policy, for example, is one area that lends itself to this socio-historical approach to comparative analysis. Fundamental to the development of anti-doping policy in different countries and contexts is a conceptual determination as to why, if at all, that nation, state or region is concerned about doping in sport. In developing policy, the World Anti-Doping Agency must then convert what is essentially a political question into a pragmatic question that can be informed by 'evidence', to return to some of the concerns from before.

In his cross-country analyses of doping policy, Houlihan (1999, 2011) has been particularly adept in applying these political questions to this second model of comparative policy analysis in order to illustrate some of the difficulties in applying consistent anti-doping policy across countries. Examining the regulation of doping within the European Union, Houlihan (1999) maintains that the issue of doping has moved from being perceived as a discrete problem in individual countries that could be addressed by individual sporting federations within that country to one that now requires extensive cooperation and 'policy harmonization' between federations and governments of the kind described in the previous chapter. To return to the question of evidence-based policy-making, this methodology for cross-country evaluations has been adopted by the World Anti-Doping Authority when assessing compliance with regulation by the different signatories of the World Anti-Doping Code (WADA, 2009).

That said, while the global 'traffic' of policy enables greater cross-country comparison and lesson-learning from countries and jurisdictions, this is not without its problems, or indeed its critics. It is argued that the 'comparisons' tend to be from countries that are so similar – in language, political structure, economic stability and the like – as to make meaningful comparisons difficult; we are, for the most part, comparing 'the same'. Equally, problems with policy 'translation' (transferring policy learnings from one country to another) may not always work in practice. That is, the trajectory of policy may resonate with local communities in different ways and questions of compliance and uptake need always to be thought of as questions of interpretation. Equally, Nicholls, Giles and Sethna point to the biases inherent in the 'evidence discourse', maintaining that 'academics and development agencies in the Global North have consistently had the privilege of shaping what … constitutes relevant and valid evidence of success' (2011: 251).

Beyond these practical concerns about policy travel and translation, there are broader epistemological concerns about the analytical utility of comparative sports policy. Henry (2007), for example, argues that the overriding privileging of Western views of the world suggests an irreconcilable difference between Western and non-Western ways of approaching the analysis of sports policy. 'Epistemological difficulties have become so intransigent that comparisons of policy systems and contexts is no longer feasible; "Western" ways of viewing the world are incompatible with non-Western perspectives such that comparisons become impossible' (Henry, 2007: 5).

Henry's argument has merit. However, rather than shy away from these difficulties, better policy analysis needs to acknowledge them and respond to the challenge. My discussion in the following chapter extends these debates about the Western-centric view of policy, and explores the tension in relation to the use and application of social theory in policy studies so as to challenge Northern theories of globalization (Connell, 2006, 2009). In the context of 'travelling' policy, adopting a transnational rather than a cross-national comparative approach to policy analysis may come some way to addressing the shortcomings in these analyses of sports policy.

Equally, my discussion in Chapter 2 about the 'hybridities within' – the fine-grained cultural nuances within countries and communities – can extend conceptualizations of comparative sports policy. In searching too sharply for similarities and differences between nation states, we may miss exemplars of policy learnings *within* countries, states or cities that we may equally learn from to inform 'best practice'. Rather than looking for exogenous policy sources, programmes and contexts, examples within may provide equally useful cases for comparative policy. Again, new and emergent technologies can help facilitate the exchange of policy ideas, examples or triggers for policy change at local, state, national and supranational levels.

MEDIATED MOBILIZATION AND POLICY CONSUMPTION

I mentioned at the start of this chapter that new media and new technologies have facilitated what Lievrouw (2006) calls 'mediated mobilization' against policy decisions and initiatives. Advances in technological communications have given rise to critical consumers of public policy who are now able to harness dissent about policy decisions in relation to sport and other public policy concerns. As others have noted, the Internet is a medium favouring subversive, extra-institutional and loosely formed groups (Bennett, 2003; Clark & Thermudo, 2006; van de Donk et al., 2004). As I develop in this section, global technologies have accelerated communication of the political dimensions of sport, and the opportunities this offers for particular forms of activism in relation to policy decision-making. As Wilson points out, 'recent developments in communication technology have contributed to a situation in which there is immense revolutionary potential in sport-related contexts' (2007: 457).

The use of new media to harness dissent against the instruments of sports policy alerts us to one of the central themes of this chapter; the increasingly mediated social relationships that are part of the globalization of public life, political culture and policy debate. In 1986, Benedict Anderson showed how the spread of print capitalism could create 'imagined communities' of people who were never in face-to-face contact, which was the prerequisite for the formation of nation states. In 2011, new technologies have produced forms of communication that far exceed the potential of the printing press to bond communities and nation states. Importantly for what follows, the kinds of technologies described in this chapter have the potential to move 'communities' beyond shared imagination to collective action.

Such notions resonate with the work on 'new social movements'. Differing from 'old social movements', such as worker movements that formed around particular economic concerns, new social movements are more disparate, and built around a collective consciousness. Diani, for example, defines a social movement as a 'network of informal interactions between a plurality of individuals, groups and/or organizations, engaged in a political or cultural conflict, on the basis of a shared collective identity' (2000: 165).

It is here that the ideas of Jürgen Habermas (1962/1989) are particularly instructive. Habermas conceived of the 'the public sphere' as being a 'space where citizens can deal with matters of general interest without being subject to coercion; thus, with the guarantee that they may assemble and unite freely; and express and publicize their opinions freely' (1991: 398). For Habermas, the public sphere can be seen as 'a theater in modern societies in which political participation is enacted through the medium of talk' and 'a realm of social life in which public opinion can be formed' (1991: 398). Critically, new media outlets such as the Internet, blogs and 'flashmobs', provide arenas where radical agency and subjectivity can be both cultivated and expressed with regard to policy decisions and directives (Savigny, 2002). In such notions of participatory democracy, public opinion becomes political action.

I mentioned earlier that the Conservative–Liberal Coalition government in Great Britain instituted a programme of drastic public spending cuts. In response, in March 2011, more than 250,000 people assembled in London in what was described as 'the largest public protest since the Iraq war rally in 2003' (BBC, 2011), with details of where to meet, what to wear and which slogans to chant all being communicated via social media. Adding his comments to the BBC website, one supporter of the protest submitted the following post:

> I won't be there, as I am one of the many disabled people concerned by the impact of cuts in money and services but unable to cope with a march. I hope our 'virtual march' will be added to the numbers of protesters. (BBC, 2011)

New media has accelerated the potential for protest and dissent, opening up the potential to engage with political protest for those previously excluded from participatory democracy. That is, participatory democracy has moved 'online', whereby technological developments and the democratization of the Internet and the 'digital normalisation' (Garrett, 2006) of communication through mass social media have created a space for contention in which policy decisions can be challenged and subverted (Lombardo et al., 2002; Wall, 2007; Wilson & Hayhurst, 2009). In other words, a consequence of globalization has been the rise of 'e-dissidence' (van de Donk & Foederer, 2001; van de Donk et al., 2004), where the 'social electricity of globalization' (Giulianotti & Robertson, 2007b: 62) has created a 'technologically empowered, deliberative public culture' (Gilchrist, 2005: 130).

Participatory Democracy and Sports Policy

These arguments about the role of new technologies in changing people's relationships to political protest are by no means unique to policy, but they are, I would suggest, unique to the processes and consequences of globalization. From the turn of the century, sociologists began to take more notice of anti-globalization resistance movements (Appelbaum & Robinson, 2005; Eckstein, 2002; Mann, 2001), and we have seen a range of resistant practices that draw on the products of global culture to express dissent, usually to the very products of global culture themselves. The 1990s, for example, were characterized by the practices of 'culture jamming'[4], 'ad-busting' and 'billboard banditry', in which billboards and other places of public advertising were hijacked and the original message parodied. T-shirts featured messages proclaiming 'Nookie – Just Did It', a parody of the 'Nike Just Do It' campaigns, or that had the ADIDAS logo redesigned as the word 'Adihash', complete with marijuana leaf. Following the unveiling of the logo for the 2012 Olympic Games, alternative media sites soon promoted counter-images of the logo and subversive commentary on the design, with the geometric and cartoon-like figures soon being likened to, among other things, the image of Lisa Simpson performing oral sex on her spiky-haired brother (*The Guardian*, 2007).

To turn now to the implications of e-dissidence and participatory democracy for sports policy, there is a growing body of literature that argues for the use of sport to advocate for and promote humanitarianism and human rights. These are the subjects of the chapters in the second section of the book. For the moment, my concern is to chart the potential of new technologies to provide a space for contentious policy. As Giulianotti notes 'sports participation enables the dissemination of ... contemporary policy initiatives' (2005: 216).

Certainly, sports policy has a long history of dissidence to do, primarily, with gender and race-related policy issues. As far back as 1922, women joined together to create the *Fédération sportive féminine international*, which was responsible for the organization of the Women's Olympics in 1922 and the Women's World Games in 1926, 1930 and 1934. The success of these games forced the male-dominated IOC to overturn policy and allow women to participate in the Olympic Games (Harvey & Houle, 1994). More recently, the American feminist movement has been active with regard to Title IX[5], arguing that the implementation of this policy has been instrumental in increasing female participation in sport, while in Canada, the Canadian Association for the Advancement of Women in Sport lobbies the national government for policy changes around greater equity in sport.

Elsewhere, racism – and racist policy – has been subject to critical scrutiny. The Anti-Apartheid movement was effective in changing the governance of sport in South Africa and anti-racism movements have been instrumental in lobbying for policies and programmes such as 'Kick Racism Out' in football in the United Kingdom or the Anti-Racism and Religious Vilification Law in Australian Rules football, discussed in Chapter 2. Critically, these latter policies have involved athletes in the policy-making process, a shift more recently being evidenced in relation to anti-doping policy, where current and former athletes play a key role in the development and review of policy (Bloodworth & McNamee, 2010).

In terms of policy dissent and the role of 'athlete advocates', we have seen challenges and critiques coming, notably, from professional cyclists in relation to several policy decisions initiated by the Union Cyclistes Internationale (UCI). In 1991, riders in the Tour de France staged a protest when they were instructed by the UCI to wear helmets.[6] The UCI relented until 2003 when Andrei Kivilev was involved in a fatal crash in the Paris–Nice race, dying of massive head injuries. Since, the UCI has insisted that cyclists wear protective headgear. As part of the 'Festina Affair' in 1998, in which the Festina squad was expelled from the Tour de France, five further teams left the race in protest at what they perceived to be a 'witch hunt' by French authorities, while in 2011, riders protested at what they regarded to be the excessively dangerous conditions of the race route.

As a professional body, cyclists are clearly well versed in the politics of participatory democracy (Thibault, Kihl and Babiak, 2010). Working in an occupational environment that is not without risk, cyclists have mobilized action around their working conditions in order to determine the rules and policies that regulate their sport. As Thibault et al. note 'in recent years, an important group of stakeholders in sport – high performance athletes – have started to play an increasing role in the development of sports policies and decisions affecting them' (2010: 277). In 2011, for example, the UCI banned the use of radio communications in cycling races, sparking further protests within the peloton, with riders delaying the start of the first stages of the Tour de San Luis, the Giro di Regio Calabria and the Challenge Mallorca. The International Association of Professional Cycling Teams (AIGCP) has written to the UCI, outlining their concern with this unilaterally imposed policy:

> The radio ban is one rule that we disagree with. Teams represent the largest segment in terms of revenue and employees in professional cycling. We contribute over 5M [Euros] to the UCI annually in licensing fees and anti-doping contributions. We feel that we should be represented accordingly. It is not the desire of the teams to be disruptive or negative. However, we do need to be strong and unified until we garner the correct representation in the governance of our sport. We will not stand for rules being imposed on us without appropriate representation. As the largest shareholder in professional cycling, we ask for nothing more than to be a part of democratic governance. (*Cycling News*, 2011)

As such comments suggest, professional cyclists are a technologically empowered, politically astute part of the 'deliberative public culture' that is emblematic of global sports policy more broadly. This is not to suggest that all athletes are equally able to participate fully in representative policy-making. Athletes are 'still not fully able to voice their opinions on all matters' (Thibault et al. 2010: 297). The human rights record of China in the run-up to the Beijing Olympics is a case in point here, where athletes were instructed on what they could say verbally or electronically before, during and after the Games; a position recanted following public outcry – further evidence of the increasing public sphere of connected, global participatory democracy.

CONCLUSION

This chapter has been fundamentally concerned with the 'doing' of sports policy against a backdrop of new media and the 'network society' (Castells, 1996). While Castells tracks the impact of the networking logic on almost every level of social experience, from work, crime, education, the media and gender relations, sport (and sports policy) are, as Hutchins, Rowe and Ruddock point out, 'absent from his sociological vista' (2009: 96). As I have argued in this chapter, new technologies have changed our consumption habits, and they have also changed our relationship to policy. New technologies now enable the rapid dissemination of policy, the wide availability of data and policy documents from all continents enables the comparative study of sports policy on an unprecedented scale, and the public availability of policy documents via new forms of media has led to a growing interest in and critique of the nature of 'evidence' that informs particular policy decisions as they relate to sport and indeed to other aspects of public life. Equally, technological changes and the growth of an international policy context have led to the widening of the space for contentious politics and contentious consumption. As Wilson argues, 'the Internet is a space where ... interventionist critiques can be, and are, distributed and consumed in unprecedented ways' (2007: 466).

The plurality of the public sphere, and the contradictory uses of media (to promote both hegemonic and counter-hegemonic discourses), returns us to the central theme of this chapter: the concept of 'connectivity'. The 'connectivity' that is embedded in these new technologies is, in fact, highly uneven, often exclusionary, and gives rise to 'disconnectivity'; that is, the mediated mobilization that develops in response to policy-making and governance of particular kinds. Connectivity, in other words, can only be experienced in relational terms. In any case, connectivity, contentious consumption and the expectations of public availability of policy, as it relates to sport or anything else, alerts us to the systematic character of global power and it is an examination of this in relation to social theory and sports policy that is the subject of the following chapter.

BOX 4.1   QUESTIONS FOR DISCUSSION

- What are the key features of 'connectivity' (Tomlinson, 1999) and how are they expressed in policy production, dissemination and reception?

- In what ways has evidence-based policy altered the relationship between policy makers and policy audiences?

- To what extent is comparative policy analysis possible in the context of globalization?

- What are the key features of 'mediated mobilization' (Lievrouw, 2006), and what role do they play in the policy cycle?

SUGGESTED FURTHER READINGS

Colebatch, H. (2006) Mapping the work of policy. In H.K. Colebatch (ed.), *Beyond the policy cycle: The policy process in Australia*. Sydney: Allen and Unwin (pp. 1–19).

Dahlgren, P. (2005) The Internet, public spheres, and political communication: Dispersion and deliberation. *Political Communication*, 22(2): 147–62.

Francoli, M. & Ward, S. (2008) 21st century soapboxes? MPS and their blogs. *Information Polity*, 13(1–2): 21–39.

Leonard, D. (2009) New media and global sporting cultures: Moving beyond the clichés and the binaries. *Sociology of Sport Journal*, 26: 1–16.

Lievrouw, L. (2001) *Alternative and activist new media*. Cambridge: Polity Press.

Tomlinson, J. (2002) Interests and identities in cosmopolitan politics. In S. Vertovek & R. Cohen (eds), *Conceiving Cosmopolitanism*. Oxford: Oxford University Press (pp. 240–53).

Notes

1 In April 2011, administrators announced the closure of sixteen Borders bookshops in Australia while in May of the same year the British government tasked 'retail guru' and television presenter Mary Portas to undertake an independent review into the increased number of vacancies in the country's high streets.

2 In 2011, armed conflict broke out in the North African state of Libya, successfully deposing the country's *de facto* ruler Muammar Gaddafi.

3 In addition, a network of 450 school sports partnerships set up across Britain and administered by the Youth Sport Trust to forge sporting links between schools and local clubs is to be scrapped. It was also announced that the government would no longer provide ring-fenced funding for the country's 3,000 specialist schools, many of which are sporting academies, offering a saving of £450 million for 2010–11 (*The Telegraph*, 2011).

4 Borrowing from old citizen band radio slang for the illegal practice of electronically interrupting radio shows, 'jamming' has developed into a range of tactics which involve inverting, editing, augmenting and unmasking advertising messages in an attempt to lift an image or a message out of its original context in order to create a new and contradictory meaning for it.

5 Title IX was a law passed in 1972 that required gender equity for boys and girls in every educational programme that receives federal funding from the US government.

6 Policy dictates that cyclists may remove their helmet at their own risk during the final climb to a summit, if the climb is at least 5 kilometres long. A Tour course marker designates the point in the race where cyclists can remove their helmets.

5

SOCIAL THEORY, GLOBALIZATION AND SPORTS POLICY IN A RISK SOCIETY

THIS CHAPTER

- introduces key political theories of policy analysis;
- applies social theories to sports policy analysis;
- introduces theories of 'risk' as a framework for understanding sports policy;
- critiques the Western-centric focus of social theory through the lens of sports policy.

INTRODUCTION

I mentioned in the Introduction that this book grew out of what I saw to be a gap in how we think about sports policy. Despite sport itself being an increasingly global phenomenon, there has been no real attempt to locate the study of sports policy within a broader consideration of global processes, practices and consequences. An additional gap in how we think and write about sports policy is the virtual absence of social theory to make sense of, interpret and analyze sports policy. Certainly, sports policy analysts draw upon theory that is drawn primarily from the political sciences (Green & Houlihan, 2004; Greener, 2002). As Hudson and Lowe recognize, 'policy analysis is a sub-field of political sciences that tries to understand and build up knowledge of the whole process of public policy' (2004: 3). In terms of sports policy analysis, however, we are hesitant to use the kind of *social* theory that colleagues in the social sciences more routinely draw upon to engage with and interpret the human behaviours they are interested in knowing more about.

Given that policy-making is fundamentally a social endeavour – that is, it is the product of cultural work by individuals, organizations and institutions – our reluctance to use social theory is a deficit in our approach to sports policy. As I argue in this chapter, our analyses of sports policy on a global scale can be strengthened by the application of social theory. As such, this chapter outlines some of the key theoretical approaches that can be used to study global sports policy and practice. The example of risk theory is used to illustrate how social theory can be applied to sports policy studies, drawing particularly on the issue of 'children at risk' as it relates to sport and play. To develop this, the examples of child protection in the United Kingdom, the 'play safety' and public liability debate in Norway and the broad issues of the rights of child athletes in China are explored. There is an extensive literature on risk in sport more generally, and it is not my intention here to repeat that discussion.[1]

THEORIES OF SPORTS POLICY ANALYSIS

Although the application of social theory to analyses of sports policy is under-utilized, several theoretical frameworks have been developed for analyzing sports policy that have emerged from the political sciences. Largely evaluative in nature, these frameworks provide a useful way through which to measure the effects and outcomes of policy initiatives and developments and are a necessary point of departure for this chapter.

By way of background, policy analysis tends to develop in response to changing government priorities and agendas. From the 1970s, policy analysis developed apace around the world, where it was seen as facilitating the agenda of democratic governments at a time when many capitalist democracies were experiencing the effects of a more interventionist involvement from the State (Houlihan, 2005: 165). The policy focus at this time was on problem identification that led to policy formulation and then an evaluation of the effects of that policy on the policy problem. Towards the 1980s and 1990s, problem identification moved to a concern with understanding the process of implementing policy, again with an evaluative focus at the end. As outlined in the previous chapter, the growing concern with 'evidence-based' policy-making has led to the evaluative dimensions of policy analysis being built into the policy cycle at a much earlier stage. The shift from 'street-level bureau-crats' to 'cosmocrats' in the policy process also led to a shift in the priorities for policy analysis but, in essence, approaches to policy analysis remain embedded within a tension between a neo-Marxist position in which policy is developed to reflect and defend the interests of capitalism ('the cosmo-cratic' argument espoused in Chapter 3, for example) and a more liberal position which argues that values like equity, democracy, respect for human rights and the like cannot be excluded from the process of policy analysis. That is, particular values, biases and assumptions are already built into the policy process and are crucial to the making of sports policy – a theme running more broadly through the book.

Houlihan (2005) argues that much of the analysis of sports policy analysis has taken place at the 'meso-level'; that is, at the level of national organizations such as ministries, national sports organizations (NSOs) and national governing bodies (NGBs). Accordingly, a discussion of the main meso types of policy analysis that have developed out of political studies follows.

Paul Sabatier (2007) has been particularly influential in developing frameworks for public and social policy analysis. Taking his point of departure as the need to simplify the 'messiness' of public policy (in which sports policy is situated), Sabatier argues for a need to reduce the complexity of public policy through the use of theoretical frameworks that can help orient or filter the subject of analysis. Sabatier outlines a range of theoretical frameworks for policy analysis, each of which orients or interprets the subject matter differently. This is a point to which I will return. For the moment, my discussion below picks up on just two of these frameworks, as they have been the two most readily adopted to theorize sports policy at the meso-level.[2]

Advocacy Coalition Framework

Developed by Sabatier and Jenkins-Smith (1988, 1993), the Advocacy Coalition Framework (ACF) has been 'applied to over 30 case studies across a range of policy areas mainly in the United States, but also in Canada, the UK, Italy, and Poland' (Houlihan, 2005: 173). The ACF is based on five key assumptions:

1 A time perspective of at least ten years is required for the analysis of policy change;
2 A focus on policy sub-systems/policy communities;
3 Sub-systems involve actors from different levels of government and increasingly from international organizations and other countries;
4 The possession and use of technical information is important; and
5 Public policy incorporates implicit 'sets of value priorities and causal assumptions about how to realize them' (Jenkins-Smith & Sabatier, 1994: 178).

Essentially, the ACF 'focuses on the interactions of advocacy collations – each consisting of actors from a variety of institutions who share a set of policy beliefs – within a policy subsystem' (Sabatier, 2007: 9). The ACF argues that policy change is a function of both competition within the sub-system (conflicting interests of the members of the coalition) as well as events outside the policy sub-system (broader social or structural change). That is, the ACF has a concern with both endogenous and exogenous processes, and has a particular interest in the values and beliefs held by the coalitions as well as the conditions under which policy-making occurs by and within those coalitions.

In terms of sports policy analysis, use of the ACF has been relatively limited, and has focused mainly on elite sports development, predominantly in the United Kingdom, as well as in other English-speaking countries such Canada and Australia. To summarize the main studies, Green and Houlihan's (2004, 2005) analyses of elite sports development policy in Australia, Canada and the United Kingdom found some evidence of the application of the ACF. In their 2004 analysis of elite sports policy change in two sports (swimming and athletics) within their respective national sports organizations (NSO) in Canada and national governing bodies (NGB) of sport (Great Britain), Green and Houlihan (2004, 2005) argued that the ACF can help illuminate the nature of policy change in these countries. In both countries, there has been a perceptible change in the commitment of national governments to elite sport, largely driven by the promise of hosting major sporting events or, in the case of Australia and Great Britain, under-performance at elite events, such as the 1976 Montreal and 1996 Atlanta Olympics, respectively.

To return to the tensions between endogenous and exogenous factors, the ACF helps emphasize the role of the State in controlling the resources that then shape the context and conditions of the debate about elite sport in which NSOs and NGBs are centrally implicated and in which policy is then developed. For Green and Houlihan (2004), the ACF proved useful in drawing attention to culture change that, in turn, effected policy change as well as to exogenous or external factors that may also influence elite sport development. In other work, Parrish (2003) has applied the ACF to sports regulatory policy in the European Union, and Houlihan and White (2002) have developed a modified version of the ACF to analyze sports development policy in the UK, reaching similar conclusions to the Green and Houlihan (2004, 2005) research.

Each of the studies, when assessed against the four criteria for the ACF, demonstrate how stability and change are instrumental to the development of sports policy, how values and beliefs are played out by the actors within the coalitions (in the case of elite sports development, these are typically NSOs and NGBs), as well as the need for a medium to long-term policy commitment by government in order determine and analyze the effects and success (or failure) of the policy over time.

Multiple Streams Framework

The Multiple Streams Framework was developed by John Kingdom (1984) and is based on the 'garbage can' model of organizational behaviour (Cohen, March & Olsen, 1972), whereby 'various kinds of problems and solutions are dumped by participants as they are generated' (Cohen et al., 1972: 2). The Multiple Streams Framework views the policy process as consisting of three streams of actors and processes: 'a problem stream consisting of data about various problems and the proponents of various problem definitions; a policy steam involving the proponents of solutions to policy problems; and a politics stream consisting of elections and elected officials' (Sabatier, 2007: 9). For Kingdom, these three streams usually operate autonomously, except where a 'window of opportunity' enables policy entrepreneurs (to return to an earlier idea) to bring together two or more of these streams. When this happens, the results are usually a major change to public, sports or social policy.

In terms of its application to sports policy analysis, Kingdom's model is useful for highlighting that the policy process is far from straightforward or rational, involving, instead, a series of competing actors and problems (a theme developed in the previous chapter). The Multiple Streams Framework remains under-utilized in sports policy analysis, despite its analytical power to reveal the complexity of policy-making. That said, the Multiple Streams Framework is useful for conceptualizing the role of the policy entrepreneur, a presence we will see more of with the rise of global 'cosmocrats' and the influence that they are increasingly exerting in sports policy-making. In 2011, the 'FIFA crisis', in which allegations of corruption and vote rigging were levelled at two FIFA officials with regard to the awarding of Qatar the 2022 World Cup, erupted. While time will tell if 'a window of opportunity' will open up to effect policy change with respect to the governance of FIFA, 'the crisis' and the subsequent re-election of Sepp Blatter as President of FIFA is nonetheless suggestive of the increasing influence of policy entrepreneurs as powerful intermediaries in the policy process.

In terms of existing studies, Green and Collins (2008) have applied the Multiple Streams Framework to their comparative study of sport in Australia and Finland and, prior to this, Chalip (1996) used it to inform his analysis of sports policy in New Zealand. Bergsgard (2000) also adopted aspects of Cohen et al.'s (1972) 'garbage can' approach to his discussion of decision-making in Norwegian sport. There is clearly a gap, given such limited studies, yet the Multiple Streams Framework can explain policy change, particularly that of considerable significance worldwide (the development of the World Anti-Doping Code would be a prime example here), and it can highlight the role of agency through the influence of policy entrepreneurs, which, in turn, alerts us once more to the socially constructed nature; that is, to the role of human intervention in policy-making and analysis.

SOCIAL THEORY AND GLOBAL SPORTS POLICY

While these typologies are useful for explaining particular kinds of policies (such as those relating to elite sport), and the ideological assumptions underpinning those policies, they are nonetheless fairly limited in terms of their ability to locate the development, analysis, implementation of and compliance with sports policy in a *global* context. That is, they are less useful at mapping change and continuity across time and geographical contexts. Social theories – explanations for human behaviour – by contrast, have greater analytical utility for helping us to make sense of how people use and respond to particular policy initiatives that develop on a global scale, in response to global phenomena such as 'risk'.

Borrowing from Wildavsky, who defines policy analysis as 'an applied subfield whose content cannot be determined by disciplinary boundaries but by whatever appears appropriate to the circumstances of the time and the nature of the problem' (1979: 15), I adopt a 'bricoleur' approach to policy analysis, applying those theories that are most adept to explain the context, circumstances and behaviours under study. As Waddington and Smith have noted, 'there is nothing as practical as good theory' (2009: 8), and sports policy, I suggest, has been restricted in the kinds of theory it adopts. Building on the theories, just sketched, of policy analysis that have developed from political studies, the following section outlines the potential application of social theories to policy studies and analyses.[3]

Why Theory?

One of the premises of this book is that 'policy' is not a neutral or a value-free exercise, but has fundamental social and political consequences that are linked to the 'work', often invisible, through which policy is 'made' to happen. The labelling of 'policy problems' – for example, the populations who are targeted for policy intervention ('deadbeat dads', 'teenage mothers') or the topics that are given greatest precedence on the policy hierarchy, such as widening participation, creating legacy or developing elite sport – do not happen 'naturally' but are, in fact, a political calculus based on the values and assumptions of both policy makers and the audience to whom policies are directed. In such a formulation, images, stereotypes, and the attribution of values to people, places and events, serve to direct and operationalize policy. Thus, social construction emphasizes the contextual richness of what Hajer (1993) calls the 'policy domain' or what Hoppe (2002) refers to as the 'critical cultures of public policy problems'. Moreover, these notions of contextual richness and critical cultures allude to a range of interpretative possibilities – what we know as social theory – as to how we may understand policy, its effects or consequences. By drawing on social theory, it is possible to explain policy behaviour or events in different ways or for particular effect.

Theory filters the world in particular ways; as such, it unavoidably compels a researcher, policy analyst or adviser to establish a series of priorities in research and policy-making, such as the kind of 'evidence' that is gathered in order to inform policy and practice, to return to some of the ideas from the previous chapter. By providing a framework – what Crotty (1998) calls 'scaffolding' – theory allows a researcher, a policy analyst or adviser to make certain choices by organizing key concepts and highlighting and emphasizing particular phenomena, and by excluding others. This is fundamental to the policy process and the role of human intervention in decision-making and the transfer of policy learnings.

These ideas of filtering the world and gathering and explaining 'evidence' through different lenses raise central, epistemological concerns for social theory, social research and social policy about the nature of 'truth' and 'knowledge' which fundamentally constitute 'evidence'. Social theory is premised on a central question: 'how do we know?' This epistemological concern allows us to see the tensions within the field of policy analysis, for it enables us to fore-ground concerns, it reveals biases and assumptions, and it privileges certain research methods over others. Discussions about epistemology and the structure of knowledge, however, usually happen in a separate box from discussions about globalization and sports policy, and it is this divide that this book, in part, attempts to reconcile.

Key Theoretical Approaches and Sports Policy

To turn now to the application of social theory to sports policy, there are essentially six major theories that have been used to study sport. As summarized in Coakley (2004), these are:

- Functionalist theory
- Conflict theory
- Interactionist theory
- Critical theory
- Feminist theory
- Figurational theory

These theories have more traditionally been used to study the social or socio-logical (rather than the policy) aspects of sport. Nevertheless, they have resonance for the analysis of sports policy. There are points at which these theories overlap and, while I provide an overview of each in turn, it is important to note that there is some fluidity to these theoretical categories. A further caveat, although I refer to 'theory' in the singular, this is done for reasons of analytical simplicity. There is, in fact, a diverse set of interpretative frameworks within each theoretical category; there is no 'one' Feminist theory or Critical theory, for example, and the suggested Further Readings at the end of the chapter provide a more comprehensive discussion of the variations within each theoretical category.

Functionalist theory

In brief, then, Functionalist theory works from the assumption that it is possible to study society and develop a system of 'social laws' that can be used to under-stand that society. 'Functionalists' view society as being an 'organized system of interrelated parts held together by shared values and social processes that tran-scend differences and promote consensus among people' (Coakley, 2004: 35). That is, Functionalist theory stems from the premise that all social systems (soci-eties, communities) share certain 'functional prerequisites' that must be met if the system/society is to operate efficiently.

In terms of sport and sports policy, Functionalist theory is most readily applied to analyses of how sport as an 'institution' can contribute to stability and change across a society or community. Clearly, this resonates with the Advocacy Coalition Framework, although the notion of building consensus is extended further in Functionalist theory. Functionalist theory, for example, may be used to explore the extent to which sport contributes to health, well-being and resilience within a community; that is, to shared, functional prerequisites. This has obvious implications for sports policy. What kinds of initiatives may facilitate this shared resilience within a community? How have previous policy initiatives hindered this? These are central policy questions that can be explored through Functionalist theory. Table 5.1 provides a summary of Functionalist theory, with some further examples of its application to sports policy.

Conflict theory

Conflict theory works from the assumption that social relationships are ultimately shaped by economic forces. That is, Conflict theory espouses the view that society is ultimately shaped by money, wealth and economic power. In the context of globalization, such a theory has much merit. Wallerstein's 'World System' approach to globalization, discussed in Chapter 1, very much adopts the underlying premises of this Marxist-based social theory. As covered in Chapter 1, the World System approach to globalization stems from an emphasis on the economic determinants of cultural activity in which globalization is reflected in particular forms of economic life rather than in terms of political power or social relations, which are explored through Critical and Interactionist social theories.

Such a focus on globalization as an economic activity has a clear resonance when thinking about sport and sports policy. Conflict theory assumes that sport ultimately promotes the interests of those with wealth and power, widening the gap between the 'haves' and the 'have-nots'. These arguments were developed in previous chapters in relation to 'cosmocrats' and the economic (and political) power they wield. While I did not explicitly address it there, it should be evident here that Conflict theory can usefully be applied to develop an analysis of their ascendancy and dominance in world sport. This is just one example of how Conflict theory may be applied to sports policy. Equally, questions such as 'how do the processes of commercialization influence sport?' are ones that could be answered using Conflict theory. Table 5.1 provides a summary of Conflict theory, with some further examples of its application to sports policy.

Interactionist theory

Interactionist theory emphasizes the social relationships that develop between people. It has a particular concern with identity and culture, and the meanings people place upon the relationships they have with others. Importantly, Interactionist theory works from the assumption that people do not simply respond 'automatically' or without thinking to the world around them, but that we are actively aware of the decisions we make and the consequences our actions will have on the social world in which we live. In other words, as we interact with others, we create culture and society.

While Interactionist theory in sports research is most commonly used to analyze how athletes and fans interact with each other – in team settings, as members of a sporting subculture, for example – the premise of Interactionism also returns us to one of the central themes of this book – the notion of social construction. I have argued that 'policy' is not a neutral exercise, but the product of cultural work in which there is a high degree human involvement and social agency in the *making* of sports policy. Table 5.1 provides a summary of Interactionist theory, with some further examples of its application to sports policy.

Critical theory

Critical theory is fundamentally concerned to explain culture, power and social relations. While this may seem to be what Functionalist, Conflict and Interactionist theories do, the key distinction is that Critical theory seeks to explain where power comes from, how it operates in social life and how it shifts and changes as people negotiate it, and their relationships with others. In other words, Critical theory is useful for explaining the historical dimensions of sport, and sports policy, or how the dynamics of relationships of power may change over time.

Critical theories are essentially theories about action, political involvement and collective empowerment, and have much resonance with the ideas discussed in the previous chapter, where the capacity of sport to mobilize political dissent was reviewed. This notion of political dissent will also be encountered in the second section of this book, where the use of sporting mega-events to organize protest around human rights and other forms of abuse is particularly powerful. Table 5.1 provides a summary of Critical theory, with some further examples of its application to sports policy.

Feminist theory

Feminist theory stems from the assumption that to understand people's actions, beliefs and interactions, we must understand the meanings that people give to gender, and the ways in which those meanings are then incorporated into social experience and the organization of social life.

There is no shortage of uses of Feminist theory in sports research. Essentially, Feminist theory and research is concerned with how gender relations privilege men over women (disparity in pay between male and female athletes, or in media coverage, for example), or how gender ideology (ideas about masculinity or femininity) may be produced and reproduced in certain sports or in certain sporting contexts ('gender appropriate' sports for women or violence against women by male athletes would be cases in point here).

Table 5.1   *Using social theories to study sports in society: a summary and comparison*

Functionalist Theory	Conflict Theory	Interactionist Theory
ASSUMPTIONS ABOUT THE BASIS FOR SOCIAL ORDER IN SOCIETY		
Social order is based on consensus and shared values, which hold the interrelated parts of society together.	Social order is based on economic interests and the use of economic power to exploit labour.	Social order is created from the bottom up as people interact with each other.
All social systems tend towards a state of balance.	Social class shapes social structures and relationships.	Social life is grounded in social relationships.
MAJOR CONCERNS IN THE STUDY OF SOCIETY		
How do individual parts of social systems contribute to the satisfaction of major system needs and the overall operation of the system?	How is economic power distributed and used in society?	How are meanings, identities and culture created through social interaction?
	What are the dynamics of social class relations?	How do people define the reality of their own lives and the world around them?
	Who is privileged and exploited in class relations?	
MAJOR CONCERNS IN THE STUDY OF SPORT		
How does sport fit into social life and contribute to social stability and efficiency?	How does sport reflect class relations?	How do people become involved in sports, become defined as athletes, derive meaning from participation and make transitions out of sports into the rest of their lives?
How does sport participation influence personal and social development?	How is sport used to maintain the interests of those with power and wealth in society?	
	How has the profit motive distorted sport?	
MAJOR CONCLUSIONS ABOUT THE SPORT–SOCIETY RELATIONSHIP		
Sport is a valuable social institution, which benefits society as well as individuals in society.	Sport is a form of physical activity that is distorted by the needs of capital.	Sports are forms of culture created through social interaction.
Sport is a source of inspiration on both personal and social levels.	Sport is an opiate that distracts attention away from the problems that affect those without economic power.	Sport participation is grounded in the decisions made by people in connection with their identities and their relationships.
SOCIAL ACTION AND POLICY IMPLICATIONS		
Develop and expand sport programmes that promote traditional values, build character, and contribute to order and stability in society.	Raise class consciousness and make people aware of their own alienation and powerlessness.	Allow individuals to shape sports to fit their definitions of reality.
	Eliminate profit motives in sports and allow sports to foster expression, creativity and physical well-being.	Make sport organizations more open and democratic.
		Focus on the culture and organization of sports when trying to control deviance in sports
MAJOR WEAKNESSES		
It does not acknowledge that sports are social constructions.	It ignores that sports can be sites for creative and liberating experiences.	It fails to explain how meaning, identity and interaction are related to social structures and material conditions in society.
It overstates the positive consequences of sports.	It overstates the influence of economic forces in society.	It ignores issues of power and power relations in society.
It ignores that sports serve the needs of some people more than others.	It assumes that people who have economic power shape sports to meet their interests.	

Critical Theories	Feminist Theories	Figurational Theories
Social order is negotiated through struggles over ideology, representation and power. Social life is full of diversity, complexities, and contradictions.	Social order is based primarily on the values, experiences and interests of men with power. Social life is gendered and based on patriarchal ideas.	Social order is based on interdependencies among individuals and groups. Connections between people take the form of social figurations.
How is cultural ideology produced, reproduced, and transformed? What are the conflicts and problems that affect the lives of those who lack power in society?	How is gender ideology produced, reproduced and transformed? How do dominant forms of gender relations privilege men over women and some men over others?	How do social figurations emerge and change? How do power balances within figurations influence relationships between individuals and groups?
How are power relations reproduced and/or resisted in and through sports? Whose voices are or are not represented in the narratives and images that constitute sports?	How are sports gendered activities and how do they reproduce dominant ideas about gender in society? What are the strategies for resisting and transforming sport forms that privilege men?	How did modern sports emerge and become so important in society? What are the social processes associated with the commercialization of sports, expressions of violence in sport and forms of global sports?
Sports are social constructions. Sports are sites where culture is produced, reproduced and transformed. Sports are cultural practices that repress and/or empower people.	Sports are grounded in the values and experiences of powerful men in society. Sports reproduce male power and distorted ideas about masculinity. Sports produce gendered ideas about physicality, sexuality and the body.	Sports are exciting activities that relieve boredom and control violence and uncivilized behaviour Sports celebrate masculinity and male power. Global sports are complex activities with local and national significance.
Use sports as sites for challenging and transforming forms of exploitation and oppression. Increase the range and diversity of sport participation opportunities. Challenge the voices and perspectives of those with power.	Use sports as sites for challenging and transforming oppressive forms of gender relations. Expose and resist homophobia and misogyny in sports. Transform sports to emphasize partnership over domination.	Develop a fund of valid knowledge, which can be used to enable people to control expressions of violence, exploitation and the abuse of power. Increase access to sport participation among those who have lacked power through history.
They have no clear guidelines for identifying and assessing forms of resistance and the value of ideas and actions across situation. They have no unified strategies for dealing with problems, conflicts and injustice.	They have no clear guidelines for identifying and assessing forms of resistance and the value of ideas and actions across situations. They give little attention to connections between gender and some other categories of experience.	It gives too little attention to problems and struggles that affect day-to-day lives. It understates the immediate personal consequences of oppressive power relations. It gives little attention to the experiences of women and to gender inequities.

Sports in Society: Issues and Controversies, 8/e, Coakley, J. © The McGraw-Hill Companies, Inc.

In terms of sports policy, Feminist theory (and the political 'work' that sits behind it) has been particularly influential. Policies relating to equity and inclusion, or policies relating to the behaviour of men towards women in sporting contexts are particularly noteworthy here. These are the subjects of Chapter 8, where the trafficking of women for the purposes of sexual exploitation is discussed in relation to sporting mega-events. This is just one example of how Feminist theory may be applied to sports policy and I return to this later in the chapter when considering child sexual abuse and child protection in sport, for it is argued that similar dynamics of power extend to girls and young boys as well as women. For the moment, Table 5.1 provides a summary of Feminist theory, with some further examples of its application to sports policy.

Figurational theory

Figurational theory is based on the premise that social life consists of networks (figurations) of interdependent people. Figurational theory assumes that people are 'more or less dependent on each other, first by nature, then through social learning, through education, socialization, and socially generated reciprocal needs' (Elias, 1978: 261).

In the context of sports policy, Figurational theory and analyses are useful for explaining issues of governance, for example. That is, how the various networks of policy actors and national, supra- and sub-national levels converge and diverge around policy interests and objectives. Figurational theory, for example, can be used to explain the complex networks that have developed in response to anti-doping policy or to elite sport – two of the themes that this book has concentrated on so far. Table 5.1 provides a summary of Figurational theory, with some further examples of its application to sports policy.

Each of the theories in Table 5.1 is useful in, at times overlapping, ways for understanding the development, implementation and analysis of sports policy in a global context.

BOX 5.1   QUESTIONS FOR DISCUSSION

- In what ways can social theory help strengthen approaches to research in sports policy?

- How do theoretical approaches influence the questions asked in research or policy?

- Of the theories outlined above, is there one that is more or less relevant to studies of sports policy?

NORTHERN SOCIAL THEORY AND GLOBALLY INCLUSIVE POLICY?

While I have argued for a greater use of social theory in sports policy, an emerging but trenchant criticism of social theory in the context of globalization is that 'modern social theory embeds the viewpoints, perspectives and problems of metropolitan society, while presenting itself as a universal whole' (Connell, 2007: viii). Uncorrected, Connell contends, 'these imbalances severely reduce our chances of understanding the world we actually live in' (2011: 288). Connell's critique, namely that 'much of current sociological thought is based on a great fantasy – that the world of the metropole is all that matters' (2011: 288), has a particular resonance with global sports policy. With 'metropolitan society' taken to be the 'Global North', the relationship between theory and policy is immediately problematic in the context of globalization. To what extent can we truly speak of 'global sports policy' (or global any other kind of policy), given the biases inherent within this political geography of knowledge?

Certainly, Connell's argument resonates with much of this book. I discussed some of the problems of this skewed representation of 'the global' in the previous chapter in relation to comparative sports policy analysis. Henry (2007), also in the previous chapter, argued that the overriding privileging of Western views of the world suggests an irreconcilable difference between Western and non-Western ways of approaching the analysis of sports policy. My intention here is to extend these debates about the Western-centric view of policy, drawing on the emerging discourse around 'Southern Theory', so as to explore what it may contribute to debates about global sports policy in ways that enable a globally inclusive approach to policy analysis.

Connell defines 'the metropole' to mean 'the group of rich capital-exporting countries that are at the centre of the world economy and the main holders of worldwide political power. That principally means Western Europe and North America' (2009: 57–8) and, without question, the organizational structures of sports policy and sports sociology reflect this orientation. The *International Review for the Sociology of Sport*, for example, has only recently concentrated its efforts in attracting publications from the Global South, while Klein notes that:

> The International Sociology of Sport Association (ISSA) envisions itself as transnational, but remains primarily European; while the North American Society for the Sociology of Sport (NASSS) is unable to venture even into Mexico and has repeatedly failed to attract scholars from outside kinesiology and sociology. No true organization has yet been formed that operates globally. (2007: 886)

This, invariably, skews the nature of the empirical research that is presented through these flagship organizations and publications, for it reflects the locations of the membership base itself.

To take just one example to illustrate, there is a growing interest by Western scholars (myself included) in Muslim women's experience of and participation in sport (see Hargreaves, 2000, 2007; Kay, 2007, 2008; Palmer, 2008, 2009). While glossing somewhat, collective academic interest in Muslim women and sport has tended to focus on (i) religion, (ii) patriarchy and male power, or (iii) veiling and the body. Certainly, Muslim women have been interviewed for research projects, in some cases acted as co-researchers, and in others been the principal researchers on projects. To my knowledge, however, none of this research was produced with reference to *social theory* from Iran, Algeria, Somalia, or other countries within which this research is either referenced or located.[4] I am not suggesting that this is 'bad research', but I am suggesting that this is just one example that reflects our theoretical bias towards the 'Northern metropole'. Iranian theorists such as Al-e Ahmad (1982) or Shari'ati (1986), for example, offer powerful arguments about the cultural dimensions of gender relations within Islamic societies, including notions of domination and resistance – key tropes in Western writings about Muslim women in sport.

I am as guilty of this oversight as anyone else, and, for this reason, I share Connell's view that anyone committed to debates about inequity and oppression, or relations between the centre and the periphery, should at least be attune to a 'world social science' that is attentive to thinking from scholars in 'the South'.[5] Connell (2007) alerts us to many of the biases and assumptions inherent in contemporary social sciences, and her analyses of social theory that are drawn from the world periphery (Africa, Latin America, South and South-West Asia, Australia's Indigenous people) have relevance for the application of theory to policy in the context of globalization, particularly the nature of the production of knowledge and 'evidence' that are among the central projects of policy-making. Moreover, Connell's intellectual project alerts us to the inequities and uneven distribution of power, as well as knowledge, across the world. Such observations chime with those of Massey (1991), who argues that the globalization of social relations is yet another source of (the reproduction of) geographical uneven development, and this needs to be acknowledged in any analysis of social relations, of which policy-making and compliance are key elements.

THEORIZING RISK

To provide a more extended case study of the application of social theory to sports policy, I turn now to particular theories of risk that emerged out of and in response to particular global developments. I have chosen the example of risk because much policy is formulated around populations 'at risk' – children at risk of obesity, risk factors for chronic health conditions, for example, and the concept has become central to how social relations are organized and governed through social and public policy. Here, Foucault's concept of 'governmentality' helps frame the logic of risk-based policy-making. For Foucault, governmentality refers to the 'art of government' in which government has 'as its purpose not the act of government itself, but the welfare of the population, the improvement of its condition, the increase of its wealth, longevity, health etc.' (1991: 100).

While risk, fear and danger are by no means new concepts, the global dimensions to actual risk, perceived risk and the potential for confronting and assessing risk are far more recent and have particular implications for sports policy. The German sociologist Ulrich Beck (1992, 1999) maintains that there is now a 'world risk society', triggered by the spread of modernity across the world, in which risk is played out on a larger and, ever increasing, geographical scale. As Beck argues:

> Unlike the factory-related or occupational hazards of the nineteenth and first half of the twentieth century, these [risks] can no longer be limited to certain localitites or groups, but rather exhibit a tendency to globalization ... and in this sense brings into being *supra*-national and *non*-class specific global hazards with a new type of social dynamism. (Beck, 1992:16, emphasis in original)

Risk Constructs

Theorizing 'risk' has become a burgeoning area of interest in the social sciences, with risk now a key part of our analytical lexicon. In broad terms, 'risk' can be conceptualized in one of three ways: (i) risk avoidance, (ii) risk-seeking, or (iii) risk reasoning. Each conceptualization has resonance for sports policy, particularly for understanding the social relations that underpin policy-making.

To briefly sketch each, Beck (1992), in his seminal account *Risk Society: Towards a New Modernity*, argues that part of the fall-out of globalization has been the emergence of a number of environmentally based risks (global warming, air and water pollution, nuclear radiation, Mad Cow disease, avian and swine flu) that have triggered particular forms of social engagement with these external and unwanted risks. Public and policy responses to these kinds of risks are couched in terms of *risk avoidance* – steer clear of eating particular foods, stay indoors – which, in turn, contributes to the notion of crisis-driven policy-making noted previously.

From Beck's gloomy view of 'everyday life as an involuntary lottery of misfortune' (Beck, 1999), there has been an evolution in understandings of risk from being calculable, external and unwanted to self-generated and manufactured uncertainties, such as terrorism, or voluntary risk taking through 'dangerous' lifestyle choices and decisions. Indeed, a countervailing perspective is that the active search for risk is as much a feature of the global order as evading or preventing risk. That is, *risk-seeking* sits alongside risk avoidance. Lupton and Tulloch have been particularly influential in attempting to insert 'the everyday'

LIVERPOOL JOHN MOORES UNIVERSITY
LEARNING SERVICES

into these cultural analyses of risk, arguing that people engage with, interpret and respond to risks of all different kinds simply by going through the business of being human (Lupton, 1999; Lupton & Tulloch, 2002a, 2002b). In their evocatively titled paper: 'Life would be pretty dull without risk', Lupton and Tulloch (2002a) maintain that voluntary risk taking has its own particular pleasures that cannot be denied. Drug taking, driving fast cars, having unprotected sex and taking part in extreme sports are among the 'pleasure pursuits' that Lupton and Tulloch identify, suggesting that experiences of risk are selfish and hedonic; risk-seeking is about satisfying personal urges and desires, a view that sits in opposition to the de-personalized interpretation of risk espoused by Beck. Drawing on the theoretical basis of Douglas (1966, 1992) and Douglas and Wildavsky (1982), this cultural approach to risk suggests that responses to risk, threat and uncertainty are made in prescribed ways that serve to maintain the boundaries and membership of particular groups and organizations (Le Breton, 2000; Palmer, 2004).

At the mid-point between risk avoidance and risk-seeking, a third form of risk operates, namely 'risk reasoning' or assessing the potential for risk. In the twenty-first century, risk assessment has become a growth industry, with a number of 'risk experts', in Beck's (1992) terms, charged with determining the probability with which risk is likely to result in damaging or fatal consequences. Risk reasoning profoundly influences sports policy in terms of socio-legal conditions, such as the rise of public liability insurance, that are designed to mitigate these consequences.

As these different interpretations of risk suggest, risk is understood as an important social and political construct that is employed in different ways through history. The assumptions that are embedded within each 'risk construct' are mobilized to effect particular forms of political change so as to achieve policy outcomes that may be either realized or thwarted (O'Malley, 2001, 2004). As Rose (1996) and Shamir (2008) maintain, risk is an important facet of how regimes of policy are rationalized over time and in different social contexts.

CHILDREN 'AT RISK'

I have chosen to focus on children in sport as most of the literature is given over to examining the risks taken, experienced or feared by adults. From a policy perspective, however, children are fully embedded in the discourse of risk in some quite crucial ways. Children are frequently subject to the risk vocabulary in terms of being 'at risk' of the supposed obesity and inactivity 'epidemics' (McDermott, 2007; Saguy & Riley, 2005), of being snatched (Backett-Milburn & Harden, 2004; Furedi, 2002) or injured through dangerous play or neglect. The three examples that follow – child protection and child sexual abuse, children's play and child athletes – all foreground the notion of risk within a broader policy discourse of children's rights.

Child Protection and Risk Avoidance

To start with a caveat, it is not my concern to document the prevalence of child [sexual] abuse in sport, or to suggest that 'efforts to combat abuse [are] a defence against such forms of exploitation' (Brackenridge, 2004: 322). Instead, it is to sketch out the policy response to the protection of children and young people within sport.[6]

The issue of child protection and child sexual abuse in sport sits within the wider discourse of risk avoidance; of putting in place policies and practices that can prevent the sexual, physical and emotional abuse of children by others in positions of authority and power. Informed by a broader literature on harassment and discrimination in sport, child sexual abuse is thus conceptualized as one form of sexual violence (Fasting, Brackenridge & Walseth, 2002; Fasting et al., 2011; Kirby, Greaves & Hankivsky, 2000; Palmer, 2011) in which gender and power relations are underscored. To return to the application of theory for policy analysis, some Feminist sociologists argue that the notion of consent in a sexual relationship is rendered invalid by the structural power differential between the (usually male) coach and the (usually female) athlete (Brackenridge, 2004).

Despite the abuse of children chiming with ideals such as 'innocence' that have a powerful cultural resonance, particularly in Western countries, child protection in sport has only fairly recently occupied a place on the policy agenda. Policy examples are somewhat limited, with the bulk of empirical research being done in the United Kingdom. As Brackenridge notes:

> Policy responses to child sexual abuse vary widely from county to country, with some – notably former Eastern bloc countries and many developing countries – still being in denial about the possibility that such a phenomenon exists in sport. Others, however, have put in place extensive procedures, codes of conduct and training programs. (2008: 42)

In the United Kingdom, where there has been substantial progress with regard to the development of policy, the appearance of child sexual abuse on the policy agenda was precipitated by a series of public scandals in swimming during the early 1990s (Brackenridge, 2001, 2004, 2008).[7] Once child abuse was acknowledged in the UK, it was followed by the formation of a dedicated Child Protection in Sport Unit (CPSU), established jointly by the National Society for the Prevention of Cruelty to Children (NSPCC) and Sport England in 2001, offering a 24-hour helpline, advising sporting organizations, setting national child protection standards and developing policies and procedures (Brackenridge, 2001). Much of the policy response to child abuse and protection in the UK has since been progressively developed in terms of risk avoidance, yet it remains a messy and 'wicked' policy problem for the reasons outlined below.

Brackenridge, arguably the leading advocate for policy reform (it was her empirical work in the late 1980s and 1990s that led governing bodies to acknowledge the problem and implement policy reform), notes several difficulties with terminology that impact upon successful policy and practice. The notion of 'child' is itself a contested concept, drawing on both legal and developmental interpretations:

> The legal age of consent varies from country to country, from as young as 12 to as old as 21. In sport, junior/senior distinctions also vary, with adults treated as children (told what to eat, when to go to bed and so on) and children expected to 'step up' in terms of the demands placed on them, meaning that there is 'no simple correspondence between chronological, developmental and "sport" age'. (Brackenridge, 2008: 41)

In a broader policy context, such age-related confusion of rights extends to country-level differences in laws relating to smoking, marriage, voting and gun-use, and the 'permissive context of child exploitation arises from the symbolic separation of sport from social and legal regulation' (Brackenridge, 2008: 41). These are points to which I return in my discussion of children's rights and risk in sport.

Furthermore, the virtual autonomy of the voluntary sports sector has effectively 'shielded it from external scrutiny and from the regulatory systems that characterize workplace industrial labour relations' (Brackenridge, 2004: 326). This self-regulation of sporting organizations speaks to some of the notions of governance described in Chapter 3, but here it is underpinned by a broader concern with organizational accountability. Fingers are quickly pointed at clubs and organizations when abuse goes undetected. While ethical codes such as those developed by UNESCO or the CPSU extend to governments, sport and sport-related organizations as well as those individuals working with young people (i.e. coaches and parents), and seek to both constrain the behaviour of those within sport and exclude those who are unable or unprepared to conform to these codes, voluntary codes of conduct are, by and large, treated as self-enforcing and subject to infrequent external monitoring.

The protection of children from abuse or harm is thus located within the twin discourses of risk avoidance and innocence; of putting in place strategies that can prevent harm to those with lives ahead of them. Alongside child abuse in sport, we see this in societal responses to environmental disasters. Digel, for example, notes that following the Chernobyl disaster, 'children were suddenly not allowed to play in their sandboxes anymore ... tennis courts were closed, sporting activities in community sports facilities cancelled and outdoor physical education disallowed' (1992: 259). Following the 2011 earthquake in Japan, Fukushima city issued radiation dosimeters to children to monitor levels of radiation they might be exposed to following the meltdown of the tsunami-hit Fukushima Daiichi nuclear plant, despite the city being outside of the 20-kilometre (12-mile) evacuation zone (AFP, 2011). While clearly a reaction to global environmental disasters, such responses nonetheless speak to a broader discourse around the protection of children from external and unwanted threats and risks.

To return to the notion of risk avoidance, it is clear how the protection of children from sexual (and other forms of) abuse sits within this particular 'risk construct', which in turn influences policy and debate. Policy developments such as the formulation of codes of conduct and the setting of national standards are about putting in place mechanisms whereby attempts are made to 'head off at the pass' the people likely to offend and abuse. As is well documented in Brackenridge's work, this is not without flaws, faults and limitations, and has had significant ethical, legal and political consequences. As Furedi notes:

> Risk avoidance has become an important theme in political debate and action. The issue of safety has become thoroughly politicised. Governments and officials are routinely accused of covering up a variety of hidden perils and of being complacent in the face of a variety of threats to people's safety. (2002: vii)

Risk Assessment and Children's Play

The rise of risk assessment and risk management has seen the concept of 'risk' take on increasingly litigious overtones. With its origins in maritime insurance in the nineteenth century, assessing risk – that is, determining the probability of risk – is now an intractable part of public policy and discourse as it relates to sport. Some sporting organizations, mindful of the possibility of insurance claims in relation to the injury of athletes in their care, are advising their coaches to seek insurance cover for liability, and there is a rise of dedicated insurance brokers, such as 'Sportplan', offering specialized insurance services to those involved in coaching or officiating. Equally, waivers, insurance premiums and disclaimers are part and parcel of participation in various sports, such as white water rafting, canyonning or bungee jumping. It is here that I return to Douglas's formulation of risk subcultures whereby communities of risk takers mobilize their shared experience of risk to symbolically construct a sense of identity and difference (Douglas, 1985, 1992; Palmer, 2002a).

In terms of policy-making, this marking out of risk communities or 'affinity groups', in Lash's (2000: 47) terminology, is crucial. I've mentioned at several points that policy often develops in response to a crisis or to the emergence of a 'problem' group. In the case of risk assessment and liability, the fact that individuals will voluntarily seek out sports where there is some possibility of injury or even death creates the problem to which policy then develops in response. In a risk society, liability considers the distribution of harms and transfers them from corporate entities to individuals (Ericson & Doyle, 2004), thus providing a particular socio-legal context to the construction of risk in which danger is actively sought out.

While the voluntary risk-seeking involved in lifestyle sports is implicated in judicial admonitions about potential liability, community sports, particularly those that are serviced by a volunteer base, are increasingly subject to institutional protocols designed to mitigate blame and liability. Verity (2004, 2006) has documented the impact of rising premiums on the volunteer sector, arguing that 'unquantifiable', 'objective' risks have, in some cases, been financially ruinous for community-based clubs and organizations in Australia. Here, instrumental risk reasoning is used to identify and calculate potential risks, and actuarial techniques are used to gather 'evidence' that can 'make known' the likelihood of potential risk.

Risk assessment and risk management are particularly prevalent in relation to children's play where safety legislation for children's play equipment and environments has seen the enforcement of laws and policies relating to 'maximum fall height, impact of absorbing surfaces, unstable equipment and the likelihood of being pinched, crushed or struck' (Hansen Sandseter, 2009). This is based on Scandinavian research showing that the majority of playground injuries result from falls from swings, slides, climbing frames or bicycles (Ball, 2004; Little, 2006). To return to the notion of risk avoidance, the supervision or surveillance of children at play is commonly believed to reduce the likelihood of injury, and is a key consideration in any risk assessment of children's play environments.

The construct of risk reasoning or assessing the potential for risk is articulated in the notion of 'play safety' that underpins early childhood policy in Norway (and other countries, like England). Determining 'precautionary risks' (Haggerty, 2003) is critical to the play safety debate. Here we see 'safety legislation, litigation, worried parents and child care workers' (Hansen Sandseter, 2009: 17) brought together to try to manage risk in play provision, which extends to play areas, playgrounds, adventure playgrounds, play centres and holiday play schemes, among others.

Such policy responses, however, are problematized by children being innate 'risk seekers' or 'risk takers', and the challenge for the play safety movement is to reconcile the tension between the objective determination of risk in risk assessment and the subjective experience of danger in the risk-seeking behaviour of children at play. As Hansen Sandseter notes, 'much of children's play is related to fear and young children actively seek out the thrills of fearful situations such as swinging and jumping from high places' (2009: 7).

Thus, risk is not experienced, conceptualized or, indeed, assessed universally, further highlighting its socially constructed nature. As Adams acknowledges, 'the problem for those who seek to devise objective measures of risk is that people to varying degrees modify their level of vigilance and their exposure to danger in response to their subjective perceptions of risk' (2001: 13).

Risk and Children's Rights

In his analysis of child labour in sport, Donnelly (1997; Donnelly & Petherick, 2006) describes a series of exploitative practices that would never be tolerated in educational or employment settings, arguing that such laxity with which children's rights have been applied in sport is problematic for a number of policy areas that sit at the junction of sport and civil society. These notions of children's rights and child welfare provide a useful framework for considering the policy implications of children in sport where there is considerable murkiness with respect to understandings and definitions of 'children' themselves. Located within a broader discourse about children's rights and the child as subject (or agent) that developed first in 1989 with the United Nations (UN) Children's Charter as an international expression of the rights of the child (as an extension of the Universal Declaration of Human Rights), it appears that many child athletes 'have lost their rights to play like a child. … They are too young to understand that they should have the rights to enjoy their innocent ages. They are too young to defend themselves when faced with sexual exploitation' (Hong, 2004: 341).

The most extended work on child athletes and child/human rights has been done by Hong (2004) and Hong and Zhouxiang (2008), using the elite training system in China as their focus of analysis. Hong maintains that sports policy in China has been built around patriotism and the 'three non-afraids' of 'hardship, difficulty and injury' (2004: 341). Describing long, gruelling training regimes adapted from the People's Liberation Army, Hong articulates the collapse of the boundaries between junior and senior, or between child and adult, that is so very problematic in the context of risk taking and risk avoidance. As Hong notes, 'these children are not permitted to be children. They are denied normal lives and important contacts and experience and child athletes should be regarded as "child labour" for they too work too young, too hard for very little pay and with too much responsibility' (2004: 341).

As is the case with other countries, performance at the elite level underpins Chinese sports policy. When China failed to repeat their performance at the 1984 Olympics in 1988, the then Sports Minister Li Meng Hua was sacked. While the policy trajectory for China is in line with other nations – it is fuelled by performance and patriotism – in few other policy contexts is the culture and politics of the training system so fundamentally linked to risks to child welfare, to risks of public humiliation and loss of face, and to risks to child social and physical development and care.

CONCLUSION

This chapter has been concerned with the relationship between sports policy and social theory. It has argued that analyses of sports policy could be strengthened by a greater engagement with social theory; that is by theories that have developed – in disciplinary terms – from anthropology, sociology, history, psychology, philosophy and cultural studies. Through the application of 'risk theory' to examples of children at risk, I have demonstrated how social theory can add particular insights into our understandings of the practical use of sports policy 'on the ground'.

I chose the example of risk as it suggests caution for totalizing, generalizing and politically prescriptive theoretical assertions. 'Risk' means different things, it is conceptualized and constructed differently, and different policy responses develop depending on the risk category that one is dealing with. In policy terms, however, the idea of 'risk' remains fundamentally connected to the concepts of order, control and governmentality. As the examples of child protection, playing safe and public liability, and the larger issues of risk and children's rights, suggest, risk is operationalized over time in different ways, and it effects, in different ways, the configuration of governments, institutions and the subjects who are meant to be risk categorized (Foucault, 1991; O'Malley, 2006). There is a tension between the uncertainty of risk in risk-seeking and the formal risk management and risk assessment by which sports policy has tended to calculate 'objective' risk in situations such as children at play or when competing as child athletes. In terms of policy-making, it is crucial that those who promote and regulate health, welfare and safety in sport understand how people think about and respond to risk; that is, those who appreciate the tension between subjective and objective experiences of risk. While risk is clearly a contested social construct, we live in an era that is increasingly risk conscious, and policy discourse and decision-making, in relation to both adults and children in sport, reflects this.

My focus on risk also sets up the agenda for much of the second section of this book, with its focus on global sporting mega-events. The mega-event distils the categories of risk introduced in this chapter. Mega-events connect the potential for risk, fear of risk and risk blaming in unique ways. There are clear environmental risks associated with the staging of a sporting mega-event; the spectre of post 9/11 terrorism hangs over events like the Olympic Games and there are a number of risks associated with forms of abuse that increase during the staging of a sporting mega-event, each of which is addressed in ensuing chapters.

BOX 5.2   QUESTIONS FOR DISCUSSION

- Can you explain the need for social theory in sports policy analysis?

- What role does a risk vocabulary play in sports policy?

- Of the three risk constructions mentioned, is one more or less relevant to studies of sports policy?

- How could Connell's discussion of 'Southern Theory' be further extended to strengthen analyses of sports policy in a global context?

SUGGESTED FURTHER READINGS

Coakley, J. (2004) *Sports in society: Issues and controversies*. New York: McGraw-Hill.
Connell, R. (2007) *Southern theory*. London: Polity Press.
Giulianotti, R. (2004) *Sport and modern social theorists*. London: Palgrave/Macmillan.

Houlihan, B. (2005) Public sector sport policy: Developing a framework for analysis. *International Review for the Sociology of Sport*, 40(2): 163–87.

Hudson, J. & Lowe, S. (2004) *Understanding the policy process: Analysing welfare policy and practice*. Bristol: Policy Press.

Sabatier, P. (ed.) (2007) *Theories of the policy process* (2nd edn). Boulder, CO: Westview Press.

Notes

1   See Palmer (2002a, 2004) for material on risk and lifestyle sports and adventure tourism or Giulianotti (2009) for a summary of sociological approaches to risk in sport. It is worth noting that 'risk' in sport can manifest itself in violence, public humiliation, actively 'taking a risk' through participation in extreme sports as well as a whole range of legal, managerial and financial responses to perceived or potential risks that sporting clubs and organizations routinely face. Equally, financial risks are an increasing part of the landscape of contemporary sport, with very real implications for sport policy and practice (such as the purchase of foreign players, the threat of liquidation or bankruptcy for a sporting organization). Taken together, these risks form a bundle of narrative themes that can impact dramatically on government policy-making.

2   In addition to the Advocacy Coalition Framework and the Multiple Streams perspective, Sabatier also includes analyses of nine other policy theories. I direct the reader to Sabatier (2007) for an overview of these alternative ways of theorizing the policy process.

3   On a related note, Davis-Delano and Crosset argue for the use of theory to explain social movements in sport. They 'examine theory itself, in terms of its utility or lack of utility for two social movements' and they found 'some theory more relevant than other theory to the outcomes of these movements. This approach allow[ed] them to assess the explanatory power of theory' (2008: 127).

4   A notable exception is Benn, Pfister and Jawad's (2010) edited collection *Muslim Women and Sport*, which is authored by, and details the experiences of, women from a range of Muslim countries and sporting contexts.

5   I am writing this book at the sharp end of globalization where it is easy to form an exaggerated view of how globalization affects the world and ignore the peripheral influences of these processes for much of the world – themes I addressed in Chapter 2.

6   The statistics on child sexual abuse (in sport or anywhere else) are notoriously unreliable because of the sensitivities of the subject, the political connotations of disclosure, and the likelihood that most cases are unreported, making it, as Brackenridge (2004) terms it, 'the most elusive crime'.

7   In 1995, the former British swimming coach, Paul Hickson, was jailed for 17 years for the rape and sexual assault of swimmers in the elite swimming squads he coached.

PART TWO

GLOBALIZATION AND SPORTING MEGA-EVENTS: POLICY IMPLICATIONS

6

GLOBALIZATION, SPORTS POLICY AND SPORTING MEGA-EVENTS

THIS CHAPTER

- considers the impacts of mega-events on a range of policy concerns;

- revisits debates about the Global North and Global South and the hosting of mega-events;

- explores the politics and pragmatics of studying sporting mega-events in the context of globalization and policy.

INTRODUCTION

I began the book with a recognition that in the twentieth century alone a number of public events and spectacles have emerged across the world stage, and these provide important sites through which social scientists can examine the global movement of people, values, goods and experiences. These 'special' or 'hallmark' events enable, as Horne recognizes, 'consideration of several overlapping and intersecting issues of contemporary social scientific interest' (2007: 81), and it is an analysis of these public events and spectacles that provides the focus for this second section of the book. These 'large-scale cultural events, which have a dramatic character, mass popular appeal and international significance' (Roche, 2000: 1), be they rock concerts, the inaugurations of political leaders, World Expos or, in this case, sporting events like the Olympic Games or football's World Cup, are quintessential phenomena of global modernity; 'intrinsically complex processes, which combine the interests of political and economic elites and professionals from the increasingly supranational cultural industries' (Roche, 2003: 99).

The dominant theme when writing about sporting mega-events has been to map the hosting of the event onto constructions and representations of national identity (Palmer, 1998a, 2002a, 2010; Rowe, 2003; Tomlinson & Young, 2006). An increasing body of research, however, now relates sporting mega-events both in general and by type to the processes and consequences of globalization (Andranovich & Burbank, 2004; Andranovich, Burbank & Heying, et al., 2001; Close, Askew & Xin, 2007; Horne & Manzenreiter, 2002, 2006; Manzenreiter & Horne, 2004), although the 'global' nature of these events is most frequently equated with simply scores of people watching these events on television around the world. Malcolm, in his introduction to *Dictionary of Sport Studies*, for example, notes that:

> sport is more properly a global phenomenon. An incredible 1.5 billion television viewers worldwide are estimated to have watched the [2006 FIFA World Cup] opening match and FIFA estimated that over 30 billion people would watch some television coverage of the tournament. (2008: xi)

However, the global consequences of these events for a number of *policy* concerns is often missed in analyses of the consumption of sporting mega-events, and this is the point of departure for this second section of *Global Sports Policy*.

While this first chapter is very much located in the literature on the global reach of these hallmark events, its focus is less on describing the largely self-evident nature of the contemporary sporting mega-event: the four 'knowns' of mega-events (Horne, 2007), and the costs and benefits attached to mega-events, and more on a consideration of the policy implications of staging mega-events for the cities and nations who do so, as well as for the athletes who compete at these events. The collision of political, cultural and commercial interests at mega-events makes them fruitful sites for policy development and analysis, and it is therefore surprising that a consideration of their policy implications beyond the 'knowns' represents something of a gap in research and writing on events like football's World Cup, the Super Bowl or the Pan American Games.

To briefly sketch the policy terrain, the social and economic impacts of sporting mega-events in terms of urban regeneration, tourism benefits or legacy outcomes for the cities and countries who host them have all been recognized by governments, NGOs and cosmocrats alike. Indeed, hosting major sports events has, for a number of countries, been an important element in tourism promotion (Sydney 2000 Olympic Games, South Africa's 2010 World Cup, Rio Olympics, 2016) and in urban and social regeneration (Barcelona Olympic Games in 1992, Commonwealth Games in Delhi in 2010, London 2012 Olympic Games), while 'urban revitalization' has become official policy in the European Union, in individual states and in specific cities (Gratton & Henry, 2001).

Many governments around the world have adopted national sports policies that specify the hosting of major sports events as a key objective[1], while the purported economic and 'brand' benefits for sponsors have been well noted since the 1984 'Hamburger Games', when McDonalds first became involved in the sponsorship of the Summer Olympics. Specific policy issues, as they are brought to bear on the London 2012 Olympic Games alone, include urban and social regeneration (Andranovich et al., 2001; Macrury, 2008), multiculturalism and racial diversity (as discussed in Chapter 2), human trafficking (discussed in Chapter 8), safety and security (discussed in Chapter 7), and governmental policies on legacy/participation and physical (in)activity (DCMS, 2007, 2008; and discussed in Chapter 4).

For the Beijing Olympics in 2008, issues of human rights commanded significant attention from politicians, policy makers and campaigners worldwide (also discussed in Chapter 8). The 2010 World Cup in South Africa placed wider public health concerns such as HIV/AIDS on the policy agenda in light of links to prostitution and the purchase of sex (Palmer, 2011) along with the Commonwealth Games in Delhi in the same year, which also raised the displacement and dispersal of the poor and the homeless as an area of considerable policy and (moral) concern. Thus, mega-events are 'crucial sites where populations are targeted by different forms of governmental and commercial knowledge/power, and where the recurring tensions of global politics are played out' (Tomlinson, 2011).

To interrogate the tensions between governmental and commercial knowledge/power that are at the nexus of policy production and consumption at global sporting mega-events, I begin by outlining the key defining properties of a mega-event before turning to the policy implications of staging these events. My particular concern is with the global *reach* of sports policy; that is, the extent to which mega-events offer a site for considering truly transnational policy-making, implementation and compliance. To ground my analysis empirically, I draw particularly, but not exclusively, on the Tour de France, and the policy concerns it foregrounds.

KEY CHARACTERISTICS OF MEGA-EVENTS

The term 'mega-event' gained much currency throughout the 1990s, where it was used to refer to 'specifically constructed and staged international cultural and sports events like the Olympic Games and World Fairs' (Roche, 2003: 99). Sharing many of the characteristics of a 'media event' (Dayan & Katz, 1992), mega-events are short-lived; they occur against an 'ephemeral vista' (Greenhalgh, 1998) but, nonetheless, have longer reaching pre- and post-event social dimensions. For Roche, 'they are publicly perceived as having an extra-ordinary status, among other things, by virtue of their very large scale, the time cycles in which they occur and their impacts' (2003: 99). Occurring in a specific location, with a restricted timing, a distinguishable personnel and a sizable media following, mega-events offer an overload of excitement and entertainment for the mass audience. As Roberts notes, certain events are 'mega' because they are 'discontinuous, out of the ordinary, international and simply big in composition' (2004: 82).

Adding another dimension to the definition, Close, Askew and Xin propose, somewhat self-evidently, that mega-events be defined as being 'those, and only those, events that are so large that they themselves have a global status, reach or scope' (2007: 28), while Cornelissen distinguishes between first-order, second-order and third-order mega-events, which differ in terms of 'prestige, attendance, interests and, particularly, publicity' (2004: 40). The consistent thread across such conceptualizations is that mega-events are major sites and sources of cultural imagination in the late twentieth century. Ephemeral, sensual and dominated by spectacle, mega-events are, as Paul Little concludes in his analysis of the 1992 Rio Earth Summit, 'new human phenomena that have emerged on the world stage during the past 50 years' (1995: 265).

In terms of sporting mega-events, Horne and Manzenreiter (2006) outline seven key characteristics: (1) they are cultural, commercial and sportive events on a large scale; (2) they have dramatic character; (3) they have a popular appeal; (4) they have international significance; (5) they have significant consequences for the host city or country; (6) they provoke major media attention; and (7) they represent a discontinuity in the ordinary nature of sport championships. In other words, mega-events 'symbolize, signal and substantively embody the progress of globalization as a set of processes along three basic social dimensions: the economic, the political and the cultural' (Close et al., 2007: 31). Each of the seven main characteristics suggests a range of policy potentialities, outlined in Table 6.1.

Bearing these policy features in mind, I turn now to my case study of the Tour de France. I provide, first, an overview of the race, before turning to a discussion of its implications for sports policy.

LE TOUR DE FRANCE AS GLOBAL MEGA-EVENT

I have undertaken ethnographic research on the Tour de France on and off since 1993 (see Palmer, 1996, 1998a, 1998b, 2000, 2001, 2002a, 2010). This ongoing engagement enables a discussion of the various currents of sport and social policy that meet and mingle in the production and consumption of the Tour de France.

But to provide some brief background to the Tour de France: staged annually each July since 1903, the Tour circumnavigates France, passing through 500-odd towns and covering approximately 4,000 kilometres in three weeks. Involving a capital investment of millions of francs, requiring a cast of thousands and attracting massive, international, media attention, the sheer quantity of resources that the Tour mobilizes guarantees it a certain stature as an archetypal 'first-order' sporting event. The Tour is a showcase of corporate interests, as Vittel, Carrefour, Coca-Cola, Nike, Crédit-Lyonnais, Skoda and Orange, among many others, stake their various claims upon it, as a publicity caravan transforms the French countryside into a surreal consumer world, and as an entire media industry is set in motion each July. The Tour brings to

Table 6.1   *Policy features of sporting mega-events*

Key features	Example	Policy implications
• Cultural, commercial and sportive events of a large scale	• Cultural Olympiad (all) • Sydney Olympics (2000) • Rio Olympics (2016)	• Funding for arts industries • Tourism benefits and infrastructure
• Dramatic character	• Opening ceremonies (all) • Sydney Olympics (2000) • Vancouver Winter Olympics (2010)	• Resourcing across competing policy sectors (e.g. arts and sport) • Representation of minority groups/Indigenous populations; highlight institutional racism and inequities in host countries
• Popular appeal • International significance	• All • London Olympics (2012) • Beijing Olympics (2008) • World Cup, South Africa (2010)	• National policy and 'legacy' agenda • Increasing physical activity agenda • Human rights concerns • HIV/AIDS and public health • Debates about the Global North and Global South
• Significant consequences for the host city or country	• Barcelona Olympics (1996) • Delhi, Commonwealth Games (2010)	• Urban and social regeneration
• Provoke major media attention	• All	• All
• Represent a discontinuity in the ordinary nature of sport championships	• All • Tour de France (all) • London Olympics (2012)	• Disruption to civic life and urban space (alcohol use, street space)

France an avalanche of commercial activity, which triggers a manifest transformation of social and symbolic landscapes (Palmer, 2002a, 2010).

In terms of globalization, the Tour is fully international in that transnational corporations build the bikes, they fund the event, and they sponsor the teams. American and German telecommunication companies sponsor outfits, Spanish banks finance teams, while Italian supermarkets, Belgian lottery agencies, French insurance companies and international brands of food, drink and clothing all support professional cycling squads. Largely rootless and de-territorialized – hallmarks of globalization – professional cycling teams are frequently associated with their sponsors, rather than the country where they are legally registered.

The Tour de France is also highly mediated as journalists from just about every major newspaper in the world report on its unfolding events, as mobile radio studios carry the race into the homes of people in cities and towns worldwide, and as television networks from the United States, Japan, the UK,

Holland, Colombia, Spain, Estonia, Australia and, of course, France itself beam their images around the globe.

Policy Implications of the Tour De France as a Global Sporting Mega-Event

From this brief description of the Tour, a number of concerns for sports and social policy emerge. To frame this discussion, I return to one the orienting frameworks of this book, Appadurai's (1996) conceptualization of 'scapes' introduced in Chapter 1. I do this because many of the consequences (both real and imagined) of staging the Tour include urban and social regeneration bene-fits, sporting legacy benefits, tourism and image benefits, and cultural and eco-nomic benefits (sketched in Table 6.1), and bring together the global flows of technology, finance, the media and people.

To take **ethnoscapes** first, the 'landscape of persons' encompasses, among other things, athletic migration, the geographic relocation within countries of professional sports workers, and the effects of this on partners and families as well as the growing need for inclusive sporting provision for refugees, asylum seekers and those crossing borders to flee abuses of human rights. Sporting mega-events bring these concerns into sharp relief. In the case of the Tour de France, the mega-event provides a stage at which athletic mobility can be enacted.

Professional cycling, like other sports, is characterized by considerable move-ment between teams, as cyclists vie for contracts and improved chances of career success. Indeed, the Tour de France lives out Appadurai's conceptualization of an ethnoscape as being a 'shifting world in which people live'. Professional cycling is an uncertain and precarious occupational environment, emblematic of broader trends in professional sport where athletic migration of footballers, most notably, is commonplace (Bale & Maguire, 1994; Chiba, 2004; Maguire & Pearton, 2000).

While not bound by 'Transfer of Allegiance' statements such as those used by the IAAF,[2] which document the changes in the nationality under which an ath-lete can race in international competition (IAAF, 2009), and without a pattern of migration from the core to the periphery – from countries significantly influ-enced by former colonial ties (commonly the movement of professional football-ers) – professional cycling is nonetheless characterized by a peak in end-of-season transfers of cyclists between teams, for which the Union Cyclistes Internationale's (UCI) policy regulates the transfer of athletes between teams (www.uci.ch). Unlike other forms of athletic migration in which athletes can change their country of representation and for which governing bodies impose waiting peri-ods which determine when an athlete can compete for their new country, the movement of professional cyclists is far more 'de-territorialized'. That is, cyclists are associated less with a 'national' team and more with the trade team of their sponsors. Thus, the very nature of athletic migration is embedded in a policy discourse in which commercial interests operate alongside those of the cyclist.

The Tour de France, then, becomes the front stage (in Goffman's terms) on which riders who may be out of contract, released due to poor form, or forced to look elsewhere due to the sponsor withdrawing financial support for the team, must perform. The Tour feeds directly into the politics of athletic migration, with the UCI governing the flow of movement between teams by enforcing a 'transfer window'. Contracts in professional cycling usually run annually from 1 January to 31 December, with the transfer window opening on 1 August each year (following the Tour in July), at which point announcements can be made regarding transfers for the following year. Policies governing professional cycling, embodied in the Tour de France, thus cast the sporting milieu as being one of movement, ebb and flow, in which 'the shifting world in which people live' has an annual cycle to it.

Ideoscapes represent the images, discourse and beliefs that are invested with political and ideological meaning, and it is their capacity to reflect and broadcast particular images and narratives of nation and nationhood that has much resonance for sporting mega-events. In the case of the Tour de France, very particular images of France and 'Frenchness' are selected and then progressively elaborated to the global media audience by a number of cultural intermediaries or brokers who are responsible for the image management of the race (Palmer, 2010).

This management of key images of nation and nationhood has implications for a number of policy initiatives through which mega-event planners, municipal authorities, publicists and various other cultural and policy brokers seek to present an image of city and country that positively reflects the ideologies of the State in ways that enable the reproduction of very particular imaginings of community. Indeed, sporting mega-events provide cities with what Scherer and Davison (2011) have referred to as 'anticipatory spectacles' that can dramatize their potential as places for investment in a context in which the choice of 'global cities' (Sassen, 2010) is seemingly limitless. While these 'arriviste cities' take on particular meanings when considered in the broader policy and ideological context of the Global South and the increasing presence of mega-events in countries beyond the traditional northern metropole – a point to which I return – events like the Tour de France must insert themselves into a network of global capital from which their impression as an economically viable, politically stable, image-rich nation can be broadcast (Carter, 2011b: 135). Consequently, the 'dramatization' of host cities' potential is key to the ideoscape of the event and the policy that thus develops around it.

Given the global media attention the Tour de France attracts, hosting a stage start or finish is enormously appealing for towns and villages. The riders, their entourage, media, sponsors, officials and other Tour personnel (as well as spectating tourists) require food and accommodation and they spend money in bars and on souvenirs, in doing so, injecting income into the local economy. Not surprisingly, bidding for the right to host a stage of the Tour de France is fierce. In 2008, 252 towns applied to host a stage start or finish. Of these, forty towns were chosen for inclusion in the race itinerary in 2010 (Le Tour, 2010).[3]

However, while the spatial transformation of urban landscape through the hosting of mega-events brings about what Belanger (2000) has referred to as the 'spectacularisation' of urban landscapes, whereby cities are taken over by casinos, megaplexes, cinemas, themed restaurants, stadia and sporting complexes, an important distinction in the case of the Tour de France is that these do not outlast the staging of the event itself (Carter, 2006), as the transformation of urban landscapes is through a temporary, transportable infrastructure. Thus, the legacy impacts of mega-events, often realized through urban regeneration and social development schemes implicit in domestic and foreign policy agendas of governments worldwide, does not materialize in any substantive way in the case of the Tour de France. Here, 'legacy' is more symbolic than actual, operating through forms of myth-making and narrative-building, which contrasts somewhat with the policy priorities of other governments, where hosting mega-events is about improving national sporting performance, civic regeneration and social development.

Of course, images of 'Frenchness' and the presentation of a capable, viable host country and its 'arriviste cities' (Scherer & Davison, 2011) – central to the policy discourse of mega-event making – are carried through the conflation of both **technoscapes** and **mediascapes**, and each of these can be mapped onto a grid of capital and a spread of financial accumulation; Appadurai's notion of a **'financescape'**. Economically, mega-events are generally viewed as carrying significant short-term as well as long-term benefits for the host cities. Mega-event planners and promoters are frequently at pains to emphasize the immediate revenue associated with these events, stemming from public and private sector investment and, particularly, advertising and media revenue (Alegi, 2001; Horne & Manzenreiter, 2002).

With clear links to both ideoscapes and ethnoscapes, the perceived economic and tourism spin-offs of the hosting of a mega-event make bidding for it a common activity of entrepreneurial cities. As Rowe and McKay note with reference to the Beijing Olympics:

> It is particularly important to convince locals that the massive resources involved are on balance beneficial for the host city and nation, not least by stimulating positive external impressions that will deliver tangible benefits. The justification for bidding, and the complexion of anticipated benefits for hosts and visitors, is highly variable. (2011: 119)

Despite doubts about national and worldwide economies to withstand the sheer scale and cost of the Olympic Games, cities continue to queue for the opportunity to stage the event. In 2011, no less than thirty-four cities had stated an interest in bidding for the 2020 Summer Olympics (Tomlinson, 2011). Such unbridled, often unsubstantiated, passion for hosting mega-events is not without its critics, particularly in terms of their more lasting impacts. As Atkinson et al. write with reference to London 2012, 'while a mega-event shines a spotlight on a city for a short period of time, most of the activities involve limited participation by local citizens and the legacy effects are often quite small' (2008: 420).

It is in terms of corporate involvement, however, that the transfer patterns of global capital within the ideoscape are made maximally visible. Rowe notes with respect to the 2002 Korea/Japan World Cup final between Brazil and Germany, that 'with an estimated global audience of 1.5 billion collectively exposed to the corporate logos of such global brands as Nike, Adidas, Yahoo!, McDonalds, Budweiser, Phillips and Fujifilm, it appears self evident that sport is globalization's most attentive handmaiden' (2003: 284). This is the kind of commentary one presumes Marx had in mind when he acerbically commented 'money is now pregnant'; the capital invested in the event is itself accorded the power to create money and wealth in its own right.

While corporate involvement may be, as MacNeil (1996) points out, part of the 'circuit of production', this is not without financial costs and risks. Even biding for a mega-event makes a statement that the city regards itself as a global player, that it has important, international, political status. Bidding campaigns are exclusive and allow only those cities which are not only able but also willing to undertake the fiscal risks that the hosting of such events generally pose (Cornelissen, 2008: 49). Thus, balancing the 'feel good' benefits that are embedded in ideoscapes and carried in media and technoscapes requires the ratcheting up of a linguistic performance in which financial risks are obscured in the narrative that surrounds the hosting of major events like the Olympic Games or the Tour de France, and, again, this is key to the policy discourse that surrounds mega-event making.

As such accounts make clear, Appadurai's 'scapes' are useful for analyzing the complex, overlapping and disjunctive nature of policy-making. Sports policy rarely takes place in isolation. In the case of the Tour de France, the policy directives that fall within the terrain of 'financescapes' – the use of the event to generate investment and sponsorship, for example – also have implications for ethnoscapes or technoscapes; for the ways in which people imagine their community and the technological resources they draw on to do so. Equally, this intertwining of scapes alerts us to the constructed nature of mega-events, and the role that various organizations and institutions play in orchestrating a mega-event, sporting or otherwise. Indeed, mega-events are 'typically organized by variable combinations of national government and non-governmental and international non-governmental organizations' (Roche, 2000: 1), and are managed by the combined forces of state apparatus and non-state civil society organizations (CSOs), such as the International Olympic Committee, to return to some of the ideas of previous chapters.

Moreover, the formulation of 'scapes' comes some way to redressing a persistent conceptual conundrum summarized by Close, Askew and Xin: 'one of the problems in defining a "mega-event" is in distinguishing these events in some other, perhaps more sociologically pertinent, sound and valuable way' (2007: 28). That is, the challenge is to move our analyses beyond the relatively simplistic descriptions of mega-events in terms of 'the numbers' I alluded to earlier in this chapter. Roche suggests that analyses of mega-events can 'benefit from perspectives that emphasize their explicitly ideological aspirations and potentially hegemonic impacts' (2003: 100) and a study of the 'scapes' of the Tour de France provides the ethnographic space through which to do so.

ANTI-DOPING AND ATHLETE WELFARE: THE TOUR DE FRANCE AS POLICY CATALYST

Having outlined the various policy concerns that emerge from the largely self-evident aspects of the Tour as a mega-event, I turn now to some other issues for sports policy that are embedded and expressed within the event. While it is tempting, as others have done, to focus on the policy implications of simply hosting mega-events, there are also wider policy considerations which sit outside the temporal and spatial boundaries imposed by customary definitions and interpretations of a mega-event. The Tour, as an annually occurring mega-event, represents a unique intersection of policy relating to anti-doping as well as policies of athlete welfare and workers' rights.

Anti-Doping and Athlete Welfare Policy

I've mentioned at several points that the 'Festina Affair' in the 1998 Tour de France was the trigger for the development of more rigorous, globally harmonized anti-doping policy, and the Tour continues to be the most visible site at which 'evidence' of testing protocols is made public. Every rider in the Tour is tested for banned substances prior to the race. A number of cyclists are selected for testing after each stage, according to a selection process determined before the race. Under current UCI rules, at least 180 urine drug tests are given throughout the race, including daily tests for the race leader and the stage winner and for six to eight cyclists who are selected at random from the field each day. In accordance with the rules of WADA, the UCI and the Fédération Française de Cyclisme (FFC), drug testing is done under secure and strictly monitored conditions. A purpose-equipped caravan is established near the finish line of every stage to transport drug samples to a private location following each day's racing. Drug test samples are then transported by private plane for analysis, and the results are quickly reported to Tour officials. This has become the benchmark for anti-doping policy in other cycling events and other endurance sports, which extends to out-of-competition testing and the use of biological passports.[4]

I noted in Chapter 4 that, as a professional body, cyclists are well versed in the politics of participatory democracy and have mobilized action in order to determine the rules and policies that regulate their sport and working conditions. Indeed, although the organizers of the Tour de France have long denied riders the right to unionize, professional cyclists have been hugely instrumental in changing the shape and rhythm of professional races. Concerned with their health and welfare, professional cyclists, through their union (AIGCP) and other advocacy bodies, have successfully argued for daily limits on stage lengths and the overall length of a race, and these are now enacted in policy and practice. Again, it is the Tour de France that provides the most visible site at which these policies have been developed and enforced. Concerns for rider welfare have limited the overall length of the race to a maximum of 3,500 kilometres spread over twenty-one days (including two compulsory rest days for the riders), during which a maximum daily distance of 225 kilometres cannot be exceeded more than twice. More broadly, union delegates have successfully agitated for income protection and other aspects of professional welfare and well-being in a short-lived and often precarious profession.

In addition to the broad policy implications that emerge from hosting mega-events, mega-events also raise two particular concerns for sports policy in the global order that are central themes of this book more broadly: (i) the power imbalances and inequities embedded in the processes and consequences of globalization; and (ii) the politics and pragmatics of 'studying' globalization. The growth of mega-events in non-Western or BRIC countries provides a useful backdrop to this discussion.

MEGA-EVENTS AND BRIC COUNTRIES

Since the Beijing Olympic Games in 2008, there has been a growing interest in the ways in which sporting mega-events both reinforce and enhance many of the inequities within the West and between the West and non-Occidental countries, particularly, but not exclusively, in terms of competitive success, for this is emblematic of broader issues of systematic and structural inequalities in the global order.[5] As Little writes, with reference to the Rio Earth Summit in 1992, '[mega-events] have brought the issues of world justice to the fore of an international political arena long dominated by the self-serving discourse of the world's major industrial powers' (1995: 265).

The imbalances of wealth and power made visible by the staging of global sporting mega-events provide a useful backdrop to the shift in debate about the negative effects of Western-led forms of globalization on non-Western countries, given the growing global capital that non-Western countries now exercise to successfully bid for a whole host of sporting events, including football's World Cup, the Olympic Games, Formula One Grand Prix, cricket tournaments and international athletics and cycling competitions. As Curi, Knijnik and Mascarenhas note:

> It has become common for former so-called semi-peripheral developing countries to stage sports tournaments of global significance: the 2008 Summer Olympic Games in Beijing, the 2010 Commonwealth Games in New Delhi, the 2014 Winter Olympics in Sochi and the 2014 FIFA World Cup in Brazil and the 2016 Summer Olympics in Rio de Janeiro. (2011: 141)

Although mega-events have been staged in non-Western countries for some time (the Tokyo Olympics in 1964, Seoul in 1998, Mexico in 1968, the 1992 World Cup jointly hosted by Japan and South Korea, as well as several football World Cup finals hosted by Uruguay, 1930, Brazil, 1950, Chile, 1952, Mexico, 1986, for example), the Beijing Olympics set in motion a new social, political and, indeed, research agenda for considering the increasing presence of non-Western countries on the global mega-events circuit, in particular, those countries that are referred to as 'BRIC' countries. Brazil, Russia, India and China, it is argued, are emerging as major economic power players and, according to some commentators, will 'become the most important new economic forces by 2050' (Curi et al., 2011: 141).

Since Beijing, a number of countries in the Global South or beyond the traditional economic power triad of North America–Europe–Japan have successfully bid for the right to host sporting mega-events, which has shifted conceptualizations of them (both the country and the mega-event). Qatar, for example, has carved out a global niche in hosting sporting mega-events in the Gulf States. As Campbell notes, 'state investment in technologically and architecturally first-rate facilities has helped qualify Qatar as a global participant' (2010: 49). The International Association of Athletics Federations Championships, the Qatar Moto GP, the 2011 Asian World Cup, the Tour of Qatar cycle race and the 2022 FIFA World Cup are just a few of the high-profile sporting events to be staged in Qatar, while neighbouring Bahrain is part of the international Formula One Grand Prix circuit, although this is not without its critics over concerns for human rights in that country. The economic power of the Gulf region may be a major factor in transforming global sport, and this has a number of policy implications, ranging from the impact of hosting mega-events on the environment, to the 'exploitation of imported labor for construction purposes, the inability of other nations to match the hosting bids of the Gulf States and the exorbitant salaries paid to attract elite athletes for one-off guest appearances (Tiger Woods received US$2 million just to play at the Dubai Open)' (Jackson & Haigh, 2009: 3), among others.

Elsewhere, in the bidding process for the 2016 Summer Olympics, Rio de Janeiro (Brazil), Tokyo (Japan), Baku (Azerbaijan), Doha (Qatar) and Prague (Czech Republic) were short-listed (along with Chicago and Madrid), with Rio de Janeiro eventually winning out. While one may attribute the success of Brazil to 'beginner's luck' – 'there had been no sport-related event of global or international significance in Brazil for the past 44 years when suddenly the country became a candidate for three – winning all of them' (Curi et al., 2011: 141): the Pan American Games in 2007, the FIFA World Cup in 2014 and the 2016 Olympic Games in Rio de Janeiro[6] – the success of Brazil in winning the rights to host these mega-events underscores the Eurocentric bias that has characterized previous studies of mega-events and the policy implications attached to them. Despite the growing presence of BRIC countries on the mega-events circuit, our sociological imagination is only now registering the social, symbolic, political and policy import of these 'other' events in 'other' countries. As Cornelissen notes, 'since the vast majority of mega-events are hosted by industrialized states, discourse and research on the processes and impacts of these events tends to be framed around the economic and political circumstances characteristic of the developed world' (2004: 40).[7]

Such gaps are reflective of the bias in studies of sport and sports policy discussed in Chapter 4, particularly Henry's (2007) critique of the privileging of Western views when approaching the analysis of sports policy. In terms of mega-events more specifically, Carter echoes this criticism, arguing that 'this is one of our failings so far: the almost complete absence of other "global" sport spectacles in our analyses (cf. Henry et al., 2003). Where are the Pan American Games, Asian Games, Commonwealth Games and other spectacles in our production of sociological knowledge about sport-related mega-events?' (Carter, 2011a: 132). Similarly, Cornelissen recognizes that 'to date, very little research has been done on African countries' attempts to participate in the global sport mega-event enterprise' (2004: 39). While certainly there is a gap in academic attention on sporting mega-events, my concern here is not with an analysis of any particular BRIC country-based mega-event, but rather to sketch out some of the implications and tensions for policy debates that these events are increasingly drawing to the attention of critical social scientists concerned to elaborate a more 'humane' version of globalization.

The Politics and Pragmatics of BRIC Mega-Events

In previous chapters I asked, somewhat rhetorically, whether or not we could truly speak of 'global sports policy' (or global any other kind of policy), given the biases inherent within the political economy and geography of knowledge that underpins policy production and consumption. Of concern here, the configurations of wealth and resources that are inevitable outcomes of the global movement of people, commodities and capital coalesce in very particular ways at sporting mega-events in BRIC countries. While there are contrasting poor and rich countries around the world, reflected, particularly, in terms of participation and performance at mega-events, the vast majority of people in the Global North who routinely watch and consume these events do not come in contact with the extremes of poverty in their daily lives. 'This structure is completely different in a developing country. Here rich and poor live side by side. The contrast is visible on a daily basis' (Curi et al., 2011: 145).

The staging of the 2014 football World Cup and the Summer Olympics in 2016 in Brazil will bring this into sharp relief. Commentators have already noted the juxtaposition of 'First' and 'Third' world populations living side by side in Rio de Janeiro. Millions of people live in slums or *favelas* without any welfare assistance, health care, access to education or any kind of public service (Curi et al., 2011: 153), which is a confronting image and reality for Games organizers, which the 2008 Beijing Olympics and 2010 Commonwealth Games in Delhi had to deal with as part of the image management of these mega-events. While the human rights implications of 'Third World' populations who live in cities that celebrate the political and economic interests of the First World through hosting mega-events are discussed further in Chapter 8, the point here is that for the cosmocrats who orchestrate mega-events in BRIC and developing countries there is an issue for brokerage, presentation and discursive management on a scale never encountered before. As MacAloon notes, 'the IOC has painfully understood the media and public relations cost of plonking down the Olympics amidst the world's most abject poverty. Whether realistic or not, it remains to be seen, but President Lula da Silva and the Rio bid team began last spring to position Rio 2016 as an urban poverty-alleviation project' (2011: 308).

Certainly, one of the challenges for BRIC and developing countries is to successfully stage a mega-event without falling victim to First World perceptions that they may be punching above their weight. In the lead-up to the 2010 Commonwealth Games held in Delhi, reports documenting the 'filthy conditions of the athletes' living quarters, the collapse of a pedestrian bridge and the subsequent cave-in of the roof of the weightlifting venue' (Carter, 2011a: 131) circulated around the world. While such accounts 'revelled in stereotypes about the organizational inadequacy of developing nations' (Curi et al., 2011: 141), they equally resulted in India and, by extension, other BRIC and developing nations, losing the symbolic capital that helps secure public confidence that they are as capable as cities in the Global North to host a first-order sporting mega-event. As Carter writes, with reference to the symbolic fall-out of such media portrayals of Delhi, 'even as the celebratory spectacles are held within the sporting venues and the imagery of athletic vitality is transmitted around the world, the poverty, pollution, and the rumoured and assumed corruption that so plague Dehlian and Indian governments has already been reaffirmed and solidified in the "global imagination"' (2011a: 131).

Within this popular discourse, there is an element of 'I told you so', when BRIC and/or peripheral nations exceed the budget for hosting mega-events. The 2010 Commonwealth Games is instructive here. The original estimate of approximately US$1.3 billion for the 2010 Games in Delhi mushroomed to $15 billion, making the Games seven times more expensive than the Melbourne Commonwealth Games in 2006 and 'by far and away the most expensive games in history' (Majundar & Mehta, 2010). Thus, the challenge for countries beyond the northern metropole is to convince the world, using the potentialities and symbolic capital leveraged by sporting 'scapes', that their new status as an economic power is matched by their ability to not only match, but *outdo* the Global North. While concerns for security, infrastructure and budget may be subject to increased scrutiny when mega-events are staged in BRIC countries, let's not forget Athens, which was heavily scrutinized for its ability and capacity to organize the 2004 Summer Olympics or, indeed, London 2012, whose budget continues to spiral well beyond original estimates.

In the context of globalization, mega-events hosted by BRIC countries allow us to see some of the culturally relative characteristics of globalization that are not made visible in the predominantly Western-focused sports scholarship (Campbell, 2010: 45). As well as highlighting the politically charged and uneven nature of globalization, sporting mega-events also offer a point of entry into a long-running debate, namely, whether it is, in fact, possible to 'study' globalization and, by extension, global sports policy.

GLOBALIZATION, MEGA-EVENTS AND SOCIAL INQUIRY

To briefly sketch the debate, it is contended that it is only ever possible to study the effects and consequences of globalization, not globalization itself. That is, we only ever study the 'things' of globalization – the investment, individuals and information that globalization makes possible – rather than the processes of globalization itself, for these are largely ephemeral and mercurial. In examining ethnoscapes, for example, we study the effects of the shifting landscape of people, rather than the landscape itself. Following from this, a related criticism of accounts of globalization is the 'a-spatial' vision of globalization (Massey, 2005; Mattelart, 2005; Savage, Bagnall & Longhurst, 2005) that is evoked in the popular imagery of a 'borderless world' and a 'single place'. In other words, while it is customary to talk of globalization in the abstract, studies of it can only take place in the concrete.

The mega-event provides a 'concrete' site at and through which to engage with these debates and concerns, and to come some way to redressing the tendency to reify concepts of globalization to the point of inaccessible abstraction, for they provide a bounded, time- and site-specific occasion at which to direct lines of social inquiry, in this case, into sports policy and globalization. In particular, mega-events offer a point of entry into a number of broader conceptual, theoretical and epistemological concerns that are raised by studies of the 'things' of globalization; namely, the multiple registers of interpretation through which the products and consequences of globalization are experienced worldwide, and the distinctive contribution that scholarly accounts of mega-events can offer over popular accounts from the cultural brokers described in Chapter 3. It is the implications of this for studies of sports policy that I turn to now.

Global Ethnography: Critical Approaches to Studying Mega-Events

In their book, *Global Ethnography*, Burawoy et al. (2000) outline an analytical strategy for studying the ways in which globalization impacts upon various groups, including, among others, breast cancer survivors, software developers in

Ireland, ship workers in San Francisco and homeless men. Adopting an 'extended case study' approach, Burawoy et al. identify four underlying principles that guide their analysis:

i   that the researcher must enter the field in order to appreciate the experiences of individuals;
ii that fieldwork must take place over time and space;
iii that research must extend from micro-processes to macro-forces;
iv that theory is extended and challenged as due process when assessing research findings (Burawoy et al., 2000: 26–8).

These principles provide a useful framework within which to consider the study of globalization and, by extension, global sports policy through the lens of the sporting mega-event.

The researcher must enter the field in order to appreciate the experiences of individuals

Social scientists are by no means alone in their interest in sporting mega-events. Little, for example, notes that mega-events are covered by 'thousands of journalists from all over the world who, via a wide means of electronic media (fax, satellite transmissions, radio waves, computer networks and so on), are sending their reports, stories, photos and sound bites [sic.] instantaneously to their home agencies' (1995: 282). This, then, begs the question as to what, if anything, is unique about social scientific analyses of mega-events, if they are so ubiquitously covered by other brokers reading and interpreting the event for audiences worldwide. As Little notes, 'like it or not, ethnographers must "compete" with journalistic production, since they too will be creating texts about the event, even though they are writing for widely different audiences' (1995: 282).

Following Burawoy et al.'s contention that 'the researcher must enter the field in order to appreciate the experiences of individuals', I argue that it is an ethnographic approach that offers a unique perspective on mega-events, and, by extension, global popular culture and public policy. My analysis of the Tour de France involved engaging with a local cycling community in France for more than fourteen months, with media organizations from several countries and with professional cycling teams, registered in Holland and Andorra (Palmer, 1996). As I write elsewhere:

> While the Tour de France in 1994 [the first year of my fieldwork] had nearly two thousand officially registered journalists sending their reports, stories, photos and sound bytes [sic.] around the world, I was the only anthropologist. ... The emphasis that anthropologists place on the practice of ethnography continues to privilege us as interpreters of increasingly fluid and cosmopolitan worlds within the contemporary ecumene. (Palmer, 2000: 376)

Ethnographic accounts can capture the cultural worlds of policy makers and event planners as they bring these mega-events to life. The extended field study approach enables the analysis of the lived, everyday nature of mega-events and the ways in which public spectacles become fully incorporated into a broader milieu of cultural policy and politics.

Fieldwork must take place over time and space

This, of course, does not deny the greatest challenge for studies of global mega-events and global sports policy: the fact that mega-events are experienced by multiple audiences across multiple registers of interpretation. While mega-events may take place at particular sites, what occurs there is then relayed to audiences worldwide, and there is thus a need to undertake fieldwork over time and space, over multiple sites of experience in multiple locales so as to recognize and accommodate the different vantage points from which mega-events can be interpreted. My study of the Tour de France, for example, encompassed the perspectives of French and Australian media organizations, Dutch and Andorran-registered professional teams and the local cycling community based in and around Grenoble, France, during the three weeks of the race, and then for twelve months in between Tours. Beyond, my study included the perspectives of Australian media agencies and French and Australian cycling aficionados who followed the race outside the time frame of my original period of fieldwork. In his account of the 2002 FIFA World Cup in Japan and South Korea, Rowe (2003) employs a similar strategy of including multiple perspectives and vantage points, viewing the event from Australia and briefly from the joint host nations as well.

Such research strategies, while they are not always practical, enable a unique engagement with the mega-event in ways that are beyond the brokered, largely text-based reading of the event. Conducting fieldwork over time and space provides a nuanced understanding of 'the event', and its implications, policy or otherwise, for local actors and communities (Carter, 2011a).

Pujik (2000) in his study of the 1994 Winter Olympic Games at Lillehammer shows how the focus on the mediated nature of these events is not particularly useful in 'illuminating cross-cultural communication in global media events, since it leaves out several layers of meaning and tends to operate instead as if one single meaning were generated by the event' (2000: 311). An audience in Hungary, for example, may watch hours of fencing at the Olympic Games, yet this sport scarcely merits attention in the USA's coverage of the Games. As Short notes, television coverage 'concentrates on [the local] national teams and representatives so that people in different countries will quite literally see different Olympics' (2004: 88).

The intersections between 'the local' and 'the global' that studies of mega-events over time and space afford are useful for problematizing the notion of 'global sports policy'. While the mega-event may be the most visible or public site at which various policy concerns are played out (such as anti-doping regulations), the particularities of local interpretation suggest caution for policy-making that is created with the expectation of worldwide unilateral compliance.

Research must extend from micro-processes to macro-forces

While studies over time and space allow a particularly nuanced, 'local' interpretation of the mega-event in different countries and contexts, the analysis of such events is by no means a unidirectional process. The research must also extend from micro-processes to macro-forces. As Eriksen argues, 'global symbols and globalised information are interpreted from a local vantage point and contribute to shaping that vantage point' (1995: 285).

While it can be argued that one of the consequence of studies of globalization is an overemphasis on 'the micro' or on ethnographic particularities such that complex issues and large-scale processes are oversimplified or obscured, engaged studies of mega-events, such as those I've outlined here, provide a clear indication that analyses of global or spatially disembodied phenomena pose no threat to small-scale ethnography (Robertson coined the term *glocalization* to counter such criticism), and small-scale ethnography can, in turn, shed light on macro-forces. As James Fox summarizes:

> Partly realised through global imagination, partly imagined through media exposure, these [ethnoscapes], Appadurai persuades us, require a 'macro' – or cosmopolitan – ethnography. Such an ethnography would recognise that everyday life is now lived out globally and that the small community is the end point of a cultural jet stream. (1991: 12)

Again, the mega-event provides a unique site at which to witness the tensions between the local and the global as being perhaps more abstract, reified and imagined than is actually lived and experienced. For many, the global *is* the local, and vice versa, and this cuts across the scapes within which sporting mega-events are assuredly embedded.

Theory is extended and challenged as due process when assessing research findings

I contended in the previous chapter that global sports policy analysis can be strengthened by a better application of social theory that can map change and continuity across time and geographical contexts. Social theories have much analytical utility for understanding how people use and respond to particular policy initiatives that develop on a global scale. Following on from this, studies of mega-events routinely scrutinize many of the theoretical concepts that flow from the globalization debate. Conceptual wordplays such as 'glocalization' or 'creolization' can be tested, evaluated and reconfigured through the research findings that sustained fieldwork affords. Burawoy's contention that 'theory is extended and challenged as due process when assessing research findings' is just one of the challenges to which ethnographic fieldwork can respond. Theory, for theory's sake, however, rarely translates to policy practice. Waddington and Smith have noted, 'there is nothing as practical as good theory' (2009: 8), and 'good theory' must be informed by sustained fieldwork that can capture the multiple ways in which policy can respond to local circumstances, and local circumstances can, in turn, shape global policy.

Pulling together Burawoy et al.'s (2000) four principles, ethnographic work can shed light on the impact of global forces in local settings in ways that are sensitive to multiple registers of interpretation. The sustained approach to studies of mega-events, I suggest, is what enables the study of the resources of global culture that flow through sporting mega-events; that is, that enables the study 'globalization' rather than the consequences and impacts of globalization. In the context of sports policy, understanding what people 'do' with globalization enables a more nuanced understanding of what they 'do' with policy as one of the key constituents of a public life experienced across multiple valences and registers of interpretation. Multi-sited fieldwork, such as that advocated here, is key to developing policy that is sensitive to the costs, benefits and risks of hosting mega-events. The 'scapes' of mega-events to which aspects of sports policy correspond are not experienced universally, and there is a need for a more fine-grained understanding of policy-making and its consequences when considering the policy implications of global sporting mega-events.

CONCLUSION

This chapter has sketched out the policy implications of hosting sporting mega-events; undoubtedly, the major global feature of sport and sports policy in the twenty-first century. While relatively generic policy concerns, such as urban and social regeneration, tourism and legacy benefits, or social and economic investment can be mapped onto Appadurai's formulation of 'scapes', mega-events can also reveal other policy concerns that are underrepresented in writings on the largely self-evident global consequences and reach of the kind of major sporting events described in this chapter. As perhaps the most visible display of a professional sportsperson's 'workplace', mega-events such as the Tour de France provide a context in which to consider policies as they relate to athlete welfare and workers' rights. Equally, mega-events are perhaps the most public site of testing and surveillance – for drugs and/or sex and gender 'irregularities' (Caudwell, 2011) – and 'crises' at mega-events (such as *L'Affaire Festina* or the ambiguity surrounding the sex of Mokgadi 'Caster' Semenya at the 2009 World Championship in Athletics in Berlin) have resulted in significant policy shifts in relation to both doping and sex testing.[8]

The staging of mega-events also addresses two particular concerns for sports policy in the global order that are central themes of this book more broadly: the power imbalances and inequities embedded in the processes and consequences of globalization and the politics and pragmatics of 'studying' globalization. The increasing interest in, and attention on, mega-events that are staged in locations beyond the northern metropole can and will continue to highlight many of the concerns for studies of global policy, such as global social redistribution, global social regulation, and global social provision and/or empowerment in a context of supranational and national interrelationships (Deacon, 1997: 195).

Equally, the global nature of mega-events begs the question of whether it is, in fact, possible to 'study' globalization. Mega-events like the Olympic Games, the Tour de France or the World Cup are seen 'differently in different parts of the world, through the eyes of many different national audiences' (Tomlinson, 1996), which suggests an unavoidably partial and 'local' dimension to their reception. Thus, while mega-events may be highly globalized, mediated spectacles, they remain deeply localized events that are viewed and refracted through local vantage points.

Having charted the broad terrain of the sporting mega-event, the next three chapters focus on particular concerns that mega-events foreground as key areas of policy debate. Issues of safety and security at sporting mega-events, human rights, and the environmental impact of hosting mega-events are the subject of the next three chapters, where mega-events offer crucial sites at which the recurring tensions of global policy and politics are played out.

BOX 6.1   QUESTIONS FOR DISCUSSION

- To what extent do you agree with the statement that the sporting mega-event is the quintessential feature of globalization in the twenty-first century?

- What are some of the limitations (for policy analysis) with popular approaches to studying sporting mega-events?

- How can analyses of sporting mega-events contribute to a more 'humane' approach to analyses of globalization in terms of inequities and imbalances of power across the globe?

SUGGESTED FURTHER READINGS

Close, P., Askew, D. & Xin, X. (2007) *The Beijing Olympiad: A political economy of a sporting mega-event*. London: Routledge.

Horne, J. with Manzenreiter, W. (eds) (2006) Sports mega-events: Social scientific analyses of a global phenomenon. *Sociological Review Monograph Series*. Oxford: Blackwell.

Palmer, C. (1998) Le Tour du Monde: Towards an anthropology of the global mega-event. *The Australian Journal of Anthropology*, Special Edition 10 'Anthropology and Cultural Studies: Ethnography and Culture in a Postmodern World', 9(3): 168–75.

Roche, M. (2000) *Mega-events and modernity: Olympics and Expos in the growth of global culture*. London: Routledge.

Roche, M. (2003) Mega-events, time and modernity: On time structures in global society. *Time & Society*, 12(1): 99–126.

Notes

1 In several cases, funding has flowed directly from the performance of countries at mega-events, reflecting shifting policy priorities. For example, the Australian Institute of Sport (AIS) was established following Australia's poor performance at the Montreal Olympic Games in 1976. In Canada, increased federal investment followed the Canadian team's disappointing performance at the Athens Games in 2004, while in Australia, an additional A$135 million of funding for sports performance was allocated in the three years prior to the Sydney Olympic Games in 2000.

2 The current IAAF rules on transfer of allegiance stipulate a three-year waiting period that can be reduced to twelve months with the agreement of the relevant member federations (the two countries involved) or reduced to no waiting time at the discretion of the IAAF (IAAF, 2009).

3 The grounds for selection are a combination of the town's geographical location – public expectations demand the regular inclusion of certain localities, such as the final stage being held along the Champs Elysées and stages that traverse the high mountain passes in the French Alps and the Pyrenees – as well as its capacity to accommodate the huge physical infrastructure and personnel that accompany the race each day.

4 A biological passport is an individual, electronic record for each rider, in which the results of all doping tests over a period of time are collated. The passport for each rider contains a haematological and steroid profile drawn from blood and urine samples.

5 Quite simply, richer countries can send more athletes and can afford the necessary expenditure in sports development and training that ensures success, the result being their disproportionate success.

6 Cornelissen (2004) has noted a similar trend in South Africa. In 1995, the country hosted the Rugby World Cup and in 1996 the Africa Cup of Nations. In 2003, it hosted the Cricket World Cup and in 2010 the football World Cup.

7 Cornelissen goes on to argue that this is particularly the case for the analysis of mega-events in Africa, where numerous countries (e.g. Egypt, Morocco, Nigeria and South Africa) have sought to host mega-events (2004: 40), yet an analysis of this remains largely absent from the literature.

8 After winning the 800 metre final in Berlin at the 12th World Championships in Athletics on 19 August 2009, 18-year-old Caster Semenya was pounced on by a voracious global media following concerns about her ambiguously sexed and gendered body. Critics such as Caudwell (2011) and Nyong'o (2010) have raised the lack of concern for Semenya's humanitarian rights in the IAAF sex testing protocols.

7

SAFETY, SECURITY AND THE POLICING OF SPORTING MEGA-EVENTS

THIS CHAPTER

- explores the policy consequences of safety and security at sporting mega-events;
- assesses the 'terrorism capital' of sporting mega-events;
- traces the implications of terrorism for sports policy at mega-events in the Global North and Global South.

INTRODUCTION

September 11, 2011, marked the tenth anniversary of the day the world tilted. A decade earlier, nineteen terrorists from the Islamist militant group al-Qaeda hijacked four passenger planes in the United States, crashing two of them into the Twin Towers of the World Trade Center in New York City and one into the Pentagon in Arlington, Virginia. The fourth plane, United Airlines Flight 93 (made famous in the eponymously titled movie), crashed into a field in rural Pennsylvania after passengers attempted to wrestle control before it could reach the hijacker's intended target of the White House. Nearly 3,000 people working at or visiting the World Trade Center and the Pentagon died in the coordinated attacks, from a reported 90 countries across the world. No fewer than sixty pieces of policy and legislation have been developed since. 'Anti-Terrorism Acts' were passed in Germany, Canada, Great Britain, Australia and New Zealand, among others, which related to the effectiveness of law enforcement, the powers granted to authorities to search and hold suspected terrorists and the intelligence monitoring of believed terrorist activity. The Australian Anti-Terrorism Act (2005), for example, included a 'shoot-to-kill' clause, while the Israeli Supreme

Court ruled that 'targeted killings' were a permitted form of self-defence. In the United States, the Department of Homeland Security was created, the 'Patriot Act' was passed, sky marshals were placed aboard flights and international travellers experienced long delays imposed by enhanced security measures as new forms of terrorism (such as liquid and underwear bombs) emerged as potential threats. Biometric and body scanning have also raised concerns about passenger privacy in a broader context of surveillance and people's rights.

The global enactment of policy and legislation, the global loss of life, and the global media transmission of those haunting images of 9/11 changed the ways in which citizens see the world and their lives within it. September 11 has been, arguably, the most profound, global event of our time. As a global phenomenon, 9/11 echoes Benyon and Dunkerley's claim that 'globalization, in one form or another, is impacting upon the lives of everyone on the planet ... globalization might justifiably be claimed to be the defining feature of human society at the start of the twenty-first century' (2000: 3).

As global spectacles that command the world's attention, sporting mega-events are among the most significant potential targets of terrorists. They demand unrivalled media attention, they attract huge volumes of tourists, athletes and media personnel, and they use multiple locations, including restaurants, bars, pubs and clubs and accommodation venues. All this means that mega-events provide key locales from which terrorists can potentially inflict maximum human damage.

Indeed, mega-events like the Olympic Games, particularly, but not exclusively, have become prime terrorist targets since satellite television created a 'real time' television audience for their activities in countries across the globe. As Kuper notes, 'terrorism is a form of public relations. The aim is to spread the greatest fear with the least effort. To do this, terrorists seek out the most public events and places. That means sport' (2006: 293). Similarly, Atkinson and Young argue that:

> While sport may seemingly share few conceptual links with acts of terrorism ... we cannot ignore how sports events may become targets of terrorism ... or the contexts of terrorism. ... For many reasons, individual terrorists or terrorist organisations might find suitable targets in athletes participating in games, spectators attending the events, or selected corporate sponsors of sports contests. (2002: 54)

For much the same reasons that cosmocrats are attracted to the ethnoscapes, fiancescapes, technoscapes, mediascapes and ideoscapes of mega-events, so too are terrorist individuals and organizations. The 'scapes' of mega-events are implicated in a cross-cutting set of ideological interests that bring to the foreground their 'terrorist capital' or potential. This serves to mobilize particular agendas and actions that are underpinned by the tactic of inflicting maximum psychological fear on individuals, societies and governments.

With this as introduction, this chapter explores the policy responses to terrorism that have developed in relation to safety, security and policing at sporting mega-events. Following 9/11, 'safety and security concerns have become increasingly central to the hosting of sporting mega-events and security budgets now run into billions of dollars' (Giulianotti & Klauser, 2010: 49). With the staging of each new mega-event, new policies are developed by nations and states, and these have implications for sports policy, social policy and foreign policy, particularly as BRIC countries emerge as political and economic powers on the mega-event circuit.

In this chapter, I provide several case studies of policy developments with regard to safety, security and the policing of sporting mega-events in the Global North and the Global South. The case studies provide a history of sport-related terrorism (and risk) in sporting mega-events going back to the Munich Olympic Games in 1972, as well as a prospective commentary on London 2012 and future mega-events to be staged in BRIC countries. Drawing together several key themes of the book, the chapter argues that terrorism, and risk, are cultural phenomena that are socially constructed but which nonetheless have very real consequences for policy and human life in the Global North and Global South. While terrorist-related policy may develop in response to uncertainty (you never know when, where or if at all terrorism will strike), the implications for policy are far from fragile or uncertain.

A BRIEF HISTORY OF SPORT-RELATED TERRORISM

While there is certainly a long history of the use of sport and sporting events to agitate for political ideologies or policy change (apartheid in South Africa, or the boycotts of the Moscow and Los Angeles Olympics in 1980 and 1984, for example),[1] sport-related terrorist activities have quite a different cultural resonance and history.[2] Given the seven 'knowns' of sporting mega-events (Horne & Manzenreiter, 2006), as well as the 'scapes' they cut across, sporting mega-events generate significant terrorist capital that can be constructed and interpreted quite differently to the use of sports mega-events to promote or protest broader political agendas such as apartheid or foreign diplomacy.

According to Toohey (2008), there have been 168 sport-related terrorist attacks between 1972 and 2004; that is, between the Munich and Athens Olympics. It was, of course, the Munich Olympics where the reality of terrorism both highlighted deficiencies in mega-event organization and infrastructure and created the need for more vigilant and visible policy responses to sport-related terrorism. Munich has been referred to as 'the defining growth of modern terrorism' in sport (Toohey, 2008), where terrorism and the Olympics were first coupled in popular consciousness (Cottrell, 2003).[3] As a result of the Munich massacre, 'the Olympic Games have required far more sophisticated security planning which resulted in some draconian consequences for athletes, officials and spectators. ... The security framework developed for [the 1972] Games has provided the paradigm for all ensuing operations' (Toohey, 2008: 87).

Since Munich, there have been attempted bombings at the Barcelona Olympic Games in 1992, where two Spanish terrorist groups endeavoured to disrupt the Opening Ceremony. The Basque separatist group Euzkadi Ta Askatasuna (ETA) attempted to bomb power pylons and disrupt electricity supplies (see Palmer, 2001, for ETA-related activities in the Tour de France), and the Marxist group, Grupo de Resistencia Antifascista Primo (GRAPO), exploded three bombs on a gas pipeline outside Barcelona. Both attempts were foiled by the Spanish Counter Terrorism Unit, the Grupo Especial de Operaciones (GEO). At the 1996 Summer Olympics in Atlanta, a lone American anti-abortion extremist planted a bomb in Centennial Park, where thousands of spectators had gathered to watch the Opening Ceremony on big-screen televisions, killing one spectator and injuring hundreds more. Sport-related terrorism resurfaced on 7 July 2005, following the announcement that London had won the rights to host the 2012 Olympic Games and Paralympics.[4] While each terrorist attack was triggered by a different political, geo-political or ideological motivation, each, nonetheless, has served to strike fear into the hearts and minds of people around the world and contributed to constantly unfolding policy that seeks to ensure safety and security at sporting mega-events for their host cities and nations.

SPORTS POLICY AND PRACTICE POST-9/11

Although three of the four attacks occurred prior to September 11, 2001, it was the events of 9/11 that profoundly changed the policy and practice landscape of hosting mega-events. Following 9/11, several athletes and national teams withdrew from international competition (citing security concerns after Foreign Office warnings), and a number of major events were cancelled or postponed in the days immediately after 9/11, including major league baseball games in New York City.[5]

Speaking to a broader geo-political agenda and security concerns (given Pakistan reportedly operating as an al-Qaeda stronghold), two home cricket series (against Australia and the West Indies) were moved from Pakistan, while in 2009, the country was stripped of the right to stage the 2011 Cricket World Cup following an attack on the Sri Lankan team bus in Lahore, reportedly by insurgents with links to al-Qaeda, which left eight people dead (BBC, 2009). This, in itself, is no insignificant event. It was the first attack on a national sporting team since the hostage-taking and murder of the Israeli team in Munich more than thirty years before. Less than a year later, however, the bus carrying the Togolese national football team was ambushed by guerillas from FLEC (Front for the Liberation of the Enclave of Cabinda) as it drove through Angola's disputed Province of Cabinda on its way to the African Cup of Nations.

Although attributed as 'terrorism' in press accounts, these latter attacks on sporting teams pose critical questions as to what constitutes terrorism. Neither of these attacks was a large-scale or indiscriminate public attack. Certainly, they were premeditated rather than impulsive acts, political as well as criminal, and resulted in the wanton loss of life; criteria used by governments and authorities when assessing the terrorist potential of attacks, ambushings, bombings and hostage-takings (Council on Foreign Relations, 2003). The question of whether such acts were committed with the intention of changing a broader political order and policy context, or were intended to have profound psychological repercussions for a target audience, remains unanswered. As I develop shortly, fear and intimidation are the 'stock-in-trade' of terrorism; they are among the risk categories within which terrorism is embedded, and the proverbial 'shark in the water' (Hoffman, 2002: 315) of terrorism underpins the types of policy response that have developed in relation to safety and security at sporting mega-events.

Panopticonic Policy

Without question, the experience of attending major events has changed for spectators, post-9/11. It is now dominated by what Sugden terms 'supersized security' (2011: 230). The introduction of bag and body searches, greater use of CCTV and surveillance technologies, and restrictions placed on access to and movement of people around sporting grounds now jar with the idea of a sporting mega-event as being a carnivalesque 'spectacular time' (Debord, 1967), so dominant in popular constructions of mega-events. Coaffee and Murakami Wood, writing about the 2006 Super Bowl in Detroit, offer this description of the ever-expanding reach of sport-related security post-9/11:

> Inside the ring of steel, fans were screened by metal and radiation detectors; special security forces and bomb disposal teams were on standby; computer linked high resolution CCTV was utilized along with real-time satellite imagery to allow instant response; and the area was guarded by 10,000 police and private security guards. (2006: 513)

Foucault's proclamation that 'our society is one not of spectacle, but of surveillance' (1977: 217) is particularly apt in this post-9/11 context.

In terms of government action and policy, the 2002 Winter Olympic Games in Salt Lake City – the first Olympics to be held post-9/11– reflected the US government's strategy of maintaining a highly visible security presence that was intended to reassure spectators, athletes and sponsors alike (Office of Homeland Security, 2002). As part of this approach to enhanced and obvious safety precautions, security and surveillance were tightened at domestic airports, airspace above Utah was restricted, and vehicles without clearance were prohibited from being within 300 feet of venues and selected buildings in Salt Lake City (Office of Homeland Security, 2002). Precautions were taken against the threat of bio-terrorism (the US government ordered a batch of anti-anthrax tablets in the event of the release of deadly spores into the environment), and biometric scanners were introduced in venues to identify accredited athletes, officials and other personnel. In total, over 15,000 personnel from 60 different federal, state and local agencies were involved in Games-related security at Salt Lake City, compared to the 2,400 athletes from the 77 countries who competed at the Games. It has been estimated that the 9/11 attacks resulted in an additional $US70 million being spent on Games security at Salt Lake City, bringing the total budget for the Games to $US500 million, more than double that of the 1996 Atlanta Olympics (Toohey, 2008: 88).

That security takes the greatest slice of the mega-event budget is perhaps inevitable in this post-9/11 context. Giulianotti and Klauser note that 'arguably, over the last decade, and certainly since the 9/11 attacks and the subsequent "war on terror", the strongest element of SME [sport mega-event] expansion, in terms of cost and personnel, has centred on security and risk management' (2010: 50). When considered against more recent Games, the security budget of Salt Lake City seems positively paltry. The costs at Athens in 2004 ballooned to US$1.5 billion, the Turin Winter Olympics in 2006 cost US$1.4 billion, and Beijing in 2008 cost an (as yet unmatched) US$6.5 billion (Giulianotti & Klauser, 2010: 50). It is perhaps difficult to imagine this kind of spending being justified on any other element of a mega-event, sporting or otherwise, bringing into play a critical tension as to political priorities and the policy hierarchy.

An extended quote from Samatas, describing the network and personnel of surveillance and data gathering employed at the Athens Olympics, illustrates the kinds of activities that these ever-multiplying budgets are spent on:

> Hundreds of CCTV cameras swept the main avenues and squares of Athens, whereas three police helicopters and a Zeppelin equipped with more surveillance cameras hovered overhead. ... Dozens of new PAC 3 (Patriot Advanced Capability) missiles were armed and in position at three locations around the capital, including the Tatio Military Base near the athletes' Olympic Village, to provide a full defense umbrella over Athens. Security forces also received 11 state-of-the art surveillance vans that received and monitored images from around the city. ... Authorities also got two mobile truck screening systems capable of locating explosives, weapons or drugs in trucks and other large cargo vessels. ... By August 13th the authorities had installed thousands of CCTV cameras and deployed all over Greece more than 70,000 military staff to patrol the first Summer Games since the September 11th attacks on the United States. (2007: 224)

Moreover, such details of security precautions and personnel are now fully incorporated into the discourse that surrounds the contemporary mega-event (Bajc, 2007). As Boyle and Haggerty note:

> Security practices are increasingly fashioned for public consumption through mass media templates. Specified personnel serve as media security liaisons for mega-events, and the coverage of preparations for

the Olympics, G8 meetings, or the World Cup are all now replete with details about the amount of money being spent on security, the number of officers involved, and the radius of restricted airspace around the event. (2009: 256)

However, the 'urban fortress' style of surveillance and the discourse of reassurance that underpins policy and practice presents something of a paradox. On the one hand, this 'superpanopticonic' approach to mega-event security post-9/11 has become a benchmark for safety, security and policing at sporting mega-events (Sugden, 2011: 234). On the other hand, these same advances in technology are deployed equally by terrorist organizations. Similarly adept in their use, terrorists equally mobilize this technical capacity, albeit for very different purposes. A division director within the Royal Canadian Mounted Police, Canada's federal policing agency responsible for security for the 2010 Winter Games, notes that:

> [9/11] sensitized us to the fact that terrorists will be very innovative and more sophisticated than perhaps we anticipate. 9/11 forced us to look at the broader potential risks that we face, and it brought about a whole means of reviewing our practices to mitigate those threats to Canada in general. (cited in Boyle & Haggerty, 2009)

Thus, the challenge for anti- and counter-terrorist organizations is to use this very same technology to pre-empt a strike so as to prevent it, and this implicates national governments worldwide in the 'war on terror' in a coordinated approach to data gathering and intelligence sharing. In the 'borderless' age of globalization, where risks pass seamlessly across frontiers, policy action becomes equally 'borderless'. As Beck notes:

> National security is, in the borderless age of risks, no longer national security ... national security and international cooperation are directly linked with one another. The only way to have national security in the face of the threat of globalized terrorism ... is transnational cooperation. (1992: 14)

This tracing of historical events and their consequences for policy and practice presents a challenge for the image management of global mega-events. Security risks now exceed the capacity for officials to fully manage or even identify them; thus, it becomes a pressing imperative for mega-event organizers to maintain the appearance of absolute security, or as Beck puts it, to 'feign control over the uncontrollable' (2002: 41). This particular socio-political backdrop, however, obscures a more central question: what is it about being human in the twenty-first century that makes terrorism such a powerful source of risk and fear? What does the abiding need to assess, manage and mitigate the risk of terrorism suggest about global citizenship in the twenty-first century? These are crucial concerns for social science and policy research to address as part of a broader agenda.

TERRORISM, RISK CONSTRUCTS AND GLOBAL CITIZENSHIP

Tracy Taylor and Kristine Toohey (2006a, 2006b, 2007) and Toohey, Taylor and Lee (2002), have written extensively on the links between sport, risk and terrorism, locating their analysis within a discussion of the 'risk society' I outlined in Chapter 5. However, while Toohey (2008) conceptualizes 'risk' as being a global, universal phenomenon, writing of a singular 'risk society', the complexities of policy-making that have emerged in response to sports-based terrorism demand a recasting of our understandings of risk to include the more discrete, plural 'risk constructs' introduced earlier. This is important, as policy-making does not occur universally, but is inflected with social, political, local and historical particularities, which makes it a dynamic process of human engagement. That is, there are multiple risk societies or risk registers operating at one and the same time, and sports-related terrorism cuts across them all.

In Chapter 5, I outlined three main 'risk constructions' or ways in which people actively engage with risk: (i) risk avoidance; (ii) risk-seeking; and (iii) risk reasoning. There, I made the point that risk is a key part of the social context within which many aspects of domestic and foreign policy are located, particularly, but not exclusively, in terms of how various populations (such as children) are positioned as being 'at risk' and become subjects of a range of competing policy discourses. I also argued that 'risk' is best understood as a social and political construct that is employed in different ways through history. That is, while risk, fear and danger are by no means new concepts, the global dimensions to actual risk, perceived risk and the potential for confronting and assessing risk are far more recent and, as such, have particular implications for sports policy in this emerging context of terrorism and mega-events. As is the case with other forms of policy-making, the 'crisis' of terrorism has prompted a series of policy responses that correspond to these three (at times overlapping) constructions or 'fields', in Bourdieu's (1990, 1993) terms, of risk.

Risk Avoidance and Policy-Making

To take each in turn, risk avoidance resonates greatly with both policy and popular responses to sport-related terrorism. As I discussed in Chapter 5, a 'risk-averse' approach is one adopted by many individuals, organizations and governments, fearful of the social and political, not to mention the litigious, consequences that may arise should a potential risk actually be realized. This precautionary principle governs virtually every domain of human activity. Fearful of risk, we do what we can to avoid situations that may put us at risk. Risk avoidance is, as Furedi observes, 'an important theme in political debate and social action' (2002: 2).

Without doubt, 'terrorist capital' provokes much policy action in the form of strategies of risk avoidance, which resonates with wider fears and concerns. In terms of policy and social action, risk avoidance at sporting mega-events takes a number of forms. Most obviously, people, either through legislation or their own volition, steer clear of those events and locations where the threat of terrorism is perceived to be the greatest, and much policy reflects this. Building on the bombing in Atlanta's Centennial Park in 1996, the Australian government, prior to the 2000 Olympics, passed legislation to regulate attendance at public spaces across Sydney.[6] The avoidance of major cricket events in Pakistan, post-9/11 and following the 2009 attack on the Sri Lankan team in Lahore, is a further illustration of this risk-averse approach to managing sports-related terrorism.

In this case, the policy context was one in which Foreign Affairs Departments advised caution for tourists and athletes visiting Pakistan, which in turn fed into wider public apprehension about the preparedness of the Pakistan capital to prevent a terrorist attack. The perceived risk of terrorism was also cited as a reason for low spectator attendance at the 2004 Athens Games (Cashman, 2004), as were the bombings in Mumbai in 2009, in the year preceding the Commonwealth Games in Delhi, which prompted warnings to competing teams (most often from the Global North) to avoid public places in light of concerns that Delhi would be a 'soft' target for terrorist organizations.

While a major part of the discourse advanced by bidding committees and governments seeking to host sporting mega-events is that of a 'legacy' couched in terms of enduring positive social or economic benefits, an *unintended* legacy of September 11 has been the increased scrutiny of a host city (by other governments, organizations and host cities) to determine whether they have the organizational capacity to successfully implement the necessary security measures to prevent a terrorist risk. In the run-up to the 2004 Olympic Games in Athens, for example, the security plans of the host city were criticized by competing nations who threatened to withdraw their athletes, despite the security preparations undertaken by Athens being the most expensive and extensive since 9/11, which led the IOC to publicly announce their confidence in the host city's security planning.

This need to garner public support is particularly the case for BRIC cities, and it is a point to which I will return in my discussion of risk assessment and actuarial approaches to mega-event governance. For the moment, it is important to note that such responses from governments with regard to risk avoidance are emblematic of a broader policy discourse which positions BRIC cities and countries as 'punching above their weight' when it comes to ensuring the safety and security of athletes and visitors at mega-events. As I discussed in the previous chapter, one of the challenges for BRIC and developing countries is to successfully stage a mega-event without losing the symbolic capital necessary to secure public confidence in their capacity to host mega-events, and this becomes paramount in a context in which the risk of terrorism needs to be successfully negotiated.

As such, risk *avoidance* emerges as a considerable dimension of sports policy-making. The strategy of public visibility and vigilance is the policy response that audiences, athletes, governments and authorities routinely implement in this construction of risk avoidance. In addition to the discourse of reassurance of making known the organizational capacity of the host city, strategies of 'problem removal' and social control are embedded in policy responses worldwide. Certainly, there is a history of this with regard to hooliganism and spectator violence at sporting mega-events, where risk avoidance takes the form of 'the problem' being removed from mega-events through systems of social control and urban management. Building on the Council of Europe's 'European Convention on Spectator Violence and Misbehaviour at Sports Events and in particular Football Matches', major football games in Europe are now heavily monitored and policed. At the 2006 World Cup in Germany, widespread travel bans were put in place for some 3,000 English fans, preventing them from travelling to Germany for the finals, and spectator violence continues to be a major focus of risk-avoidance strategies and legislation at sporting mega-events worldwide.

Such strategies are a means of regulating significations of public disorder. In appearing to control 'the problem' so as to reduce the risks of violence and disorder that are posed by spectator violence, authorities, in turn, project signs of 'order' to public audiences (Ericson & Haggerty, 1997). In other words, visibility and reassurance are key discursive strikes in the policy construction of risk avoidance.

Risk Reasoning and Assessment

Of course, risk avoidance works in tandem with **risk reasoning** or risk assessment; of pre-empting terrorist potentialities so as to avoid them. The management of urban landscapes through the increased use of surveillance and data-gathering technologies is a case in point here, as authorities and organizers seek to identify those threats to the mega-event before they materialize (Schimmel, 2006: 169). While there is some slippage between risk assessment and risk avoidance – monitoring airspace or movement in and out of venues can arguably be conceived as both – evaluating the *likelihood* of an attack remains fundamental to the policy-making dynamic. A whole range of security technologies and practices, as well as government policies and legislation, are concerned to assess, through particular kinds of knowledge and expertise, the possibility of a terrorist attack, and then responding pre-emptively to this threat, using what Boyle and Haggerty refer to as a 'precautionary logic' (2009: 257).

Indeed, risk management and assessment have developed apace in terms of the cost and personnel associated with hosting sporting mega-events, and the potential risks seem to know no limits. In describing the security preparations for the 2000 Sydney Olympics, the travel writer Bill Bryson noted that planners had analyzed every contingency short of an asteroid strike or a nuclear attack (Bryson, 2000: 330). Although tongue-in-cheek, Bryson's assessment of risk reasoning can no longer be ignored by Olympic security planners, following the unprecedented scale of 9/11. Thus, predicting the potential for terrorist attacks in a climate in which the types of risk posed are all the more unpredictable becomes a considerable challenge for policy makers and mega-event planners alike.

As such, an expanded security logic informs the planning of sporting mega-events. For a city to successfully secure the right to host the Olympic Games (or other mega-events), it must be able to demonstrate that it has a highly sophisticated security plan in place, and that it has conducted a thorough risk assessment of all real or potential threats to security around the city and event. In preparation for the 2004 Athens Olympics, response plans were drafted for a total of 211 theoretical terrorist attack and other emergency scenarios, and ten full-scale operational readiness exercises were staged (Voulgarakis, 2005). Equally, Olympic Intelligence Centres now exist within all Olympic Organizing Committees. Post-9/11, the USA, Canada, Italy, Greece, Australia and the United Kingdom created 'Major Event Divisions' within their police forces, which, with the Olympic Intelligence Centres, are responsible for assessing risk and crafting major-event security policy.

Predicting the unpredictable: risk experts and managing the unimaginable

One of the consequences of 9/11 has been the need for security planners to 'think outside the square'; that is, to attempt to predict the unpredictable and to base their risk assessment on a 'worst case scenario' of unlikely but catastrophic events. In the lead-up to the 2010 Vancouver Winter Olympic Games, for example, the Threat Analysis report of the Canadian Office of Critical Infrastructure and Emergency Preparedness (OCIEP) – the agency responsible for the risk assessment of the Games – warned that Canada's critical infrastructure needed to be prepared for another event equal to or greater than 9/11:

> Those events [9/11] have altered the way in which emergency management professionals, policy makers, and the owners and operators of CI [critical infrastructure] conduct their affairs because the possibility, regardless of how remote, that an event on an equally grand scale might occur again precipitates the need for robust and flexible mitigation. (OCIEP, 2003: 48)

This need to prepare for events 'regardless of how remote' reveals a burgeoning logic in the security world. Peter Ryan, the Principal Security Adviser to ATHCOS, the Athens Olympic Games Organizing Committee (and former Police Minister of New South Wales), noted that security planners for the Sydney Olympics had considered scenarios that would 'sound bizarre and outlandish to non-security experts' (Boyle & Haggerty, 2009: 262). This need to plan for contingencies, regardless of how remote and unimaginable, flies in the face of the established techniques of statistical calculation and predictability that underpin 'the science' of risk reasoning and risk assessment (de Goede, 2008: 166). It does, however, reflect the unpredictability of contemporary terrorism, which makes it so very effective and impels governments worldwide to plan for every contingency, no matter how unlikely.

To contain the incalculability of terrorism, sport-related or otherwise, this logic of expanded security has given rise to the occupational category of the 'risk expert' and increased the need for 'evidence-based' judgements, to return to the concerns of previous chapters. Following 9/11, policy-making was vulnerable to 'panic, grandiosity and overreach' (Boyle & Haggerty, 2009: 262); it was determined by risk assessments that were practised more as a craft than a science and that lacked rigorous evaluations of their practice. Drawing on a combination of prediction, probability and previous experience, risk experts are now in the business of calculating the potential for risk, wherein much of the evidence upon which risk experts base their judgements is drawn from past experience. Many mega-event organizers now utilize standardized security templates that can 'maintain continuity in security planning between events and act as institutional memory banks for lessons learned from previous events' (Boyle & Haggerty, 2009: 268). As each new, previously 'unthinkable' terrorist attack occurs, security planners and risk experts are thus further equipped to plan for the future.

Several models have been developed to assist the work of 'risk experts'. For example, a template developed by the Rand Corporation (a global research organization undertaking commissioned policy-led research) to assist in security planning efforts for the London 2012 Olympics is intended to help 'foresee, in a structured and systematic way, a range of different potential security environments that could potentially exist in 2012' (Rand, 2007: 50).

The model is composed of three factors: (i) adversary hostile intent; (ii) adversary operational capability; and (iii) potential domestic/international influences on UK security (Boyle & Haggerty, 2009; Rand, 2007). Combined, these factors produce no fewer than 400 possible future security threats, ranging from 'best case' non-violent threats through to 'worst case' scenarios of deliberate acts of technologically sophisticated mass destruction. Using this planning model, specific (hypothetical) scenarios are devised that will assess and develop the operational capabilities of LOCOG to respond to terrorist threats at the Olympic Games in 2012. Importantly, the model 'does not give any specific weight to a particular future scenario, rather, it treats all futures as equally valid' (Rand, 2007: 50), reflecting the shift in risk assessment thinking that now considers previously 'unthinkable' possibilities as now possible.

Risk-seeking

The third 'risk construction' is that of risk-seeking. This is the backdrop against which strategies of risk assessment and risk avoidance emerge. Certainly, the experience of terrorism (sport-related or otherwise) for spectators or organizers is part of Beck's (1999) 'involuntary lottery of misfortune', although the *act* of terrorism is a calculated and manufactured one that terrorist individuals and organizations actively seek out. To return to the constructions of risk outlined in Chapter 5, this active search for risk, alongside other forms of risk-taking behaviour, is as much a feature of the global order as evading or preventing risk is. The voluntary, selfish, motivations that underpin terrorism, in other words, are a powerful risk construct, which then mobilizes particular forms of policy actions and outcomes. That is, risk-seeking sits alongside risk avoidance in contemporary social life, and these collide, in very particular ways, in policy responses to sports-related terrorism.

Each of these risk constructs provides a basis for understanding and anticipating public and policy responses to hazards and for improving the communication of risk information between lay people, technical experts and decision-makers. As the shifting evolution of sport-related terrorism has illustrated – from Munich in 1972 to mega-event planning post-9/11 – risk is an important facet of how regimes of policy are rationalized over time and in different social contexts and is critical to understanding the socially constructed and constitutive nature of policy-making.

POLICY IMPLICATIONS OF SPORTS MEGA-EVENT RELATED TERRORISM: LONDON 2012 AND BRIC COUNTRIES

As we saw in the strategies of risk reasoning and risk assessment, much policy emphasis is placed on 'second-guessing', on using networks and webs of surveillance and data gathering to pre-empt, based on past experience, a possible terrorist strike, yet it is the 'unknowns' of terrorism – it is what *hasn't* happened – that continues to command significant policy responses, for the symbolic capital of terrorist uncertainty drives so much of security planning. The budget apportioned to safety and security at the Beijing Games in 2008 is a case in point here. Given China's relatively benign position on the US-led 'war on terror', to which a number of Western governments committed troops (Australia, Spain, the United Kingdom being among them), the disproportionate budget, relative to previous Olympic Games, posed a critical question. As Faligot asked in the lead-up to the 2008 Games: 'what has China done to prevent a suicide bomber blowing himself up during the finals of the hundred meters dash? The answer will come next year in Beijing' (2008: 326). It has been suggested that such elaborate spending in Beijing was really a pretext for a crack-down on domestic political dissidents, human rights activists and ethnic minority groups, particularly those associated with Tibet (Sugden, 2011), and these concerns are discussed in the following chapter. For the moment, it is the ways in which potentialities and possibilities determine the policy agenda for future sporting mega-events that commands my attention.

Implications for London 2012

At the time of writing this chapter, the 2012 Summer Olympic Games in London are looming as the next major sporting happening to appear on the global mega-event circuit. Given the effects of the Games-related terrorist attacks in London in July 2005, coupled with a longer history of the 'Troubles' in Northern Ireland,[7] the United Kingdom's support of the US-led 'war on terror', London's status as a 'global city' (Sassen, 2002), and its history of migration and multiculturalism (discussed in Chapter 2), the threat and fear of terrorism is an indelible part of the public imagination, with safety and security precautions promising to be on a unprecedented scale at the 2012 Games.

Echoing the response of the Salt Lake City Olympic Organizing Committee as they prepared for the first Olympic Games following 9/11, London has adopted the 'spectacular security' (Boyle & Haggerty, 2009) approach that has become the benchmark for ensuring the safety of host cities as they prepare to stage a mega-event. Much of the anticipated security budget for London 2012, for example, will be spent on the technology and expertise needed to assess risk, leading Morgan to write that this is tantamount to asking the British taxpayer to write a blank cheque (2008: 2). In terms of government policy and legislation, the 'security legacy' of London 2012 will have significant impacts, both at the Games itself and in years beyond, as 'test policy' becomes inscribed in legislation.

The huge budgets that are directed towards security technologies are justified by London's success in staging global media events (such as the 2011 wedding of Prince William to Kate Middleton in London's Westminster Abbey) without a hitch. The challenge for security planners is to balance the reassurance of an overt security presence with the fear that such an overt security presence exists because the threat of terrorism is very real. As Boyle and Haggerty note, 'security officials must avoid depicting a situation that would be perceived by citizens as being "too great" a security spectacle. If it becomes too egregious, security stops being reassuring and can, paradoxically, accentuate the prospect of extreme, unmanageable danger' (2009: 265). The iconography and symbolism of security must be carefully balanced, and London 2012, with its particular cultural history, will test the ability of organizers to balance these competing tensions.

Driven by a security logic that is increasingly oriented towards negating the prospects of a vastly expanded range of unknown dangers, security planning for London 2012 has undergone a dramatic expansion, particularly in terms of the personnel attached to security operations, either as risk experts or as 'foot soldiers' conducting street sweeps, bag searches, monitoring CCTV cameras and the like. The London Metropolitan Police, for example, asked to treble the police numbers through hiring 6,000–7,000 more officers specifically for the 2012 Olympics, alongside the estimated thousands more contract security agents who will be operational throughout the Games (*Sunday Times*, 1 June 2008).

As well as this increased personnel, the London Olympics will also leave a 'technological footprint' across the city. Drawing on new and existing security technologies, such as CCTV, traffic cameras and biometric screening at Olympics venues, the Games are set to realize Foucault's maxim that 'our society is one not of spectacle, but of surveillance'. London already has the world's highest number of CCTV cameras per capita, with spectator violence and hooliganism at football matches serving as the catalyst for the growth of this form of surveillance. By the early 1990s, all major UK football stadia had installed CCTV cameras, and security technologies are already in place at major urban centres across the capital, such as transport hubs and retail complexes, a legacy of the city's previous response to terrorist and paramilitary activity. As Boyle and Haggerty note, 'policing partnerships, legal changes, screening technologies, or informational databases, all have ways of being re-rationalized for other uses once their original application context has disappeared' (2009: 266).

The intensive, state-of-the-art technologies first introduced at Salt Lake City will be further showcased at London, with organizers keen to promote such technologies, in part, to justify the billowing budgets attached to securing public safety at sporting mega-events. As Boyle and Haggerty note:

> The massive budgets and cultural capital associated with Olympic involvement makes them the security industry equivalent of what Paris or Milan is to the fashion industry. The successful pilot testing of security practices and technologies – or, more accurately, the lack of stunning failures – helps to ensure that new knowledge, practices and devices emerge as 'proven' solutions to be marketed as applications suitable for other contexts. (2009: 271)

These security strategies, while they are to be tested most fully in London 2012, also reflect the transnational dimensions of security capacity and planning and their enduring legacy. 2012 security operations see British security officials working alongside the military, other national police forces and contract security companies from around the globe. Here, we see the local and the global collide. The securing of a mega-event takes place at the local level – typically, within the boundaries of the urban centre it occupies – yet, requires securing the safety of competing teams, officials, sponsors and cosmocrats from across the globe, many of whom travel with their own security personnel. As such, risk assessment and risk avoidance foster the production and circulation of sophisticated and specialized security knowledges that are shared globally. While the operational security needs of different events can vary substantially, they share the common fact that they often outstrip locally available expertise and resources. Consequently, conceptions of security have become increasingly sub-national, regional and urban in scale and orientation (Graham, 2004). In risk reasoning and risk avoidance we see Beck's (2002) notion of 'de-bounded' or borderless risks assume a new meaning. Risks are now spatially, temporally and socially de-bounded and this is fuelled by a speculative popular imagination that understands the potential for risk as being possible anywhere or anytime.

Implications for Mega-Events in BRIC Countries and the Global South

I noted in the previous chapter that non-Western and BRIC countries are now successfully bidding for a whole host of sporting mega-events. Post-9/11, these mega-events raise a particular set of issues and challenges for safety, security and surveillance: as Giulianotti and Klauser note, 'the hosting of these 21st century SMEs in the Global South will bring international sports and securitization into completely new territory' (2010: 51). While many of these challenges are yet to be borne out in practice – the Olympic Games in Rio de Janeiro in 2016 may be perhaps the first truly global mega-event that speaks to the new politics of the Global South – a speculative glance over several of the emerging issues proves indicative and instructive for global sports policy as mega-events take on a truly global significance in terms of the locations where they are held.

To return to some of the concerns raised in the previous chapter, Western-held fears for the organizational incompetence of BRIC and developing countries is particularly acute when it comes to their perceived ability to prepare for and prevent sports-related terrorism. The 2009 bombings in Lahore, for example, were described in popular media coverage of the event as follows:

> No group has thus far claimed responsibility for Tuesday's commando attack, which could easily have resulted in double or treble the fatalities. It was clearly aimed at attracting maximum international exposure – cricket is far and away South Asia's most high-profile and popular sport – and at demonstrating the inability of Pakistani authorities to secure even the country's major cities. (Jones, 2009)

As each mega-event in the Global South passes without event, such arguments become harder to substantiate. Despite fears of Delhi being ill-prepared to cope with safety and security requirements, it nonetheless successfully pulled off South Asia's biggest ever multisport sports mega-event – the 85-nation Commonwealth Games.

Equally, concerns around the organizational capacity of BRIC and developing countries extend to the extent to which they are able to adequately project the image of a safe, clean urban space in light of poverty, social divisions and urban crime that are much more a part of everyday life for residents than they are for the tourists, cosmocrats and athletes fleetingly visiting for the mega-event. As Giulianotti and Klauser note, poverty, deep social divisions and urban crime occupy a 'categorically different scale of significance [in the Global South]' (2010: 53). Underpinning such concerns is the Western-centricism I have alluded to earlier. As Nicholls, Giles and Sethna note, 'contact between the Global North and Global South is often fraught with messages of Southern cultural inferiority and northern domination ... where the politics of knowledge in bridging "the local" and "the global" is complex' (2011: 250). As such, as mega-events move to the Global South, they bring into play a particular discourse that inflects policy responses to terrorism and 'preparedness' more broadly in particular ways. In preparation for the 2010 World Cup finals in South Africa, for example, strong security concerns focused on controlling the relationships between wealthy international visitors and local populations in urban centres and in 'fan parks' where fixtures were screened on giant television screens.

This restriction of movement and contact between 'locals' and 'visitors' has a history of inscription in government policy and legislation. In the run-up to the Sydney Olympics in 2000, laws were introduced that limited gatherings in public spaces, which forced the clearance of particular population groups (the homeless, Indigenous Australians), and slum clearance and rebuilding programmes intended, in part, to remove and repopulate inner-city localities were similarly enforced at Beijing and Delhi, in the 2008 Olympic and 2010 Commonwealth Games respectively. As more and more sports mega-events are hosted in the Global South, the focus on poverty, social divisions and urban crime, and the implications for safety and security at mega-events, will become far more prominent on the policy agenda.

It would be remiss, however, to suggest that social divisions and social problems are the sole preserve of the developing countries and the Global South. These concerns are certainly relevant for mega-events in the Global North. The London Borough of Newham, for example, where the Olympic Stadium is being built, is one of the United Kingdom's most deprived and ethnically diverse areas. In Vancouver, the Downtown Eastside location of several event venues for the 2010 Winter Games has high levels of street crime, drug use and homelessness (Vancouver Organizing Committee for the 2010 Olympic and Paralympic Winter Games, 2007: 134). However, to return to notions of risk avoidance and risk reasoning, these risk constructs will be tested in the face of new 'unknowns' as mega-events occupy an increasing presence in the Global South.

CONCLUSION

Since 9/11, sporting mega-events have attracted budgets and policy agendas that reflect the global concern with terrorist capital. They are now staged against a backdrop of three key 'risk constructs' that implicate terrorism, and associated social, sports and foreign policy in very particular ways. These risk constructs have led to what Giulianotti and Klauser refer to as the 'security legacy' (2010: 53), in which a range of strategies and impacts continue to have significance beyond the life of the mega-event.

These risk constructs also offer a useful point of entry to larger concerns about global citizenship in the twenty-first century. The abiding need to assess, manage and mitigate the risk of terrorism offers a commentary on the fragility of human existence, and our need to manage the uncertainty of social life and action. The risks of terrorism, and our responses at both a societal and governmental level, are crucial concerns to address as part of a broader research agenda(s) on global citizenship and humanity. As members of 'risk societies', we perceive ourselves as being increasingly vulnerable to all sorts of risks and threats that are beyond or outside our control. While we may be sceptical of the veracity of claims made with regard to, say, the risks posed by climate change, our vulnerability to terrorism remains. As Hoffman notes, terrorism 'is used to create unbridled fear, dark insecurity, and reverberating panic' (2002: 315).

Some critics have suggested that policy responses to 9/11 are little more than a 'moral panic', yet this is precisely the capital that terrorists trade on. Indeed, acts of terrorism are frequently executed to undermine confidence in government and leadership, and policy action (or inaction), and the discourse that surrounds the staging of mega-events in BRIC countries is particularly instructive here.

There is undoubtedly, a global dimension to terrorism and risk that speaks to the comparative policy agenda. While risks like terrorism may find their roots in African or Middle Eastern countries (and indeed in the towns and suburbs of major Western countries), their effects are felt worldwide. As nations and cities in the Global South continue to win the rights to host mega-events, the security-related issues and concerns that emerge in these contexts can provide social scientists with opportunities for comparative policy development and lesson-sharing across and between the Global North and South.

Importantly, these dimensions of comparative policy learnings, when considered against the broader risk constructions, and the potential implications that surround policy-making in a culture of fear and precaution, raise some questions about the politicization of these issues. Commentators such as Coaffee and Murakami Wood (2006) are concerned that events like London 2012 may be used by governments and security-related interest groups to magnify in the public mind the 'terrorist threat' and construct a climate of fear that can be used to justify technologically driven control strategies, to counter anti-social behaviour and democratic protest and to exclude the dangerous 'other' from public space (Sugden, 2011). As Sugden notes, the upping of the ante at each sporting mega-event provides 'successive host cities and their respective governments with the licence to do almost anything in the name of counter-terrorism' (Sugden, 2011: 231). These issues of human rights, citizenship and civil liberties set the agenda for the concerns of the following chapter.

BOX 7.1   QUESTIONS FOR DISCUSSION

- To what extent do you agree with the proposition that 9/11 has altered the safety and security dimensions of staging sporting mega-events?

- Why does terrorism capital 'work' at sporting mega-events?

- In terms of safety, security, surveillance and policing, what lessons for mega-events in the Global North can be learned from those staged in the Global South? And vice versa.

RECOMMENDED FURTHER READINGS

Atkinson, M. & Young, K. (2002) Terror Games: Media treatment of security issues at the 2002 Winter Olympics. *OLYMPIKA: The International Journal of Olympic Studies*, 11: 53–78.

Samatas, M. (2007) Security and surveillance in the Athens 2004 Olympics: Some lessons from a troubled story. *International Criminal Justice Review*, 17: 220–38.

Taylor, T. & Toohey, K. (2006) Impacts of terrorism related safety and security measures at a major sport event. *Event Management*, 9(4): 119–209.

Toohey, K., Taylor, T. & Lee, C. (2002) The FIFA World Cup 2002: The effects of terrorism on sport tourists. *Journal of Sport Tourism*, 8(3): 167–85.

Tulloch, J. (2000) Terrorism, 'killing events' and their audience: Fear of crime at the 2000 Olympics. In K. Schaffer & S. Sidone (eds), *The Olympics at the millennium: Power, politics and the games*. New Brunswick, NJ: Rutgers University Press (pp. 224–42).

Notes

1 The boycott of the 1980 Summer Olympics in Moscow was initiated by the United States in protest against the Soviet War in Afghanistan. In 1984, the Soviet Union and other sympathetic countries similarly boycotted the Los Angeles Olympic Games (see Hulme, 1990).

2 The 'Tlateloco Massacre', which occurred ten days before the Mexico Olympics in 1968, when thousands of students took to the streets of Mexico City to protest at what they saw to be a waste of resources being spent on the Games, and which resulted in several hundred students being shot and killed by Mexican security forces (Sugden, 2011; Toohey, 2008), lies outside this discussion as the killings were carried out by Mexican forces trying to suppress the student uprisings rather than an ideological, political or religious group attacking the event to draw attention to their cause and inflict maximum human damage.

3 The events of Munich have been well documented, so briefly: on 5 September 1972, eleven Israeli athletes and coaches were taken hostage by members of Black September, a militant faction of the Palestine Liberation Organization (PLO), in turn the armed wing of the political movement Fatah, led by the late Yasser Arafat. The German police launched an ill-thought-out plan to take the hostages to a nearby German airfield in an attempt to secure their release. There, they were killed in a bungled rescue attempt along with all but three of the eight terrorists, prompting a series of security operations by and between the Israeli and Palestinian governments over the release of political prisoners held by each country. The events of the Munich Olympics have been subject to several celluloid treatments, including Kevin McDonald's award-winning documentary *One Day in September* and Steven Spielberg's fictionalized account, *Munich*.

4 In four coordinated suicide bombings, terrorists boarded the London Underground and one city bus, detonating bombs which killed 52 people (including the bombers) and injured 700 more. In the days following, al-Qaeda claimed responsibility in a videotaped message shown on the Arab television network al-Jazeera.

5 By contrast, in commemoration ceremonies for the tenth anniversary of 9/11, sport has been promoted as a source of healing for communities affected by the events a decade earlier (Wetzel, 2011).

6   Critics such as Lenskyj (2002) argue that this legislation was a thinly veiled attempt to regulate and monitor the attendance of Indigenous Australians in public spaces in the host city throughout the Games. These forms of the social control of minority groups are addressed further in the following chapter on human rights and sporting mega-events.

7   The 'Irish Troubles' refer to a period of ethno-political conflict over the constitutional status of Northern Ireland *vis-à-vis* Great Britain. The paramilitary organization, the Irish Republican Army, has engaged in a series of high-profile bombings against British institutions, most notably, the Grand Hotel in Brighton in 1984 where the then Prime Minister, Margaret Thatcher, was staying ahead of the Conservative Party conference.

8

MEGA-EVENTS, SPORTS POLICY AND HUMAN RIGHTS

THIS CHAPTER

- examines the policy implications of human rights as they relate to sporting mega-events;

- explores how advocacy and activist groups use mega-events to raise awareness of abuses of human rights;

- provides the example of the trafficking of women as a case study of human rights and sporting mega-events.

INTRODUCTION

Since the 2000 Olympic Games in Sydney, where a campaign argued that the State-perpetuated human rights abuses against Indigenous Australians should disqualify Australia from hosting the Games, there has been a questioning of the notion of sport in the context of social justice, a Human Rights agenda and a consideration of the dehumanizing machinery through which athletic bodies are created, monitored and controlled in the service of Olympic performance and consumption.

In particular, the 'appropriateness' of cities and nations to host (or participate in) sporting mega-events in light of their human rights record has been raised by a number of commentators (Kidd, 2009, 2010; Kidd & Donnelly, 2000; Lenskyj, 2000, 2002, 2008; Morgan, 2003; O'Bonsawin, 2010; Sugden, 2011). At the same time, sport is increasingly occupying a place on the agendas of governments and organizations such as the United Nations, the IOC and UNESCO for its aspirational hopes of achieving opportunities and freedoms for those marginalized from civic participation through gender, class, religion or disability. Equally, boycotts and sanctions of countries (or companies) with poor track records of human and civil rights are employed to pressure those regimes to revisit their modes of governance and political rule. It is this dual capacity of sporting mega-events to both *enable* and *address* abuses of human rights that forms the global backdrop against which the intertwined aspects of human rights, sport and social policy need to be considered.

Building on some of the ideas outlined in Chapter 4 about disconnectivity, a heightened global consciousness and the rise of 'e-dissidence' as public protest, this chapter explores the policy implications of sporting mega-events in the context of human rights. While Chapter 4 was concerned with the use of new technologies and social media to organize dissent, this chapter extends this idea of global protest to questions of human rights as they relate to sporting mega-events. I begin by providing an overview of globalization, human rights and sport, before moving onto two particular human rights issues that are played out at global sporting mega-events. These are: (i) the track record of host cities and nations, and (ii) cultural diplomacy and foreign policy. Having charted this broad terrain, I then turn to an extended case study of the trafficking of women and girls for the purpose of sexual exploitation. The fundamental abuses of human rights that are bound up with this form of trafficking provide an emergent issue for policy and for the planning of sporting mega-events.[1]

SPORT, GLOBALIZATION AND HUMAN RIGHTS

Resistant responses to human rights abuses in sport are fully embedded in a wider social, political and economic context of globalization and anti-globalization. In the late 2000s, the global financial crisis saw the collapse of a number of financial institutions, governments and economies in the Global North and Global South alike. This sparked uprisings in major metropoles and fuelled global campaigns such as the 'Occupy' movement and led to the ousting of governments in Greece and Italy. It is in this neoliberal context of opportunities for mass mobilization (seen in previous global movements such as 'Make Poverty History' or the 'Million March Against War') that sports activism is situated. That is, sports-associated activism, as it relates to human rights, needs to be considered within a broader discussion of consumer movements and the work that is done by citizen-consumers, anti-globalization and alterglobalization movements to bring ideological, cultural and political change by mobilizing a coherent set of political activities to reassert 'the local' or at least local mediations of the global in ways that protect the human rights of the oppressed (Auyero, 2001).[2] For many of the same reasons that cosmocrats are attracted to the 'scapes' of mega-events, so too are activist groups who use the mega-event to highlight the exploitative practices that are made maximally visible at events such as the Olympic Games or football's World Cup.

I noted in Chapter 6 that mega-events enhance and reinforce many of the systematic social and structural inequalities of the global order. The rights of women, the poor, the disabled, children, ethnic minorities and Indigenous populations are among the marginalized and disaffected groups for which advocates have worked hard to effect change, to bring human dignity and to make accountable those individuals, organizations and governments that perpetuate exclusionary policies and practices. As Wilson notes, 'to seek to isolate sport as an activity that stands alone in human affairs, untouched by "politics" or "moral considerations" and unconcerned for the fates of those deprived of human rights is as unrealistic as it is (self-destructively) self-serving' (2004: 28).

In the context of globalization, these inequities take a particular shape. On the one hand, global interconnectedness has facilitated the notion of a 'shared humanity' (Kidd & Donnelly, 2000: 133), fuelled by the 'take-off' phase of globalization (Robertson, 2002), during which we saw the emergence of global humanitarian organizations (such as the Red Cross or Médecins Sans Frontières), global competitions (such as the mega-events described in this section) and the emergence of a standardized notion of human rights through declarations such as the International Bill of Human Rights.[3] At the same time, while the transfer patterns of global capital may have encouraged trade between countries, this has had deleterious consequences for developing countries and those in the Global South who sit outside the traditional trade triad of Northern Europe, North America and Japan, and the economic safeguards that come with membership of this privileged financescape.

The deterioration of protections for weaker nations in the Global South has led to their exploitation by stronger nations. A lack of tariffs on imported goods or restricted quotas which regulate trade between countries mean that large companies in the Global North (many of which sponsor sporting mega-events) are able to offer salaries to workers in poorer nations that entice them to endure unsafe labour conditions in factories, quarries, mines, construction sites and the like. Without the protections afforded in the Global North, should manufacturing processes at worksites in poorer nations change through stricter labour laws being introduced, the company then either closes down or relocates to another nation without worker protections in place. The inequities of global labour thus shift endlessly across a landscape of exploitation and disadvantage. As Frenkel writes, 'globalization has hastened the growth of buyer-driven commodity chains that connect advanced country marketing or retail companies with contractors manufacturing in low-cost, developing countries' (2001: 531).

Sage (1994, 1999) and others (Ballinger, 2008; Connor, 2002; Connor & Dent, 2006) have noted that this is particularly the case in the sportswear industries. The American-owned company Nike (particularly, but not exclusively) has been the focus of activist groups for its treatment of factory workers in South-East Asia, while commanding more than 50% of the global market share (along with Adidas and Reebok) in sports apparel and footwear. Sage has, most extensively, examined the 'organizational dynamics, collective actions, and outcomes of a transnational advocacy network that was formed to protest the labor practices of Nike's sport shoe factories in Asia' (1999: 206), from which successful campaigns have forced 'the big three' to improve working conditions and wages for their employees.

Alongside issues of sweatshop labour, the exploitative conditions in which children are forced to work are similarly scrutinized by human rights groups keen to draw attention to the global imbalances of power that have led to children working in hazardous environments such as quarrying, salvage or cash cropping, being trafficked or forced to work in prostitution or pornography. Manufacturers in Pakistan, for example, have been subject to scrutiny for using young children to make the soccer balls used by the elite countries who contest football's World Cup. Here, activist groups have lobbied to end child labour through the formation of the Atlanta Agreement, which regulates the use of children (defined as under the age of fifteen) in the Pakistan city of Sialkot by centralizing labour and raising the minimum wage that can be earned by young workers when stitching footballs (International Labour Organization, 1997). Since, companies such as Adidas have agreed to only purchase 'Fair Trade' balls from manufacturers who comply with the Atlanta Agreement. Donnelly (1997) and Donnelly and Petherick's (2006) observations that the careful concealment of much of the 'work' of sport allows the exploitation of children through practices that would never be tolerated in educational, employment or other settings is a pertinent reminder of the junction of sport and civil society within which a debate about the rights of children is a central part.

The human rights and policy agenda in sport, however, is not simply about the rights of children or workers. Athletes are equally implicated in the discourse. For some sportsmen and women, sport provides a means through which to flee persecution and find opportunities for a new life and/or to pursue an athletics career (Darby, 2000b; Darby, Akindes & Kirwin, 2007; Maguire & Falcous, 2010; Poli, 2010). For others, however, the movement and migration of sportsmen and women across the global ethnoscape has highlighted the de-skilling of 'donor' countries, particularly in Africa and Central and South America, whose athletic base is depleted to supply leagues and markets (predominantly football and basketball) in more prosperous parts of the world, predominantly the United States and United Kingdom (Magee & Sugden, 2002), where there are few policies in place to protect 'exiles' and 'the expelled'; those who choose or are forced leave their home country for political or personal reasons (Magee & Sugden, 2002).

It would be remiss, however, to dismiss human rights and sport as being simply a discussion about the unfair distribution of wealth, resources and opportunities between the developed and developing world. Mega-events also bring together and make visible deep social divisions within *arriviste* cities in the Global North noted in the previous chapter, and the rights of athletes in 'First World' sports and countries also occupy a place on the human rights agenda. Again, mega-events provide a very public location at and through which to consider the rights of sportsmen and women. Returning to one of the recurrent themes of the book, the policies and protocols surrounding the testing of athletes for performance-enhancing drugs make visible issues of privacy and confidentiality for athletes in a broader context of the global ethics of sporting competition (Schneider, 2004).

In his discussion of testing protocols, Houlihan (2004) argues that the require-ments of the World Anti-Doping Code compromise the civil rights of athletes:

> There cannot be many occupations where part of the contract requires workers to be observed by a complete stranger, possibly two or three times a year, urinating. Nor can there be many occupations where workers are obliged to notify employers of their location dur-ing their free time. For elite athletes, such indignations and intrusions are a normal part of their participation in high-performance sport. (2004: 420)

In a context where there is already some slippage in terms of the rights of chil-dren (many elite athletes are still minors), drug testing is particularly problem-atic for human rights where 'rights' tend to embrace the protection of athletes through the Court of Arbitration for Sport when hearing disputed allegations of doping offences. The appeals framework fails to address the fundamental intru-sions that Houlihan (2004) notes, for athletes have effectively been relegated to the margins of decision-making and policy-making, the implicit assumption being that athletes, NGOs and governments are all in agreement about policy intentions and outcomes. While several professional bodies and their unions have been vocal about a lack of consultation in those policy-making processes that are ostensibly intended to protect their rights (Thibault, Kihl & Babiak, 2010), the Court of Arbitration tends to be aimed at securing individual rights and entitlements rather than the collective voice of solidarity seen with the industrial action taken by professional cyclists, for example. Thus, it is difficult to disentangle a more abstract discussion of athletes' rights from the institu-tional context of power relations within which such discussions take place. As Houlihan notes, 'rights and liberties may be capable of being defined in the abstract but it must be remembered that they are always operationalized in a context of public policy and power relations' (2004: 425).

These issues of exploitation and abuse of different kinds coalesce at the sport-ing mega-event in terms of the human rights track record of the host city or nation and the broader policy rhetoric that sees sport equally being able to address the same abuses of human rights that it allows and perpetuates.

TARNISHED TRACK RECORDS

The track records of cities and nations to host (or participate in) sporting mega-events in light of perceived abuses of human rights such as regimes of torture, racism, corruption or the silencing and exiling of minority groups or outspoken critics of political regimes has been raised by a number of commentators. Indeed, the very notion of 'Olympism' has been critiqued by new social move-ments for its implicit toleration of athletic harm and infringements of civil liber-ties. Helen Lenskyj (2000, 2008) has been a strident critic of the Olympic

Games, and the political relations it has with other global institutions. Lenskyj's analysis over several decades reveals the reproduction of systemic inequities and mistreatment at and through this particular mega-event, particularly the ways in which its Opening Ceremony adopts then misappropriates Indigenous imagery and actors. Similarly, Shaw, drawing comparisons between the Sydney and Vancouver Olympics, notes that:

> [Indigenous] Leaders could be co-opted into going along with the bids, serving as community 'representatives' ... children could be used at Olympic opening ceremonies to add local color with native music and dancing for an international audience. None of this was meant to address the glaring disparity in wealth between Aboriginal and non-Aboriginal communities. Nor was it designed to remedy the appalling levels of poverty, the lack of basic health care, educational opportunities and future prospects of Aboriginal people. (Shaw, 2008: 200)

While opening ceremonies provide a very public 'front stage', in Goffman's (1959) terms, upon which leitmotifs of (contested) nationhood can be enacted, many of the concerns for human rights are played out in the run-up to the mega-event itself. The most notable example of this 'backstage' preparation for a mega-event was the Beijing Olympics, where the practices of the Chinese government in relation to the oppression of Tibetan dissidents, ethnic minorities and environmental degradation were subject to much global scrutiny throughout the four-year Olympiad that preceded the actual Games. I will return to the specificities of Beijing shortly, but other examples of these 'backstage', anticipatory concerns have included the Formula One Grand Prix that was due to be staged in Bahrain in 2011. This event was postponed over disquiet for the human rights record in that country, with the former British driver Damon Hill lending his voice to the broader discourse that questioned hosting races in a new, largely unproven market for global mega-events. Echoing the duality of the discourse surrounding human rights and sport – as both an enabler of and an answer to abuse and exploitation – Hill, in an interview with a British newspaper, maintains:

> The ruling family in Bahrain have said they want to stage a race there, and we all do. But F1 must align itself with progression, not repression, and a lot of demonstrations in that country have been brutally repressed. You are either aware of that or you're not. It is clear, whatever anyone says, that some very violent events have taken place in Bahrain. It is not our country. It is their country. But we can't just fluff over it and pretend that the difficulties there don't exist, or that they will sort themselves out. It is an over-simplification to say that the rulers there are the bad guys and the demonstrators are the good guys. But we cannot pretend that the political situation there is not a factor, because it is. It is important that Formula One is not seen to be only interested

in putting on the show, whatever the circumstances. You can't just base
your decision to hold a race in a country on that country's ability to pay.
(*The Guardian*, 3 June 2011)

Hill's comments alert us to one of the fundamental issues and tensions for the
global growth of mega-events in a context of 'arriviste cities' (Scherer &
Davison, 2011) and anticipatory spectacles. As new countries appear on the
mega-events circuit, systems, policies and regimes that were previously 'closed'
become subject to scrutiny through the kinds of activities by activist and humanitarian movements I alluded to earlier. That is, what were once largely domestic
policy concerns are now situated within a wider milieu of exogenous policies,
politics and pressures that circulate globally.

Domestic Policy Moves 'Front Stage'

The practice of slum clearance (often couched as 'urban redevelopment') that
occurred in relation to several mega-events in BRIC countries and the Global
South brings this tension between endogenous and exogenous policies into
sharp relief. In the lead-up to the 2008 Olympic Games, Beijing underwent an
estimated US$40 billion redevelopment programme. Up to 1.5 million people
were forced to move, as homes were razed in neighbourhoods that were
redeveloped into new commercial zones, and protests against the low levels of
compensation for this displacement were broken up by the military and police
(CBS, 2008). In anticipation of the 2016 Olympic Games in Rio de Janeiro, the
favela (slum) areas of the city have been earmarked for demolition, and transport routes will slice through neighbourhoods, dividing and displacing communities (Curi, Knijnik & Mascarenhas, 2011). Gaffney notes the human rights'
costs of such activities: 'these projects tend to violate all statutes which are supposed to protect human rights, because they move people away to places where
they know nobody, to houses which are not necessarily better than theirs and
far from their jobs' (2011).
    Alongside the dislocation of residents to make way for Games infrastructure,
mega-events have been seen to precipitate the displacement of particular population groups – ethnic minorities or those already living in circumstances of dire
social and material disadvantage. In the lead-up to the 2010 football World
Cup, street children in Durban were rounded up and arrested, while ahead of
the Beijing Olympics, police initiated crackdowns on Indigenous ethnic minorities, particularly the Muslim Uighurs from far-west China, in the run-up to the
2008 Olympic Games (Giulianotti & Klauser, 2010).
    Similar practices of population displacement occurred in Delhi in anticipation
of the 2010 Commonwealth Games. The clearing of tracts of Delhi to make way
for the Athletes' Village prompted public activism from groups such as Amnesty
International, Human Rights Watch and ACORN – a collection of community-
based organizations agitating for improved standards of living in developed and

developing nations. Mobilizing the network of new media outlined in Chapter 4, letters and petitions circulated around the globe, calling for protest and collective action. Here, we see one of the key legacies of the global order, whereby online communication technologies have facilitated the functioning of social movement groups and participatory democracy in the public sphere.

It is no coincidence, however, that many of the examples that draw attention to the inequities, injustices and abuses embodied in sporting mega-events come from BRIC countries or from the Global South. As mentioned earlier, the inequities of global labour shift endlessly across a landscape of exploitation and disadvantage, and it is in the Global South where the greatest concentrations of disadvantage are found, at times blurring definitions and expectations of 'rights' that were developed and created by 'the West' and 'the North'. For this reason, there is now a moral imperative to award hosting rights to countries in the Global South in order to contribute to the making and implementation of a 'just' social policy that reflects the global embrace of rights and responsibilities.

Beijing 2008

The Beijing Olympics, it has been suggested, brought concerns of power, privilege and human rights into particularly sharp relief. As Hwang notes, 'the Games incited people in the contemporary international community to "speak" about the idea of "human rights"' (2010: 870). With a human rights record inexorably linked to (i) the 1989 massacre in Tiananmen Square, where, according to some estimates, thousands of students, journalists and foreign ministry personnel were killed after challenging the Chinese government's political rule, (ii) the treatment of Tibetan dissidents and political exiles, and (iii) a heavily monitored and censored media and communication system, it was thus unsurprising that awarding the 2008 Olympics to Beijing in 2001 precipitated myriad calls for protests and boycotts over human rights abuses in China. That said, it is not my intention here to trace the 'vigorous and, at times, violent contest over the legitimacy of China's role in the Games and, by extension, of the moral status of the nation itself' (Rowe & McKay, 2011); rather, it is to consider the broader intersections of sports policy and human rights in this context of enhanced global scrutiny and accountability.

Beijing certainly had its work cut out for it in terms of changing public perceptions that the city could embody the aspirational aims of the Olympic Charter that the 'practice of sport is a human right' (IOC, 2010). As Kidd puts it, 'human rights and athletes' rights took a beating during the Beijing Olympics' (2010: 901). It was the image of a highly repressive regime that Beijing sought to overcome when the Games were promoted under the slogan 'One World One Dream', through which BOCOG (the Beijing Organizing Committee of the Olympic Games) conveyed the 'lofty ideal of the people in Beijing as well as in China to share the global community and civilization and to create a bright future hand in hand with the people from the rest of the world' (Beijing, 2008). While others have documented the prospective impact of hosting the 2008

Olympics on China's domestic sports policy concerns against the traditional metrics of performance and participation (Close, Askew & Xin, 2007; Hong, 2004), as well as the well-rehearsed tropes of nationhood and national identity (Close et al., 2007; Xu, 2006), my concerns lie more with examining the policy implications (rather than policies themselves) of human rights as they relate to sporting mega-events, than with these other themes and debates.

In the context of globalization, the human rights implications of the Beijing Olympics return us to several of the themes addressed in previous chapters. I noted in Chapter 1 that the concerns of global sport and social policy are redistribution, regulation and social provision and/or empowerment. Questions of social rights and social redistribution are clearly raised in the advocacy and activism work of campaign groups that rally against the kinds of human rights abuses I describe here. In particular, it was suggested that the global media attention the Beijing Games would attract would compel China to conform to these expectations of redistribution, regulation and social provision and/or empowerment. As Hwang notes:

> Many parties in the international community used the Games to draw attention to various political/human rights issues that were associated with China. They argued that while the Chinese government was facing the dilemma of sacrificing either Olympic glory or its standpoint on various political issues, there was an opportunity to pressure Beijing into making concessions. (2010: 856)

Certainly, the global scrutiny faced by Beijing is testament to the kind of participatory democracy discussed in Chapter 4. Linked to this policy agenda of human rights, there is now a growing demand for participation in 'public (and organizational) policy decisions' (Thibault et al., 2010: 276). As we saw in Chapter 4, it was the use of new technologies by advocacy groups to promote their agenda that proved an effective means of communication for transnational advocacy networks, for it enabled them to 'bypass governmental laws and domestic media sources that could screen, repress and censure communication unflattering to powerful elites' (Sage, 1999: 215–16). As Katwala has argued, 'the shape of global governance and power is changing – increasingly educated, assertive and networked citizens expect to have a say on issues which they care about' (2000: 6).

The heightened public scrutiny of Beijing over a range of domestic policy concerns also brought into play a tension between policy and protest. To deflect the growing momentum of international criticism of its human rights record, the Chinese government established 'protest zones' during the Olympics – designated areas at which to express dissent. Protestors, however, were required to apply in advance for the 'right' to protest at these sites, thus declaring their opposition to particular policy and political decisions and regimes, putting themselves at serious personal risk in the process. Moreover, in such instances, it became difficult to separate the relationships between the mega-event, cosmocrats, national and international institutions, and the discursive manipulation and image management of the event. As Lenskyj states, 'the Olympic industry has the power to suppress local dissent and to promote the illusion of unequivocal support on the part of host cities and countries' (2002: 152).

HUMAN TRAFFICKING, HUMAN RIGHTS, SEXUAL EXPLOITATION AND MEGA-EVENTS [4]

Trafficking and forced labour is a human rights concern for sport and social policy. The issue has been addressed mainly through the movement of athletes across the globe. Bale and Maguire (1994) note that the highly competitive world of sport drives the global migration of athletic mercenaries, which brings me to my case study of the trafficking of women (and girls) for the purpose of sexual exploitation. The abuses of human rights that are bound up in the movement of women and girl in this form of labour are inextricably located within broader concerns of citizenship, rights and responsibilities. The need for temporary labour, auxiliary labour and forced begging are implicated in the broader issue of mercenary labour, trafficking and human rights, although in terms of sporting mega-events, my concern in the ensuing section is on the trafficking of women for the purposes of sexual exploitation, and the policy actions and directions that developed in response.

To provide some context first: although the data is patchy and inconclusive, it is estimated that 2.45 million people are trafficked for the purpose of forced labour and sexual exploitation (International Labor Organization, 2005), with the trafficking of women across the world estimated to be a US$12 billion industry (Di Tommaso et al., 2009).[5] Such forced migration is often driven by demand (Anderson & O'Connell Davidson, 2003; Bales & Soodalter, 2009). Evidence has already established that major international sporting events promote an increase in demand for paid sex, because, in part, of the temporary population growth (Future Group, 2007; Hennig et al., 2006; Toynbee Hall, 2009) through an influx of tourists, site workers, contractors, the media, and indeed the athletes themselves. It is clear that mega-events provide a context in which women may be exploited in ways that pose a threat to their human dignity, and this has had particular implications for the development of policy across a range of domestic and foreign policy concerns that relate to women's safety, immigration and labour migration and border protection, among others.

To sketch how these policy concerns transpire in sporting mega-events, I focus on the Athens Olympics and the 2006 World Cup in Germany. I do this as the same question of 'a lack of evidence' in relation to sex trafficking and prostitution at each mega-event produced two very different policy responses.

Athens 2004

While evidence suggests that human trafficking in Athens increased around 2004 as the city prepared to host the Olympic Games, the Greek government was retrospectively criticized for its lack of preventative action in addressing the issue of human trafficking prior to the event (Future Group, 2007; Hennig et al., 2006). A report from the Greek Embassy (Hellenic Republic of Greece, 2004), however, points to a number of initiatives, actions and policies proposed in anticipation of the potential rise in trafficking activity. These plans included doubling the budget for anti-trafficking actions, developing agreements with neighbouring countries and financing the education of police officers, judges and public prosecutors. Although these strategies were not specific to the trafficking of women, it was the risk of multiple impacts for women that makes sex-related trafficking of particular policy concern.

To return to the issue of evidence-based policy-making introduced in Chapter 4, the author of the Greek Embassy's report could find no evidence that could quantify, prove or evaluate the success of any of these measures. Indeed, the International Organization for Migration, cited in Hennig et al. (2006), maintains that *no* trafficking occurred in relation to the Olympic Games in Athens during 2004. Given the hidden, illegal and criminal nature of trafficking for the purpose of sexual exploitation, such reports should be read with caution. An absence of 'official' evidence is not surprising and does not provide sufficient evidence that *no* sexual trafficking took place during the Athens Games. Instead, it highlights the contested nature of the evidence base around issues of trafficking, and underscores the need for further empirical research with women who have been trafficked or involved in the sale of sex during or in relation to the staging of major sporting events that can inform ongoing policy development and practice by agencies and authorities; that is, by Lipsky's 'street level bureaucrats' (1980), to return to an earlier notion.

This is evidenced in the following account, where limited tracking data has been collected by Greece in relation to trafficking (rather than sexual trafficking specifically) since 2001. The Future Group's 2007 report highlighted that the Greek Ministry of Public Safety recorded a 95% increase in the number of human trafficking victims in 2004; a figure almost double that of the previous year. While the report notes that trafficking did decline by 24% in 2005, following the Olympic Games, the figure was still 47% greater than that of 2003. This potentially shows a connection between the Athens Games and human trafficking, although it is difficult to directly link this 'spike' to the Olympic Games, or to suggest that this increase in trafficking was for the purpose of sexual exploitation (as opposed to trafficking for labour more generally). Again, in the context of evidence-based policy-making, such data need to be interpreted with caution. The report collapses categories of trafficking, and more accurate means of data capture are needed in reporting on incidences of sexual trafficking if they are to successfully impact upon policy with regard to sporting mega-events.

Germany 2006

Unlike the policy response of Athens, which was retrospectively criticized for its lack of preparation in anticipation of an increased number of girls and women being trafficked within and into Greece for the Olympic Games, Germany explicitly planned for an expected increase of women being involved in sexual trafficking and paid sex during the 2006 World Cup (Germany Report to EU, 2007).

Such preparations were in response to the predicted rise in the demand for paid sex that gained some attention in the lead-up to the World Cup. Some months before the start of the World Cup, several organizations released estimates that the event would be likely to accelerate sex trafficking. The figures fluctuated from 30,000 to 60,000 women expected to be trafficked during the competition (CARE for Europe, 2006; Council of Europe, 2006; Hennig et al., 2006; IOM, 2006; Neuwirth, 2006; Sparre, 2006), and it was widely expected that the sale of sex would increase around the games venues in Germany's major cities. German police and authorities thus focused their efforts on preparing for this predicted increase. To meet the demand for paid sex, Toynbee Hall (2009) point to the building of new structures such as 'sex huts', 'love boxes' and a four-storey 'mega brothel' in Berlin as well as the 'car-port like structures that offered rudimentary facilities' for the sale of sex in Cologne (Toynbee Hall, 2009: 3).

To return to the notions of crisis-driven and evidence-based policy-making, the German government's report to the European Council (Germany Report to EU, 2007) after the World Cup suggests that initial expectations of an increase in sex trafficking did not materialize in practice. Milovejevic and Pickering argue that the predicted figures were a product of how 'a wide ranging coalition of interests fuelled a moral panic around sex trafficking in Europe', which was further elaborated by sensationalist media coverage of the issue of sex trafficking (2008: 24). Unlike the policy response in Athens, in which an absence of *evidence* of Games-related trafficking was taken to be evidence of an absence of Games-related trafficking, in Germany, an absence of 'evidence' was taken to be evidence of the success of a range of widespread health promotion and public education campaigns across Germany.

Upon reporting that an increase in trafficking failed to eventuate during the World Cup in 2006, the German government claimed that the measures they had put in place to counter the threat of trafficking has been successful (Germany Report to EU, 2007) – clear 'evidence' of evidence-based policy-making and implementation. Among the measures instigated was the establishment of a multi-agency approach to the prevention of trafficking. The federal and state police forces worked alongside non-government organizations (NGOs). NGOs held public events, including large discussions, press conferences and interviews, while posters and leaflets were distributed, and information was provided through radio and television, telephone hotlines and websites (Future Group, 2007) to help raise public awareness.

This comprehensive network of information and support was supplemented at the ground level by the German police; that is, by 'street level bureaucrats'. A simultaneous national and regional approach was adopted (Germany Report to EU, 2007) which saw the formation of new specialist task forces. These forces conducted raids into known areas involving the sale of sex and established contact with known 'informers' in high-risk areas (Future Group, 2007). At a national level, border controls were reinstated for people travelling into Germany for the World Cup and targeted programmes were put in place to increase the awareness of hotel and accommodation staff (Future Group, 2007).

The examples of sex trafficking at the 2004 Olympics and the 2006 World Cup raise several key issues for global sports policy. The problem of 'evidence' for evidence-based policy-making is particularly acute, where the absence of evidence (that is, claims that no trafficking occurred) presents a perennial problem for claims to effective policy-making and compliance. On the one hand, an absence of evidence is taken to be an absence of a problem, and supports a rearguard position that no policy or action is required. On the other hand, as was the case in Germany, an absence of evidence was taken to be an indicator of the success or the effectiveness of particular policies and action, and continuing strategies are needed.

The trafficking of women for the purpose of sexual exploitation at mega-events also underscores one of the themes of the book, namely that sports policy is not just about sport. The trafficking of women in relation to sporting mega-events has implications for foreign policy in terms of labour migration and border control, as well as for domestic policy that effects the policing and protection of women and girls. Indeed, the trafficking for the purpose of sexual exploitation at sporting mega-events highlights the 'backstage' context within which much policy-making work takes place. While issues such as the sale or purchase of sex may seem to have very little to do with sport, it is clear that mega-events are an enabler of these forms of abuse. At the same time, their visibility and ability to attract and command global media attention provides mega-events – and their organizers – with particular opportunities and responsibilities to address these – and other – abuses of human rights that are of concern for this chapter.

CULTURAL DIPLOMACY AND FOREIGN POLICY

To return to an earlier theme, the contentious discourse surrounding government and political action at the Beijing Olympics provides a point of entry into debates about foreign policy, cultural diplomacy and human rights. The tarnished track records of host cities and nations, and the responses from activist organizations, are fully embedded in a broader discourse of cultural diplomacy and foreign policy. Despite the very real opportunities that mega-events afford to pressure those governments and regimes with poor track records of human and civil rights to revisit their modes of governance and political rule, the *infrequency* with which this occurs is perhaps the most striking feature of the discourse. Certainly, countries have used sport to draw attention to domestic issues that have international consequences – the boycott of South Africa over their policy of apartheid is a case in point here, as is the use of athlete activists to raise awareness of drought, famine or poverty in various parts of the world, but foreign policy *action*, in the form of policy that *impacts upon international relations*, is rarely forthcoming. As the examples from this chapter have shown, activist work tends to operate at the 'form of life' level rather the level of 'the State', to return to Hannerz's (1996) earlier formulation of socio-political interactions in the global order.

In something of an indictment, Peter Donnelly (2009) contends that the only major human rights victory that can be attributed to sport, through the kind of activities associated with broader State-level cultural diplomacy (such as sanctions and boycotts), has been that of the Anti-Apartheid movement where South Africa was suspended, in 1961, by FIFA (which kept the country out of international football until 1992), and then by the IOC in 1970 (which banned South Africa from Olympic competition until 1991). Since, 'there has been a clear reluctance on the part of governments to become involved in foreign policy issues relating to sport, and it is only under extreme circumstances, such as the boycott of the 1980 and 1984 Olympic Games, that there is evidence of direct involvement' (Donnelly, 2009: 41). Echoing Hunt's (2007) claim that 'human rights are easier to endorse that enforce', governments (as distinct from sporting bodies) from the Global North have been largely silent on 'difficult' policy decisions with regard to taking effective action against fellow countries with questionable human rights records. Zimbabwe, under the political rule of Robert Mugabe, still participates in international cricket matches. Formula One Grand Prix is still contested in Bahrain, while countries with similarly contentious histories of political rule and oppression (such as Iraq, Afghanistan or Syria) remain members of the international Olympic community. Diplomatic muscle, in the form of sanctions and boycotts, is rarely flexed.

Two key reasons can be attributed to this reluctance of governments to intervene in the international and foreign policy dimensions of sport. First, the policy concerns that are international or outwardly focused are intertwined; it is difficult to separate political decisions relating to tourism, economic development or the environmental impacts of hosting mega-events, for example, from the costs and consequences for human rights. In part, this is due to the 'relationships between and influence of transnational corporations on governments and the decisions that are made about international sport' (Donnelly, 2009: 42).

Second, mega-events labour under the falsehood that international sporting competition should remain free from politics and political action. One of the main objectives of the Olympic Movement, as stated in the Olympic Charter, is to 'oppose any political abuse of sport and athletes' (IOC, 2010), yet the Games have been consistently and repeatedly influenced by politics. While not intended to offer a definitive history of boycotts at the Olympics, Australia, Great Britain and Switzerland are the only countries to send a team to every Olympic Games since their inception. Where countries have decided not to attend, most of the boycotts have been motivated by domestic political situations and policy concerns. The Olympic Council of Ireland, for example, boycotted the 1936 Berlin Games because the IOC insisted its team be restricted to what was then known as the Irish Free State rather than all of Ireland. As mentioned earlier, several African countries, in 1972 and 1976, successfully threatened the IOC with a boycott, which forced the IOC to ban South Africa from Olympic competition because of its policy of apartheid. In 1980 and 1984, the United States and Russia boycotted each other's Games due to the ongoing Cold War. In 2008, there was also a call for boycotts of Chinese goods and of the 2008 Olympics themselves in protest at China's human rights record discussed previously. Despite the sustained pressure by global activist groups, and despite the resources of e-dissidence and mediated mobilization employed by citizen-consumers worldwide, no country instigated or supported a boycott, of either Chinese goods or the Games.

This lack of political will is indicative of an uneasy tension between exogenous and endogenous – domestic and foreign – policy concerns. Cultural diplomacy is more about *inter*-national relations, rather than international relations in which historical legacies cannot be separated from contemporary policy-making. That is, cultural diplomacy is indicative of relationships between nations, rather than located within the overarching architecture of global governance that sees supranational, cosmocratic organizations and institutions wield influence that can effect policy and diplomatic change. As such, global sports policy cannot be distanced from historical shifts and expanding agendas which reflect broader political relations and social structures within which the human rights dimensions of sporting events are implicated.

CONCLUSION

This chapter has examined the policy implications of hosting sporting mega-events in the context of human rights. Sporting mega-events provide a location through which to draw global attention to abuses of human rights, while at the same time human rights are continually and routinely violated in ways that are directly or indirectly related to sport (Donnelly, 2009: 33). It is this duality that has enabled something a revolutionary moment in sport, whereby issues of human rights and human dignity are fundamentally embedded in a discourse of fair play that speaks to the notion of a 'humane globalization' with which this chapter has been centrally concerned. As Kidd and Donnelly note, 'human rights in sport cannot be achieved without all sports participants fully enjoying those rights' (2000: 131).

In terms of policy, increasing attention has been paid to human rights in domestic policy (whether of young athletes, as discussed in Chapter 5, or young people in the sports manufacturing industry, as addressed in Sage's work (1999) in this chapter). At the same time, exogenous or global sports policy concerns, such as the worldwide trafficking of women or, indeed, the intrusions that the World-Anti Doping Code makes with regard to the testing protocols of athletes, have also brought to our attention concerns for human rights through the global inequalities carried through sporting mega-events. The attention that is paid to injustices in sport and sport-related practices cannot be separated from injustices of different kinds, and sports-related activism shares many of the discursive and political connections with non-sporting protest movements such as those advocating for gender or environmental justice or Indigenous sovereignty. Indeed, sporting mega-events raise fundamental questions for rights, responsibilities, regulation and the redistribution of resources that are central to debates about global social and global sports policy more broadly.

This growing awareness of and concern with the inequities that are embedded in global sport is part of what I've termed a more humane globalization, which chimes with Robertson's formulation of a 'global consciousness' (1995). For Robertson (1995), 'humankind' is at the heart of what he terms the 'global *gemeinschaft*', which considers globalization as achievable only through establishing 'a fully globewide community' that is underpinned by a 'commitment to the communal unity of the human species' (Robertson, 2002: x). It is the future of the human species and its relationships to the environment that are the concerns of the following, penultimate chapter, with its focus on the environmental impacts of sporting mega-events and issues of global, corporate responsibility and social policy.

BOX 8.1   QUESTIONS FOR DISCUSSION

- To what extent do you agree with the statement that the politics of sport should be kept separate from the politics of human rights?

- In what ways do you think this impacts upon the development and implementation of sports policy and legislation?

- To what extent have anti-globalization and alterglobalization movements been successful in highlighting abuses of human rights in sport and mega-events?

- What are the barriers they face, and what opportunities do these kinds of groups have for effecting meaningful change to the human rights agenda in sports policy?

SUGGESTED FURTHER READINGS

Brown, C. (1999) Universal human rights: A critique. In T. Dunne & N.J. Wheeler (eds), *Human rights in global politics*. Cambridge: Cambridge University Press.
Giulianotti, R. (2004) Human rights, globalization and sentimental education: The case of sport. *Sport in Society*, 7(3): 355–69.

Notes

1   There is a large and growing body of literature that examines a broader human rights agenda in sport and physical activity as it relates to government and NGO-led policy initiatives across the globe (Darnell, 2010; Darnell & Hayhurst, 2011; Kidd, 2009, 2010; Kidd & Donnelly, 2000). These are beyond the scope of this chapter with its focus on sporting mega-events.

2   Differing from its antecedent of anti-globalization, alterglobalization refers to the large spectrum of global social movements that present themselves as supporting new forms of globalization (rather than opposing all forms of globalization), urging that values of democracy, justice, environmental protection and human rights must be put ahead of purely economic concerns. Harvey, Horne and Safai (2009: 383–6) provide a useful overview of the broad terrain that alterglobalization covers, including civil rights; ecological concerns; women's rights, antiracist issues; peace; lesbian, gay, bisexual, transsexual and queer rights; human security; workers' rights; children's rights and Aboriginal rights. Drawing on social movement theory, Davis-Delano and Crosset (2008) further conceptualize the movement in relation to Indigenous rights and the appropriation of mascots and imagery for use at sporting mega-events.

3   The cornerstone of any discussion of human rights is the 1948 Universal Declaration of Human Rights (www.unhchr.xh/udlhr/lan/eng/htm). The Declaration set out the ambition to achieve 'a common standard' of basic freedoms and human rights. It draws upon the great liberal traditions of individual freedoms in its affirmation of 'life, liberty and security of person, equality before the law and the freedoms of thought, expression and peaceful assembly and association, and its prohibition of discrimination, slavery or servitude, arbitrary arrest, torture or cruel, inhuman or degrading treatment or punishment'. It is these rules, which protect the civil liberties of individuals, that are the cornerstone of our understandings of human rights, and it is within this broad definition and understanding that my discussion of sporting mega-events and human rights is located.

4   Parts of this section have been previously reported in Palmer, C. (2011) Violence against women and sport: A review. www.endviolenceagainstwomen.org.uk/data/files/evaw_violence_against_women_and_sport_.

5   Our knowledge of trafficking for the purpose of sexual exploitation remains exceptionally limited. This is due, in part, to the criminal and hidden nature of the activity (Agustin, 2005; Albanese, 2007; Doezema, 2000; Kelly, 2002; Kempadoo, 2005; Laczko & Gramegna, 2003; London Councils/GLE, 2011).

9

MEGA-EVENTS, THE ENVIRONMENT AND CORPORATE RESPONSIBILITY

THIS CHAPTER

- examines environmental impacts on the policy and practice dimensions of staging sporting mega-events;

- explores the roles and responsibilities of sports governing bodies and mega-events' organizers for managing the environmental impact of sporting events;

- introduces notions of 'green washing' and corporate responsibility to debates about sporting mega-events and environmental policy.

INTRODUCTION

The late twentieth century has seen a resurgence of interest in environmental values in social and political life. The development of 'green politics' and political parties (such as the Australian Greens, the Popular Movement for the Environment in Switzerland or the Finnish Green Party), the growth of environmental movements (such as Greenpeace, Friends of the Earth or the World Wildlife Federation), and a commitment from governments to tackle global ecological concerns, place the environment at the forefront of policy development and the decision-making processes (Butcher, 2003; Collins & Flynn, 2007; Stubbs, 2008).

The impact of sport on the environment is, in the context of global debates about climate change, the pricing of carbon emissions, resource depletion and environmental degradation, an increasingly important dimension of domestic and foreign policy. A growing body of evidence (and public opinion) suggests that the production and consumption of sport impacts on the environment, whether it be from the unregulated use of natural resources, the destruction of habitats, the emission of greenhouse gases, or from urban development programmes such as those in London, 2012, Delhi, 2010 or Beijing, 2008. These issues are all part of an emerging agenda for sport and social policy.

Equally, concerns about the carbon footprint associated primarily with air travel to 'world class' *arriviste* cities have been noted (Scherer & Davison, 2011; Whitson & Macintosh, 1996), with the environmental action group 'Plane Stupid' using the London Olympics to draw attention to the significant environmental costs of vast numbers of people travelling across the globe to attend this mega-event. In other words, there is a growing conscience about the potential environmental impacts of the unmanaged growth and development of sporting mega-events, tourism and leisure activities around the world, which echoes the work of the sports-based political activist movements discussed previously.

Drawing on much of the conceptual material presented in this second section of *Global Sports Policy* (the properties of sporting mega-events and their appropriation by activist groups), this chapter focuses on the environmental impacts and consequences of hosting sporting mega-events, and their wider links to a social discourse of corporate environmental responsibility. The chapter traces the time period between the staging of two Winter Olympic Games – Lillehammer in 1994 and Vancouver in 2010. The increased attention of sports activist groups throughout this period has shifted the policy discourse to one of greater public accountability and legislation, and the regulation of host nations for the environmental impacts of sporting mega-events.

The ensuing chapter proceeds against this background. Several key questions ground the discussion. What responsibilities, if any, do governing bodies have for the impact of their sport on the environment? To what extent should the IOC or other transnational organizations regulate the impact of mega-events on the environment? Should those sports that have a negative impact on the environment be removed from international competition? Should those countries with poor environmental track records be removed from international sporting competition? To help frame these questions, the chapter draws on the concepts of 'green washing' and corporate social responsibility in the context of global sporting mega-events.

THE EMERGENCE OF THE ENVIRONMENT AS A POLICY CONCERN

Since the mid-1970s, the environment has emerged as a major policy platform for political parties around the world. To return to one of the themes from Chapter 3 – globalization and governance – the environment poses a significant challenge for developing and enforcing transnational policy. By their very nature, environmental issues and debates transcend states, regions and nations, which often have conflicting structures and expectations of policy compliance. Unlike anti-doping policy (the main example used in Chapter 3), which developed (not unproblematically) out of the perceived need for global policy harmonization, the level of interdependence needed to endorse and ensure compliance with environmental concerns requires a level of political interaction across policy areas and between nations, states and governments that exceeds the limits of global governance. As Cantelon and Letters note:

> Difficulties exist in the adoption and implementation of universal standards of environmental management. World championships and Olympic Games are highly mobile affairs and are constantly staged in different locations. And herein lies the difficulty. ... Different cross-cultural interpretations of environmental protection constitute a serious challenge to transnational sporting organizations even if they are committed totally to environmental responsibility. (2000: 295)

As one of the building blocks of an imagined world, to return to Appadurai's formulation of 'scapes', the notion of an 'enviroscape' (my formulation) seems something of an omission in how we conceptualize the interdependence between human society – both built and social – and the imagined world on a global scale. Operating in a diasporic public sphere, the policy implications of the environment are contentious and disjunctive in equal measure.

The Environment and Sport and Physical Activity

As is the case with much of the material covered in *Global Sports Policy*, the relationship between sport and the environment is a paradoxical and contradictory one. On the one hand, healthy and supportive environments are necessary for the promotion and performance of sport at both everyday and elite levels. On the other hand, sport has the potential to degrade the very same natural and physical environments on which sports participation and performance depends.

The role of the environment as being conducive towards social health and physical activity has been consistently documented as part of a broader research and policy agenda on the social determinants of health. In particular, the role of the physical environment in terms of civic infrastructure is recognized as an important part of health promotion. Abraham, Sommerhalder and Abel (2010), Forrest and Kearns (1999), Kingsley and Townsend (2006), Macintyre (2007) and Satariano and McAuley (2003), among others, suggest that amenities like shops, community halls, community gardens and sporting and recreational facilities provide a social focus which, in turn, affects people's perception of their neighbourhood and contributes to their quality of life.

In the context of the broader social justice agenda which informs much of this book, it has been suggested that people's experiences of the physical environment of their neighbourhood matter more to those with fewer resources, both financial and social (Baum & Palmer, 2002; Coalter & Allison, 2000; Ellaway et al., 2007; Forrest & Kearns, 1999; MacDougall et al., 2002; Stafford et al., 2008). As Forrest and Kearns recognize:

> The neighbourhood environment still matters ... to these disadvantaged communities. The elements of the neighbourhood conceived in early planning concepts are still ... desired though not always present ... residents would prefer their neighbourhoods to satisfy a range of residential functions, but changing social patterns of shopping, leisure and recreation, together with the significant costs involved in providing facilities, meant that these neighbourhoods were no longer self-sufficient for many of the functions people sought from them. (1999: 36)

While most of the research connecting quality of life to the quality of the physical environment has been undertaken in deprived urban areas in the Global North – notably Glasgow – the extremes of poverty and social divisions in the Global South present new challenges for developing policy and providing opportunities and infrastructure that can contribute positively to a community's understandings and experiences of health and well-being, where unmanaged economic growth and unregulated development have already contributed to the destruction of natural habitats. It was reported, for example, that in the run-up to the Beijing Olympics, a state-owned Chinese business planned to invest $US1 billion to construct a processing plant in Indonesia designed to harvest 800,000 cubic metres of rare merbeau timber for the floor in the Bird's Nest Stadium (Friends of the Earth International, 2006; Jackson & Haigh, 2009: 2).

That said, I would not want to overstate the social divisions between the Global North and the Global South at the expense of social divisions *within*. The events in New Orleans following Hurricane Katrina, where thousands of the most underprivileged people in the United States sought refuge in the city's Super Dome, suggests that the 'use of sporting facilities is deeply implicated in issues of social justice, exclusion, development and power' (Mincyte, Casper & Cole, 2009: 104).

With the provision of sport and recreational facilities playing important roles in promoting the social and physical well-being of individuals and communities, it is not surprising that environmental and recreation-related improvements occupy a place on the domestic sports policy agenda of many developed nations (Book & Carlsson, 2011). Sport England, for example, through PPG 17 (Planning Policy and Guidance) – Open Space, Sport and Recreation – maintains that open space is a valuable sporting and recreational resource in towns and cities, whether as formal areas for activities such as playing fields, cycle paths, walking trails and playgrounds or more informal multi-function areas such as parks. In a response to changes to the National Planning Policy Framework mooted in 2010 by the Department of Culture, Media and Sport, Sport England contended that they 'would not want to see the successful key principles and policy guidance of PPG 17 to be lost in the new NPPF'. In short, these are:

> The recognition that sport and recreation underpins people's quality of life, and is fundamental to delivering broader Government objectives such as urban renaissance, rural renewal, social inclusion and community cohesion, health and well-being and promoting sustainable development. (Sport England, 2010)

As noted in the previous chapter, many sports-related projects have reclaimed derelict tracts of urban space – home to many of the world's poor and destitute – as part of development programmes in anticipation of the arrival of a sporting mega-event, and this needs to be considered in any discussion of environmental development aimed, ostensibly, at improving the physical and visual amenities of urban areas. In the United Kingdom, for example, redundant military bases have been converted into water sports centres, which now offer training facilities for international teams contesting the canoe and kayak slalom events at the 2012 Olympics. Clearly, the redevelopment agenda is linked to the performance agenda, but the social costs and consequences of such activities remain a persistent undercurrent. As Mincyte et al. note, 'as major stadiums are built ... what happens to the people who live and work in the area? What happens to entire cities, economies and industries, but also to animals, plants and wildlife living in and nearby stadiums?' (2009: 104)

As such observations suggest, the 'city favors the consumer over the citizen' (Sze, 2009) in ways that mean the human dimensions of racism, colonialism, power and privilege cannot be separated from sport, sporting mega-events, poverty and development.

The Effects of Sport on the Environment

The flipside of the positive association between sport, the environment and quality of life is that sport is also hugely destructive of the environment, both the urban environment discussed above and the natural environment in which many sports are played. The sculpting of mountains to provide for ski runs has the potential to disrupt fragile ecosystems. Artificial snow-making diverts natural waterways through alpine environments. The maintenance of pristine golf courses consumes huge volumes of water and chemicals. The construction of sporting venues and stadia eat into built environments. Recreational fishing impacts upon declining fish stocks, while sewage spews into waterways, affecting many water-based sports. In other words, the risks and consequences of 'when sport meets nature' (Mincyte et al., 2009: 103) are acute.

In particular, the environmental impact of golf (and its not unrelated association with a particular demographic profile) has been subject to public scrutiny.

During the 1990s and early 2000s, the environmental effects associated with the development and maintenance of playing greens was the focus of public questioning when:

> The public began to wonder about the chemicals used on golf courses and whether they may pose a health risk to humans and wild life; about the water consumption that aids the production of the lush green courses so many players desire; and about the effects of course construction on the environment and the social ramifications that seem to be so often linked with golf courses. (Wheeler & Nauright, 2006: 428)

One of the themes of this book is that the inequities of globalization shift endlessly across a landscape of exploitation and disadvantage. As was the case with labour associated with the sportswear industry in South-East Asia, when faced with opposition, golf course developers simply shifted their operations to the new and largely unregulated markets of India, South-East Asia and the Gulf States. 'Developers are finding it harder to find areas where course construction does not meet public opposition. ... As a result, many are turning their attention to underdeveloped countries where the means to halt projects is less readily available, thus ensuring sustained profit generation' (Wheeler & Nauright, 2006: 428).

ENVIRONMENTAL SOCIAL MOVEMENTS AND SPORTS POLICY

This concern with the inequities of sports-related expansion in developing nations forms part of the global humanity agenda of the new social movements described in the previous chapter. Informed by discourses of Feminism, Socialism and Human Rights, groups such as Greenpeace, Friends of the Earth and the World Wildlife Fund for Nature, among others, form a broad range of interlinked networks that seek to draw attention to global environmental concerns. As we saw in the previous chapter, sports-related activism is a more recent addition to this broad portfolio of social movements, and the environmental impact of sport has emerged as an even newer dimension of the global expansion of this activist agenda.

Importantly, in the case of environmental issues, sports-based activism shifted from the margins to the mainstream as it gained popular and political currency. While this is a point to which I'll return in my discussion of corporate social responsibility and the policy implications for sporting mega-events, the point here is that while environmental activism was once most typically associated with subcultural groups and 'alternative' lifestyles, it has been subsumed or complemented by a more mainstream discourse, wherein we are 'witnessing a formalisation of green politics and the establishment and legitimation of global environmental social movements' (Mansfield & Wheaton, 2011: 383).

Throughout the 1990s and early 2000s, the advocacy work of sport-related environmental movements was associated with the rise of 'lifestyle sports' such as surfing, skateboarding, climbing, mountain biking and *parkour* (Atencio, Beal & Wilson, 2009; Atkinson, 2009; Heywood & Montgomery, 2008; Robinson, 2008; Wheaton, 2007, 2008). Concerns with land use and traffic pollution soon gave rise to groups such as the cyclist advocacy movement Critical Mass, while ocean pollution was instrumental in the formation of Surfers against Sewage. Much of the identity politics of this 'recreational activism' (Erickson, 2011) was associated with the 'alternative', 'green lifestyle' of environmentalism and, in the initial stages of promoting environmental issues and concerns, this association operated as a barrier to policy development and uptake. That is, environmental concerns were regarded as part of an antagonistic political identity of a counter-cultural minority (Horton, 2006) rather than having mainstream appeal that would resonate with broader policy concerns.

While it is not my intention to document in detail the shift from the margins to the mainstream, environmental politics have, throughout the late twentieth century, nonetheless gained legitimacy and led to the development of public policy across several government portfolios in most developed and, to a lesser extent, developing nations. As Cantelon and Letters note, 'the legitimacy extended to the global environmental movement has impacted upon those organizations responsible for international sports events' (2000: 295).

This movement of environmental concerns from the margins to mainstream, or from the local to the global, has been critical in taking forward a policy agenda in relation to sport and the environment, particularly around the notion of environmental sustainability. In 1994, the UN Environmental Programme (UNEP) created a Sport and Environment programme, and charged it with promoting environmental awareness through sport, as well as with the design of sustainable sports facilities and equipment. Alongside this, sport and physical activity have been linked to sustainable transport through initiatives such as 'walking buses' designed to encourage children to walk to school, as well as policy encouraging the very public cycling cultures of Denmark and the Netherlands, where cycling exceeds the use of private cars and other forms of public transport in municipal areas (Pucher, 2008; Pucher & Bueler, 2007). In other words, although domestic policy in developed nations has responded well to the issues raised by hitherto marginal environmental groups, when these shift to the environmental impacts of sport at a *global* level, this becomes problematic.

ENVIRONMENTAL POLICY AND SPORTING MEGA-EVENTS

To return to the primary focus of this section of *Global Sports Policy*, sporting mega-events bring together many of these policy-related concerns about the impacts of sport on the environment, and have been on the 'environmentalist agenda' since 1974 when 'Denver held a referendum and subsequently turned down the IOC's offer to host the upcoming Winter Games on the grounds that they posed too great a threat to the environment' (Lenskyj, 1998: 343). As Tranter and Lowes note, 'mega-sport events strain local resources, increase traffic and pollution, displace local communities, consume scarce resources, dramatically increase waste and, in doing so, pose public health risks associated with mass consumption' (2009: 151).

Citing several sporting mega-events, Schmidt goes on to contend that:

> The 2006 Super Bowl in Detroit produced 500 tons of the greenhouse gas carbon dioxide (from transport and utility usage), while the 2004 Summer Olympics in Athens produced half a million tons in two weeks – roughly comparable to what a city of 1 million people would emit over a similar period. Each match during the 2006 World Cup will use up to 3 million kilowatt-hours of energy (similar to the annual consumption of 77 European households), and produce an estimated 5–10 tons of trash. (2006: 114)

Not surprisingly, 'organizations responsible for international sports events ... have been pressured to respond to questions concerning the relationship between their mega-events and the impact they have upon the natural environment' (Cantelon & Letters, 2000: 295). Environmental campaigners such as Greenpeace and Friends of the Earth, for example, used the heightened scrutiny of the 2008 Olympics to alert a global audience to the impacts of unregulated heavy industry in China's capital on air and water pollution levels, greenhouse gas emissions and the rights of humans to live in healthy environments (Brajer & Mead, 2003; Close, Askew & Xin, 2007; UNEP, 2008).

In light of growing public pressure on host cities to clearly articulate the environmental impacts of mega-events along with the social and economic impacts described earlier in the book, several took 'adaptive', proactive courses of action. The 2006 World Cup in Germany, for example, strived for 'climate neutrality' in Frankfurt, through off-setting the estimated 100,000 tons of greenhouse emissions associated with the event and channelling rainwater run-off for use in cleaning and in public toilets (*Green Goal: Environmental Goals for the FIFA 2006 World Cup*). Coca-Cola, one of the major sponsors of the event, agreed to use recyclable drinking cups at the event as part of the World Cup's public commitment to corporate and environmental responsibility.

THE GREENING OF THE OLYMPICS

It is against this backdrop that the International Olympic Committee began to explicitly address environmental concerns as part of its broader policy agenda:

> Concerned about the levels of expenditure needed to stage its mega-events and perhaps chastened by its acquiescent embrace of

commercialism in the 1980s and 1990s, the IOC recognized sustainability as being allied to its core philosophy of 'Olympism' – thereby partly justifying the value of the Olympics by reference to their lasting impact upon the quality of life of their host cities and their citizens. (Gold & Gold, 2009: 1982)

Given their reliance on the alpine environment, the Winter Olympics present arguably greater challenges for a 'green games', and host cities are perhaps subject to more intense public scrutiny of the environmental impacts, in part because of their location in a (subjectively) beautiful alpine environment. Described as a 'huge fridge in the mountains', the tracks used for bob sled and skeleton competitions demand the artificial regulation of an alpine environment, while the snow and ice-making needed to keep ski runs safe and with comparable conditions for all competitors, along with the construction of spectator facilities and viewing platforms in mountain environments, all present considerable practical challenges for hosting an environmentally responsible global sporting mega-event.

Lillehammer, 1994

This commitment to a 'Green Olympics' is attributed to the 1994 Winter Games in Lillehammer. Returning to one of the themes from earlier, local environmental activist groups 'put forward the environmental issue' (Lesjø, 2000: 290), successfully campaigning for Norway's Olympic Organizing Committee to build the Games infrastructure in ways that would be 'in harmony' with the surrounding landscape (Lesjø, 2000: 289). The speed skating rink, for example, was designed to avoid potential effects on a nearby bird sanctuary, and Games officials agreed to an environmental plan that incorporated waste recycling, renewable building materials and the use of energy efficient lighting and heating at Games venues (Lesjø, 2000; Schmidt, 2006). In an exaltation that would be similarly echoed six years later in Sydney, the then President of the IOC, Juan Antonio Samaranch, declared the Lillehammer Games to be 'the best Winter Games ever' (Lesjø, 2000).

To return to one of the orienting frameworks of the book, the 'greening' of the Lillehammer Games did not occur naturally, but was the result of considerable cultural work and human intervention in which a 'Green Games' was made to happen. In his analysis of the Lillehammer Olympics, Lesjø (2000) picks apart the planning process by which the Green Games came into being. Drawing on the figurational sociology of Norbert Elias outlined in Chapter 5, Lesjø (2000) maintains that bidding and planning for events like the Winter Olympics are a 'game' between several players with different power ratios, an observation that echoes my own analysis of the role of cosmocrats and cultural intermediaries in the governance of global events like the Tour de France. As Lesjø (2000: 284) notes, the planning process for Lillehammer was far from rational, and was cross-cut instead with conflicts and compromises among interest groups that saw a discursive shift in how Lillehammer presented the Games it was to host in the bidding process for the 1994 Winter Olympics.

Lesjø's empirical data suggests that Lillehammer's original bid was premised on the notion of the 'Compact Games', in which everything – venues, events, etc. – would be located in the one small city. Over the ten to 15-year timeframe within which planning for mega-events typically takes place, this tagline of the 'Compact Games' was replaced with that of the 'Green Games'. In a case of the margins meeting the mainstream, environmental issues were initially put forward by grassroots activists and were then taken up by the Norwegian government. The Norwegian Ministry of the Environment wanted 'the Olympics to highlight environmental politics and to show the world that Norway took the recommendations for the UN report [*Our Common Future*, a 1998 report arguing for sustainable development in Third World countries] seriously' (Lesjø, 2000: 290). It was the ideological convergence of activist groups such as the Norwegian Environmental Organization (NEC) and the local Olympic organizing committee that led the IOC to deploy the marketing strategy of 'corporate environmentalism' (Lesjø, 2000: 292), whereby the Lillehammer Olympics transformed into the Green Games. Although critics such as Lenskyj (1998) contend that the approach taken was a 'light green' one, rather than one that changed the IOC or the Olympics in any substantive way, the ideological imperatives that drive forward a policy agenda in relation, in this case, to the environmental impacts of sporting mega-events are constantly shifting, shaped by and responsive to the normative, often conflictual, political priorities.

IMPLICATIONS FOR GLOBAL SPORTS POLICY

On the back of widespread international claims of environmental damage and mismanagement from the staging of the 1992 Winter Olympics in Albertville, the IOC was pressured to rethink its position on environmental issues. 'In two short years, the IOC went from an organization with no environmental policy to one with a policy fully integrated into its philosophy of Olympism' (Cantelon & Letters, 2000: 295). A year after the Lillehammer Games, the International Olympic Committee, in conjunction with the United Nations Environmental Programme (UNEP), established 'the Environment' as the 'third pillar' of the Olympic Movement, along with Sport and Culture:

> The IOC objective is not only to see to it that the staging of the Games does not have a negative impact on the environment, but also to help improve the environment and leave a green legacy. ... The Games can be used to provide sustainable environmental legacies, such as rehabilitated and revitalized sites, increased environmental awareness, and improved environmental policies and practices. (IOC, 1998: 1)

As VanWynsberghe, Kwan and Van Luijk note, 'the IOC's adoption of a third pillar of the environment marked the prospect of a new standard in sustainable mega-events' (2011: 370). The 'local initiative of Lillehammer has become the global policy that all future Olympic Games organizing committees must follow if they are to win the bid to organize an Olympiad' (Cantelon & Letters, 2000: 294). Any country wanting to host the Olympics needs to produce an environmental assessment to accompany its bid that follows strict and specific guidelines describing energy use, water consumption, waste generation and sustainable building construction, in addition to a 'social commitment' to include local communities in the planning process (IOC, 1998; Schmidt, 2006: 116).

A brief timeline of those Olympic Games that have been held since the addition of 'the third pillar' is instructive for the development of environmental sports policy.

Nagano, 1998

The Winter Olympics at Nagano, Japan, in 1998 was the first Games at which the IOC's environmental protection policy was to be followed by the organizing committee (Cantelon & Letters, 2000: 294). When Nagano bid for the 18th Winter Olympics, 'Coexistence with Nature' was its theme and its tagline was that of 'the Environmental Olympics'. The Games venues included land designated as a national park, so managing the demands of running the event without destroying this protected area was key to the environmental strategy put forward by the bidding team. Following the selection of Nagano, the strapline of 'Coexistence with Nature' was carried through in the design of venues and courses, where the Games attracted notoriety for, among other things, introducing low-emission vehicles and adopting staff uniforms made from recycled materials.

While it is tempting to attribute this commitment to environmental protection and sustainability to the after-effects the Lillehammer Olympics, there were a range of broader environmental and social justice activities taking place that the IOC could not afford to distance itself from. In some cases, these predated the inclusion of the third pillar of the Olympic Movement. The UN Conference on Environment and Development (more popularly known as the Rio Earth Summit) took place in 1992, which proved a catalyst for a number of sport-related environmental initiatives that were then played out at subsequent mega-events. At the Summer Olympics in Barcelona in 1992, the IOC urged all national organizing committees in attendance to sign the Earth Pledge, an initiative borrowed from the Rio Earth Summit, and the IOC Sport and the Environment Commission was created in close affiliation with the UN with the purview of bringing about policies of sustainable development in sport.

Importantly, in the year following the 'Environmental Olympics', the IOC adapted Agenda 21 to the Olympic Movement. Originally developed by the United Nations at the Rio Earth Summit, the Declaration on Environment and Development and the Statement of Principles for the Sustainable Management of Forests was adopted by the Olympic Movement as the Sport for Sustainable Development programme, or 'Agenda 21' as it was more commonly known.

Agenda 21 operated as a sustainable development plan that itemized a series of actions that cut across every aspect of human interaction upon the environment and which were to be taken globally, nationally and locally by members of the United Nations, by national governments and by major sporting organizations and governing bodies. Some 178 governments signed up to Agenda 21, which had three main goals: (i) improving socio-economic conditions; (ii) the conservation and management of resources for sustainable development; and (iii) strengthening the roles of the main groups in environmental protection (IOC, 1998). In short, Agenda 21 offered sports governing bodies a mechanism through which to integrate sustainable development into their policies in ways that would allow them to play a key role in promoting the environment in connection with their sports.

Sydney, 2000

Just as the addition of the Environment as the third pillar of the Olympic Movement was the catalyst for the explicit agenda of the Nagano Winter Olympics, the mandate of the Olympic Movement's Agenda 21: Sport for Sustainable Development formed part of the policy backdrop to the Sydney Summer Olympics in 2000. As an island nation with a 'fragile ecological balance, unique flora and fauna, and regular extremes of weather – droughts, floods and bushfires – Australia can hardly afford to ignore the environment' (Lenskyj, 1998: 344). In an economy that is historically dependent on agriculture, the protection of farming lands and livestock is a key concern, and many overseas visitors express surprise at Australia's strict quarantine regulations, which until recently included spraying with pesticide all passengers disembarking from international flights.

Thus, it was not unexpected that the principles developed by the Sydney Bid Committee, following the introduction of the third pillar of the Environment to the Olympic Movement, stated a commitment to energy and water conservation, to protecting human health with appropriate standards of air, water and soil quality, and to safeguarding significant natural and cultural environments (Lenskyj, 1998: 346). That said, the Sydney Games attracted criticism for its policies of displacing or 'moving on' homeless and Indigenous populations from around the high-traffic tourist areas of The Rocks (Lenskyj, 2000), discussed in the previous chapter, while the inaugural triathlon in Olympic competition was contested in the busy Sydney Harbour, which raised concerns about the quality of the water the athletes would be swimming in, given the stated commitment of the Bid Committee to protecting human health with appropriate standards of water quality.

Torino, 2006

As environmental issues gained popular and political currency, addressing the longer-term environmental costs and impacts became an increasingly important dimension of the Olympic Movement's Agenda 21. Host cities needed to ensure sustainability that went beyond the relatively short duration of the mega-event. As the first Games to embrace this policy shift, the 2006 Torino Winter Olympics, for example, was required to articulate a plan outlining the ways in which the skating rinks and other facilities would be used beyond the life of the Games. To do this, the organizing committee embraced the HEritage Climate TOrino (HECTOR) project, which had the ambitious aim of making the Torino Games entirely carbon-neutral. By supporting energy efficiency and renewable energy schemes, both locally in the region of Piedmont and globally in Sri Lanka and Eritrea, the Torino Olympics sought to offset the estimated 300,000 tons of greenhouse gases released during the two weeks of the Games (TOROC, 2006a).

The agenda of 'evidence-based' policy-making discussed in Chapter 4 was part of the broader context in which bid criteria for the Olympics were subject to growing accountability and the need for more rigorous systems of measurement. That is, Games organizers needed to *substantiate* their claims to environmental sustainability. The Torino Organizing Committee thus adopted an environmental management system that conformed to the Eco-Management and Audit Scheme (EMAS), which was regulated by the European Union and used across industry and construction. Companies and contractors registered through EMAS could monitor and evaluate their environmental performance, and twenty-nine Olympic sites were built by companies registered through EMAS (TOROC, 2006b), reflecting the need to 'evidence' environmental sustainability and accountability.

As part of this need for increased accountability and 'evidence', an extensive monitoring plan of sixteen environmental indicators was developed by TOROC. These included water and air quality, soil use, energy consumption, waste production, ecosystems, landscape, and the urban environment. Suppliers of goods and services involved in the Games were also selected on the basis of the ecological quality of their products. In line with the European 'eco-label' for hotel services, TOROC promoted an eco-label trademark for the tourist sites and hotels in the Olympic areas and provided technical support necessary to obtain certification (TOROC, 2006b).

This movement towards including companies, contractors and suppliers with 'eco-friendly' credentials reflected an environmental agenda that the companies and sponsors associated with sporting mega-events were increasingly embracing. Two of the official sponsors of the Torino Games, the McDonald's Corporation and the Coca-Cola Company (along with Unilever), were part of 'Refrigerants, Naturally!', a scheme supported by UNEP and Greenpeace that promoted alternative point-of-sale refrigeration technology in the food and beverage industry (TOROC, 2006b).[1]

The increasing buy-in of corporations and sponsors to the philosophy of environmental sustainability is a point to which I'll return in my discussion of 'green washing' strategies to promote an environmentally friendly public image of global social responsibility, and certainly critics such as Levermore (2010, 2011) have drawn attention to the paucity of evidence as to whether such environmen-tally based corporate social responsibility strategies actually work, especially over time. The point here is that, in the climate of public accountability, meas-urement and transparency afforded and demanded by the broader context of evidence-based policy-making, such transnational companies and sponsors could scarcely afford not to be involved in the very public 'green' activities wit-nessed in Torino.

Beijing, 2008

In the Games following Torino, concern was raised over air pollution from large industries based in Beijing, particularly the impact this might have on athletes' breathing in training and competition. As part of their bid, the Beijing Organizing Committee of the Olympic Games promised to achieve 230 'blue sky' days per year (Brajer & Mead, 2003). To do this, the city ordered the Shougang Corporation (a major steel producer) to move its coal-fired smelters – and some 120,000 employees – to a small island in the neighbouring Hebel province (Schmidt, 2006).

Such concerns with heavy pollution and what seem to be the heavy-handed relocation of people and industry return us to some of the human rights dimen-sions of staging mega-events in cities and nations beyond the northern metropole discussed in the previous chapter. While there is, arguably, a moral obligation to award hosting rights to cities in the Global South in order to contribute to the making and implementation of a 'just' social policy, we must also recognize the realities of the social, political and economic circumstances faced in the Global South and BRIC countries, and the impacts these have on environmental and related policy and practice.

Vancouver, 2010

Continuing the agenda of evidence-based environmental policy-making appar-ent at the Torino Games, the bid for the 2010 Winter Olympic Games embraced the need for accountability, transparency and bid criteria measures, which are now included in the Olympic Movement's Agenda 21: Sport for Sustainable Development. The organizers of the Vancouver Games (VANOC) worked with UNEP for three years prior to the event, and every venue was designed to meet Canadian Green Building LEED's (Leadership in Energy & Environmental Design) 'silver' designation. Waste wood was chipped, composted and diverted from local landfill and rain was captured to irrigate landscaping. Nearly 70% of the heating for the Olympic Village came from waste heat recovery systems (including from sewage and used bath water), and transportation initiatives encouraged the use of public transport, bicycling and other alternatives to com-muting by cars. Vancouver's efforts provided its sponsors, government and the media alike with bragging rights that Vancouver would be the 'the greenest Games ever', in something of an ascending discourse of environmental supremacy as each new event appears on the global mega-event circuit.

In keeping with the growing politics of environmental activism, the Vancouver Olympics were greeted by strident criticism. The measurement of the 'minimal impact' of the Games (one of Vancouver's selling points) was perceived, by those communities most directly affected by the Games, to be superficial or 'light green', to return to Lenskjy's (1998) formulation. In particular, there was a lack of meaningful consultation of local Indigenous populations and regard for the cultural and natural environments so important to Canada's First Nation peoples.

Speaking out against the environmental impacts of the 2010 Games and its corporate sponsors, Clayton Thomas Muller, of the Indigenous Environmental Network, maintained that:

> When we look at the assessment of the carbon footprint of the Games, the reality of it is that they only looked at very surface issues; they only looked at the flights. ... They did not look at the forest loss, the tree loss, the impact on wetlands. They did not look at the construction CO2 imprint of all of the machinery that has been going 24/7 for the last year in preparation for the Games. When we calculate all of that the games represent a much larger carbon and ecological imprint than what has been publicly stated by VANOC. (cited in Saunders, 2010)

Adding to these criticisms, the environmental activist group Whistlerwatch, along with the Council of Canadians (an Indigenous Rights Coalition), maintained that the focus of environmental sustainability had been on the initiatives that were undertaken in the main host city, Vancouver, although other Olympic sites, including the ski resort of Whistler, some 125 kilometres north, had seen environmental impacts such as the loss of thousands of trees that were felled as part of Games preparation. This sort of periphery development was of similar concern to Indigenous communities, as evidenced in the following statement by Kanahus Pelki of the Secwepemc First Nation

> Gordon Campbell [the then Canadian Prime Minster] has been quoted as saying that the spinoffs of the Olympics are something that BC [British Columbia] can't even imagine. These investors and industries are creating major negative impacts on our territories. The territories that we continue to depend on for our traditional food and medicine harvesting. We depend on these glacier areas for our water. The Canadian Government is using the Olympics as a big advertisement that our lands are open for business. But we want the world to know that our lands are not for sale here in BC. Our lands here are unsurrendered, unceded indigenous territories – we have never given up our land. (cited in Saunders, 2010)

Certainly impassioned, such claims by Indigenous elders are increasingly the stuff of policy consequence. More and more mega-events are staged in parts of the world that are home to Indigenous populations and ethnic minorities – Catalan groups in Barcelona, Aboriginal Australians in Sydney, Uighurs in Beijing, First Nation Canadians in Vancouver (and Montreal). As part of a global human rights agenda, the dovetailing of the environmental consequences of mega-events for minority groups with a growing awareness of the capacity of mega-events to operate as sites of contentious politics is an increasingly pressing concern for Games' organizers who must now plan for events in a context where expectations of global humanity are gaining popular and political currency as mega-events move into new territories.

EMERGENT ISSUES FOR GLOBAL SPORTS POLICY

This sixteen-year timeline of the sport–environment nexus, when situated in a rapidly changing policy environment, highlights the political will of environmentalists in taking forward a particular policy agenda. It also underscores the importance of human interaction in the creation of global sports policy and the primacy of local initiatives in effecting policy change (Cantelon & Letters, 2000: 294).

Building on some of the key policy developments identified in this timeline, some of the prospective issues for forthcoming mega-events are worth summarizing. Clearly, environmental concerns have shifted beyond simply 'nature', and the implications of urban development, the built environment, social dislocation and unregulated industry in BRIC and developing nations are part of the wider discourse of environmentalism within which the planning of mega-events is now situated. Moreover, there has been a move from an 'adaptive' mode of policy-making, in which Organizing Committees of Olympic Games (OCOGs) implemented a series of steps that they would take in order to ensure compliance with both IOC and stakeholder expectations during the staging of the Games (i.e. energy renewal, waste management and pollution reduction schemes), to an 'incremental' approach, in which OCOGs were more proactive, e.g. by proposing 'Games-time' adherence to environmental standards (i.e. Torino agreeing to build games structures in accordance with national laws and regulations that had been co-signed by the IOC) (Paquette, Stevens & Mallen, 2011: 361).

One of the 'legacy promises' of the London 2012 Olympics was to 'make the Olympic Park a blueprint for sustainable living' (DCMS, 2007). It remains to be seen how realistic this promise was, yet the anticipatory redevelopment agenda that surrounds the Games brought together several key themes for mega-events and the environment.

Many of the Games venues were built in the East End of London, on land that was earmarked for remediation and redevelopment. This forms the core of the

2012 regeneration strategy that linked economic growth with long-term sustainability, one of the key reforms of the Olympic Movement's Agenda 21. The strategy was, in the words of Robert Harding, the Olympic Project Officer at the United Kingdom's Environmental Agency, a regeneration for the whole area up to and beyond the Games:

> The London 2012 Games have been a catalyst for major investment in that part of east London and to regenerate the whole area up to and beyond the Games. ... The Olympic project has brought that land back into long-term use. Lots of money has been invested in the clean-up to enable the London 2012 Olympic Delivery Authority to create something to behold for the future. (Olympic.org, 2011)

Such allusions to the long-term impacts and environmental sustainability of activities associated with the Summer and Winter Olympics are now fully implicated in the discourse of mega-events. The organizers of the 2014 Sochi Winter Games have already indicated their commitment to leaving an 'environmental legacy of having a carbon neutral and zero waste games' in ways that can contribute to and enhance the quality of life of residents beyond the short life of the event. With echoes of Lillehammer's original planned bid, Sochi purports to be the most compact Winter Olympics, with Sochi, where the ice events will be contested and the mountain venues, where the skiing and sliding events will be held, being less than 30 minutes apart, reducing the impact of travel between locations.

In anticipation of the 2016 Games in Rio de Janeiro, we are already witnessing the displacement of people from the slums and *favelas* in the city, and the social costs and consequences of such actions, alongside the human rights to live in safe and healthy environments, remain a persistent undercurrent to policy that will continue to develop in relation to sporting mega-events where the 'local' environmental consequences for a city or a region cannot be represented in isolation from the rest of the world. Indeed, environmental policy that has developed around mega-events shows that that racism, colonialism, poverty and development – hallmarks of globalization – are intractable elements of the environmental impacts of sporting mega-events.

CORPORATE SOCIAL RESPONSIBILITY AND 'GREEN WASHING'

I've maintained at several points that sporting mega-events are largely steered by power elites and cosmocrats in pursuit of their own interests. In this chapter, I have suggested that those interests have largely ignored environmental and ecological needs and concerns, or have acknowledged them in response to political pressure from environmental movements. Increasingly, however, those cosmocrats, policy brokers and cultural intermediaries charged with staging mega-events cannot afford to ignore their 'footprint' or be reactive in taking action to minimize the environmental impacts of their events. As we have seen in relation to the management of global environmental disasters – the 1989 Exxon Valdez oil spill off the coast of Alaska, the 1984 gas explosion at the Union Carbide Factory in Bhopal, India, or the 2010 Deepwater Horizon oil leak in the Gulf of Mexico – poorly orchestrated disaster response strategies can be catastrophic to the 'brand'. The consequences of environmental disasters are global, and this is frequently played out in public responses to them, given the accelerated communications discussed earlier in the book. There is thus a need for corporations to respond responsibly to offset negative perceptions to preserve the brand and consumer confidence and, indeed, the environment.

This nexus of the environment, responsibility and corporate/consumer confidence raises a number of questions for sport and sports policy. A growing agenda of corporate social responsibility (CSR) has emerged that sees sportswear companies, sponsors of mega-events and developers of sporting infrastructure enter into a dialogue of environmental politics that simultaneously legitimates and problematizes the involvement of global sports interests in environmental justice.

Corporate social responsibility and mega-events

In terms of legitimating involvement, it has been argued that, as most global sports corporations operate as 'social institutions'; they must not only actively pursue but take the lead in corporate social responsibility initiatives (Babiak & Wolfe, 2006). Those companies that are in the business of the environment, such as Patagonia, Lowe Alpine or The North Face, provide instructive examples of this green consumerism: the 'retail face of a broader trend in green liberalism' (Erickson, 2011: 480). Certainly, there is some self-interest here – greater brand profile and perceptions of 'brand integrity' or 'brand sincerity', whereby social values are embedded in products, exemplified throughout the 1980s and 1990s in the work of The Body Shop or Starbucks (Žižek, 2009), or opportunities for cross-promotion with other market segments, such as Cricket Australia lending support to national Breast Cancer Awareness campaigns, as well as the potential cost-saving benefits of taking on in-house waste-reduction and energy saving schemes. The adoption of CSR campaigns, however, also exposes organizations to a range of ethical concerns such as those I've alluded to already. More specifically, Berglind and Nakata (2005) argue that CSR initiatives can blur the lines between corporate identity and social and environmental activism, begging the question as to whether companies are authentic champions of the cause they lend their name to or are simply, and disingenuously, presenting a particular image of corporate social responsibility for economic gain. That said, it is not my intention to answer the question here, but to suggest how it may play out in terms of CSR, sporting mega-events and the potential implications for sports policy more broadly.

The first point is that the commercial media has been crucial in enabling a wider discourse of corporate environmental responsibility in sport, leisure, tourism and recreation. Coupled with the appropriation of environmentalism by mainstream consumers, this has led to environmental concerns occupying a relatively benign place in the market. As Mincyte, Casper and Cole note, its 'currency has accelerated in corporate headquarters, marketing departments, and advertising storyboards' (2009: 104).

Certainly, the global sports mega-event provides a case in point here. I noted earlier that, since the Lillehammer Winter Games in 1994, environmentalism has become inseparable from the Olympic brand, with each successive Games promoting itself in terms of its green credentials. As we look to the London 2012, it too will be the 'greenest games in history', according to the British government and Games organizers. A key factor in London securing the 2012 Games – as was the case with previous games – was its plan for sustainable development and a green legacy, its promises to address climate change, waste, biodiversity, inclusion and healthy living (London, 2012, 2011; Olympic.org, 2011).

The greening of London 2012?

This ongoing appropriation of mega-events to promote a commitment to environmental justice is clearly by no means new. What *is* new, in the context of heightened reflexivity, consumer activism and a commitment to global social justice, is a growing scepticism about what is perceived as a duplicitous corporate agenda, or what is known as 'green washing' (or 'greensheen'); the public relations exercise engaged in by governments and corporations to promote an environmentally friendly public image while failing to measure up to standards of best practice (Athanasiou, 1996; Beder, 2002; De Bois, 2008; Lenskyj, 1998).[2] Presenting cost cuts as reductions in the use of resources, for example, or enticing investors who associate environmental performance with financial performance, are among the practices whereby companies disingenuously 'spin' their products and policies as being environmentally friendly (Johnson, 2005; Munshi & Kurian, 2005).

The London 2012 Olympics provides several examples of this green policy 'spin' and the involvement of the French-owned EDF Energy is noteworthy. As the 'major sustainability partner' of the London 2012 Games, EDF adopted various advertising, marketing and public relations strategies to promote their association with London 2012, many of which revolved around the imagery of a 'Green Britain' and a 'Green Team Britain'. In July 2009, EDF launched their 'Green Britain Day' campaign, aimed at 'bolstering its green credentials, with a heavyweight advertising campaign, majoring on its status as the "sustainability" partner for the 2012 Olympics' (McCallister, 2009). The advertising campaign was carried in television, radio and print media and backed by British Olympian James Cracknell and the Olympics Minister, Tessa Jowell.

LIVERPOOL JOHN MOORES UNIVERSITY
LEARNING SERVICES

Importantly, in this context of greenwashing, the key, iconic image used in the television and print campaigns was that of a green Union Jack flag, ostensibly symbolizing an environmentally friendly Great Britain. The flag, however, was already the logo of Ecotricity, a UK-based alternative energy company, who used a green Union Jack in their own advertising and promotional campaigns. The appropriation of an already established image opened EDF and, by proxy, the London Organizing Committee of the Olympic Games (LOCOG) to accusations of green washing, the logic behind the accusation being that any organization which borrows another's icon may also be just borrowing its values for the sake of a strong image (Newlands, 2010a, 2010b). Indeed, the founder of Ecotricity, Dale Vince, accused EDF of hijacking not just his company's logo, but also the British identity, claiming 'to most people, a green Union Jack represents something or someone green and British. And to most people, EDF are neither, being both nuclear and French' (Murray, 2009). The broader context of the escalating costs of the Games during the global financial crisis did not help public perceptions of this kind of corporate sleight of hand which 'fostered negative reporting on a variety of fronts, one of which was the accusation of "greenwashing"' (Newlands, 2010b: 2).

The practice of greenwashing, in this context of corporate social responsibility, raises several concerns for policy, which beg the question of corporate accountability. Because companies are not required by law to publish environmental policy statements or to verify their statements by independent third parties, there is little way of knowing whether a published commitment to a policy translates into actual implementation of that policy (Book & Carlsson, 2011). Thus, environmental policy, like policy in relation to human rights, becomes easier to endorse than enforce in the context of sport and sporting mega-events.

CONCLUSION

There is no question that we are faced with environmental issues of global proportions and sport is by no means immune to environmental change. While environmentalism typically appeals to a social discourse that is local (our beaches, our waterways), 'the human activities that impact upon these local natural environments influence the cultural, economic and/or political life in communities far beyond the local' (Cantelon & Letters, 2000: 298). That is, the discourse of environmentalism is a key part of the global order.

The environmental dimensions of sporting activities and industries are contradictory and paradoxical, enhancing participation in sport, yet contributing to all manner of environmental impacts and consequences at one and the same time. Indeed, human activities such as sport are fundamentally altered by environmental conditions and processes, and humans fundamentally alter environmental conditions and processes. Thus, the environment is woven into human activities and 'the movement of human bodies through space and time can and do deeply affect the environment' (Mincyte, Casper & Cole, 2009).

Importantly for this book and the themes it develops, the relationship between sport and the environment highlights the socially constructed nature of 'the environment' as cultural phenomenon and policy concern. As we saw with the development of a new discourse of the 'Green Games' at Lillehammer, it is impossible to separate the 'work' of policy construction from the 'work' of image-making and public reception. As the Lillehammer, and subsequent Winter Olympics have highlighted, the sport–environment relationship is dependent on a set of relations that includes human, natural and technical dimensions. We see this, particularly, through the cultural practice of 'greenwashing' and the social–ethical concerns that are raised by sport-related corporate responsibility.

I began this chapter by posing a series of questions that are raised by the nexus between sport and the environment. Since the UN's Environmental Programme and the 'Green Games' at Lillehammer, there has been an acknowledgement that sports policy and the planning of mega-events must be attentive to environmental impacts, although issues of global governance make true responsibility and accountability difficult to monitor. Certainly, governing bodies and transnational organizations must take action to regulate the impact of sports and mega-events on the environment, although those sports that have a negative impact on the environment remain a part of international competition, as do nations with poor environmental track records. The 'green washing' of sport highlights the corporate responsibility towards the environment in the context of global sporting mega-events, and the difficulties with realizing true global environmental equity in sports policy.

BOX 9.1   QUESTIONS FOR DISCUSSION

- Can you identify five key environmental concerns/impacts of sporting mega-events? What are they? Consider both built and natural environments.

- What responsibilities, if any, do governing bodies and the organizers of mega-events have for monitoring and minimizing the impact of sporting events on the environment?

- To what extent do you think 'greenwashing' occurs at sporting mega-events?

- Do you think this is an alternative to corporate responsibility or the same thing?

SUGGESTED FURTHER READINGS

Brajer, V. & Mead, R. (2003) Blue skies in Beijing: Looking at the Olympic effect. *Journal of Environment Development*, 12: 239.

Cantelon, H. & Letters, M. (2000) The making of the IOC environmental policy as the third dimension of the Olympic movement. *International Review for the Sociology of Sport*, 35(3): 294–308.

Lesjø, J.H. (2000) Lillehammer 1994: Planning, figurations and the 'green' Winter Games. *International Review for the Sociology of Sport*, 35(3): 282–93.

Paquette, J., Stevens, J. & Mallen, C. (2011) The interpretation of environmental sustainability by the International Olympic Committee and Organizing Committee of the Olympic Games from 1994 to 2008. *Sport in Society*, 14(3): 355–69.

Notes

1 Under this initiative, Coca-Cola deployed more than 1,000 beverage machines at the Torino Games that used carbon dioxide as the refrigerant instead of the ozone-damaging chlorofluorocarbons (CFCs) and hydrofluorocarbons (HFCs) (TOROC, 2006a).

2 The term was coined by the environmentalist Jay Westervelt in the mid-1990s as a critique of the hotel industry's practice of placing green notices in each room, promoting the re-use of guest towels, ostensibly to 'save the environment'. Westervelt noted that, in most cases, little or no effort towards waste recycling was being implemented, due in part to very little costs being actually saved by the practice. Westervelt argued that the motive of this 'eco-friendly' initiative was, in fact, increased profit, and he monitored this and other outwardly environmentally conscientious acts that had a greater, underlying purpose of increased profit (Hayward, 2009).

10

REFLECTIONS ON GLOBAL SPORTS POLICY

From the previous chapters, it should be evident that this book has been centrally concerned with the impact of globalization upon sports policy, defined here as public and/or social policy as it relates to sport. It has essentially been about the making and contestation of sports policy and in adopting this focus I have attempted to locate the study of sports policy within a broader consideration of global processes, practices and consequences. My interest has been, fundamentally, to take the concepts and debates about the impacts of globalization on social life that are prevalent in the social sciences more broadly and apply these to analyses of public policy as they relate to global sport. That is, I was concerned to foreground the *social* aspects of globalization in the context of sports policy.

THE RATIONALE REVISITED

As such, I deliberately chose to do two things. First, I chose to consistently refer to sports policy in the plural. The 'interstitial' (Bhaba, 2004: 3) nature of sports policy – encompassing many sports, and intersecting with a range of other social policy contexts (education, employment, the environment, health, and so on) – meant that my approach to writing this book focused on no single sport, nor on any single approach to policy. Readers may be disappointed with my lack of coverage of football, widely referenced as the archetypal exemplar of global sport: 'the game the world plays'. Given that there is no shortage of analyses of football in relation to globalization – athletic migration, sponsorship, fan bases and consumptive practices, the standardization of rules, governance and administration, among other themes pursued – I have not sought to add to this substantial literature, mindful of Houlihan's warning that 'there is always a temptation among social scientists to overextend and overanalyse a concept until it dies of exhaustion' (1994: 372). My intention instead has been to broaden thinking about globalization to consider other sports and other ways of engaging with the debates that underpin scholarly thinking about globalization. I also adopted a fairly fluid approach to my interpretation of 'policy'. Policy has been defined variously, as government aspiration or government inaction, and while acknowledging those positions, I have also wanted to include discussion of the role of 'cosmocracies' – the IOC, FIFA and the like as well as street-level bureaucrats – in influencing the global sports policy agenda.

That said, I could not, and did not, hope to cover all sports, all policies or indeed all countries that are implicated in the conditions of globalization. As such, the material assembled is an inevitably eclectic selection that reflects my previous, current or emerging research interests in relation to sport, sports policy and social policy. I have been at pains, at times, to move away from the traditional analysis of the effects of globalization on non-Western countries or, in Connell's (2007) terms, of the northern metropole on the Global South. For this reason, several of the examples I have included have explored the impacts of globalization on policy-making and compliance within Western contexts. That is, I have wanted to explore the hybriditites of relationships that take place within a particular set of intra-country relations, not simply those that take place between countries.

Second, I chose not to write a book that focused on comparative sports policy; that is, that compared and contrasted particular policy examples or concepts such as elite sport or 'sport for all' across different countries and policy contexts. Certainly, the work of Henry (2007), Henry and Uchiumi (2001), Collins (2007, 2010) or Green and Collins (2008) illustrates and evaluates the major approaches to comparative and transnational analyses of sports policy, focusing, in the main, on the effects of exogenous policy on domestic sports. In doing so, they highlight the major theoretical and methodological weaknesses, such as the overriding 'Orientalism' inherent in most Western studies of sport and sports policy. While in agreement with colleagues' assessment of this interpretative bias, my focus has been more on using debates within studies of globalization to try to generate an understanding about the social, constructed and 'disjunctive' nature of sports policy in a global context than it has been on comparing policy concepts. Debates about the local and the global, tensions between homogeneity and heterogeneity and concepts such as flow, scapes, the glocal and the grobal, I argue, can as usefully inform our understanding of the policy process as they can our understanding of social relations within a global order.

Throughout the book, I have been concern to include examples that both render problematic and come some way to redressing the diminishing significance of 'the local' within debates about globalization when viewed through the lens of sports policy. My discussion in Chapters 2 and 6, which respectively interrogated the relationships between the global and the local (and the bits in between) and perhaps the single most dominant sporting feature of the global ecumene, the sporting 'mega-event', is an attempt to penetrate the complexities and tensions that are inherent in debates about the impacts of globalization on local cultural processes in which sports policy is assuredly implicated. Following Rowe's (2003) call to repudiate the global, I have, in Hay and

Marsh's terms, been concerned to demonstrate how local practices can construct or reform global practices (2000), as well as to illustrate the contested impacts of the global on the local as it manifests itself in relation to policy development and compliance.

I have been at pains to emphasize the constructed nature of policy-making. Using Hannerz's framework of 'cultural flow' as a point of departure, I suggested in Chapter 2 that human agency and intervention are fundamental to understanding the interstitial relations between the local and the global, and the social and spatial dimensions that underpin conceptualizations of local–global relations. Inserting 'the social' into an understanding of policy implementation and compliance underscores my central point that the policy process does not occur 'naturally' or without human intervention and social agency. Pushing this argument further, I argued in Chapter 3, Globalization and the governance of sports policy, that the production of sports policy is the result of considerable cultural work on the part of a whole range of key individuals, agencies, organizations, governments and departments at sub-national, national and supranational levels, and this has significant implications for the management and administration of sport. Indeed, one of the central themes to run through this book is that policy-making is not a neutral or value-free exercise, and the two main conceptual frameworks for theorizing globalization introduced in Chapter 1 – as the product of either the spread of capitalism or of cultural relationships and exchanges – alerts us to the role of human involvement and social agency in the *making* of sports policy.

Equally, the broad sweep of topics that are included in the umbrella of 'sports policy', coupled with the very different organizational structures within which sport is located (everything from Departments of Health to Youth to Ageing to Education), as well as shifting policy agendas and competing tensions around the funding of sport, underscores the contested and constructed 'work' of sports policy-making. The point I made with respect to the governance and administration of global sports policy was that very particular definitions, understandings, biases and privileges are imposed in the development and implementation of sports policy. Nowhere is this more evident than in the governance of anti-doping policy, where nuanced notions of morality, ethics and fair play influence the uptake of and compliance with a universally standardized policy across countries, sports and jurisdictions.

My particular concern throughout the book has been, in Ong's words, 'to put human agency at the centre of analysis and situated interactions as the process that mediates global flows' (2009: 89). Although I have used expressions like 'the impact of globalization on social life' and 'the cultural consequences of globalization', I have been at pains to stress that globalization is not a process that operates outside culture. A constructionist at heart, I contend that culture, of which policy is a part, is not an inert category that people simply experience, but is one that they themselves produce and shape. As Hannerz notes: 'to keep culture going, people as actors and networks of actors invent culture, reflect on it, experiment on it, remember it (or store it in some other way), debate it, and pass it on' (1996: 5).

One of the consistent themes throughout this book has been the pervasive nature of policy. We live in a policy-saturated world. Irrespective of the country or the culture in which we reside, almost every aspect of our lives is defined by policy, from the amount of tax we pay, to welfare provisions by the State, to medical provisions for gastric banding for the morbidly obese, to the numbers of asylum seekers a given country will allow entry, through to military involvement in the world's 'trouble spots', such as Iraq and Afghanistan. While some of these are by no means new – there have been US-led invasions of Arab countries long before the 'War on Terror' – the ways in which we confront these issues now have a different form. In other words, the centrality of policy takes a particular shape in the context of globalization.

As I outlined in Chapter 1, sports policy fits within the broader category of global social or global public policy and, as such, it can ask and answer the same kinds of questions that are asked and answered by these more traditional forms of policy analysis. Sports policy, like public policy and social policy, is made in the public realm, in terms of certain public issues, and in terms of particular social concerns. As I have, perhaps implicitly, addressed, issues of rights and responsibility, issues of equity and access, issues of inequities between developed and developing nations (and within countries as well) all manifest themselves in different ways (and through different policies and policy responses) across sports policy, social policy and public policy.

Sports policy, like other forms of social policy, I would argue, must fundamentally undertake work of consequence. It must, as C. Wright Mills urges, 'be of relevance to public issues and insistent human troubles' ([1959] 2000: 20). Following Burawoy's call for a public sociology that can address the divide between the 'sociological ethos and the world we study' (2005: 7), and Jarvie's challenge 'for today's sociologists of sport and others not to accept the narrow job description of the academic but instead to ensure that the social study of sport is one of these very public, visible forms of activity and engagement' (2007: 411), I hope my discussions of human rights, child exploitation, athlete welfare, environmental justice and corporate responsibility in sport has pricked a global social conscience that can contribute to wider work of policy consequence.

The book has also attempted to engage with some of the methodological and intellectual challenges that emerge from the relationship between research and policy in the context of globalization. I argued in Chapter 3 that the increasing public scrutiny of government investment in sport demands robust evidence to ensure the delivery of a government's policy goals. This, in itself, is not particular to globalization, but the staging of increasingly extravagant global sporting mega-events brings it into sharper relief. The aspirational claims that London 2012 will leave a tangible, sustainable legacy for current and future generations when set against a backdrop of spiralling budgets and an economic downturn provides perhaps the most obvious example of the need for an improved evidence base in sports policy for the deliverables of sports policy beyond the nebulous 'feel good factor' of hosting major sporting events.

Equally, emergent technologies have changed quite dramatically the dissemination of policy decisions and policy-based initiatives. Applying the concept of 'connectivity', I have been keen to 'examine the rapidly developing and ever-densening network of interconnections and interdependences that characterize modern life' (Tomlinson, 1999: 2), and its impacts on the reach of and response to public policy in the context of global sport. As I addressed at several points, new forms of telecommunications enable the rapid transmission of research findings and policy directives, while the wide – and increasingly public – availability of data and policy documents from all continents enables the comparative study of sports policy on an unprecedented scale. These technologies also enable the global sharing of resistant and subversive critiques of, most notably, the human rights and environmental track records and practices of cities and nations in relation to the hosting of sporting mega-events, through the rise of anti-globalization and related social movements. This reflexivity of the heightened connectivity that globalization now affords is the Janus face of 'disconnectivity' which, as Giulianotti and Robertson (2007a) note, allows individuals and communities to raise awareness of the unevenness of global flows, and the inequalities and social differences that are embedded within them.

THE GLOBAL RESEARCH IMAGINATION – REFLECTIONS ON 'DOING' SPORTS POLICY

Globalization and these new technologies open up new possibilities for 'doing' global sports policy. As Connell draws our attention to:

> There are new arenas and social spaces that we need to research … we now have new structures of power in the world in the form of transnational corporations, the international state and international media that are on a different scale than before. This involves new issues of accessibility – different from what we are used to on a national scale. (2009: 68)

These issues raise questions for how, if at all, we can realistically study 'globalization'. Drawing on my own research on the Tour de France, I argued at several points in the book that studies of global or spatially dis-embedded phenomena which, ultimately, is what globalization is really about, pose no threat to small-scale ethnography, and indeed, small-scale ethnography can add power to our analyses and understanding of the free-floating phenomena or 'stuff' of global life. Ethnography's fine-grained explorations of cultural practices and social relations, which reproduce (and are reproduced in) transnational processes across diverse, often distant, sites and locations, has much to offer here.

It is in this context of new and different arenas and social spaces that a discussion of the global research imagination sits nicely. As academics ourselves, we are inherently global – products of what Kenway and Fahey refer to as 'the travelling research imagination' (2009: 10). Ours is a transnational occupational category, for as Konrad observes:

> Intellectuals are the ones who know most about one another across the frontiers, who keep in touch with one another, and who feel that they are one another's allies ... they hop across seas to discuss something with their colleagues; they fly to visit one another as easily as their counterparts two hundred years ago rode over to the next town to exchange ideas. (1984: 208–9)

Kenway and Fahey note that epistemological and geographical travel is the 'arch wherethrough' experience is shaped. As scholars of globalization, and global sports policy, we may come from different places in the social sciences and we frequently move across disciplinary boundaries. To return once more to Hannerz, we are both cosmopolitans and locals (1990: 237) in equal measure.

WHAT ABOUT THE ANTHROPOLOGY?

Although a book on global sports policy, it has nonetheless been informed by my background as a social anthropologist, and I hope something of this has come through in what I've written. I am a strong advocate for the contribution that anthropology can make to studies of policy, if only to inject critical questions (and methods) from the discipline into studies of sports and other forms of social and public policy.

I have endeavoured to explore policy issues from an anthropological perspective. My starting point was to ask, perhaps rhetorically, and certainly implicitly, 'what is policy and can it be studied anthropologically?' Throughout the book, I have explored several questions of relevance to anthropologists and policy analysts alike, such as 'how do (or can) policies work as instruments of political intervention and social change?' My discussion of the ways in which policies and policy decisions produce resistant and counter-hegemonic critiques of the politics of sporting mega-events, and their governance, attempts to answer this question. I was also keen to examine the question of whether an analysis of policy could offer insight into transformations of systems of governance, and my analysis of the institutional architecture of the governance of sport in Chapter 3 comes some way to contributing to that debate. Finally, I wanted to explore whether ethnographic accounts could capture the critical dimensions of policy-making, and the cultural worlds of policy makers themselves. My work on cultural brokers and policy entrepreneurs extended the work and questioning around these questions of the socially constructed nature of policy-making and governance.

Essentially, I was keen to challenge the often-held assumption that policy is a top-down, linear and rational process and to suggest, instead, that it may be more complex, messy and disjunctive as it is played out at local, regional, national and supranational levels. That is, policy is a site of constant contestation, negotiation and construction.

This intersection of anthropology and policy, I suggest, returns us to 'the problem of polarity' (Robertson, 1992), this time through the lens of interdisciplinarity. There is much to be said for raiding disciplines – methods, theories, concepts and approaches – while recognizing the distinct contributions that the disciplines can make to the object (or subject) under study – in this case, policy and policy-making. As Hannerz observes, the development of clusters of ideas and practices associated with different disciplines are 'best served by their having their own institutional power base' (2010: 41).

FINALLY

Ken Robinson, in his book on creativity, *The element*, describes 'being British' as 'driving home in a German car, stopping off to pick up some Belgian beer and a Turkish kebab or an Indian takeaway, to spend the evening on Swedish television, watching American programmes on a Japanese TV' (2009: 111). While playing to some of the stereotypes of local–global relations that I have been quick to dispel, it is nonetheless this sense of mingling and movement that is at the heart of this book and provides a bookend to the Hannerz quote I began with. I have attempted to broaden out the notion of the social in globalization to both ask and respond to a series of questions that can interrogate the relationship between globalization, sport and policy.

These include questions such as:

- What is the theoretical link between globalization, sport and policy, and how does this relationship differ from other aspects of the globalized nature of sport? That is, between, say, studies of globalization and national identity, for example.
- Which case studies, from which countries, can help us to understand the contested and constructed relationship between globalization, sport and policy? That is, which empirical examples can help generate an understanding of the role of social agency in the policy process?
- In what ways do sporting mega-events generate or even distort the perception that we are part of a global community sharing a global conversation? That is, how can mega-events like the Tour de France, the Olympic Games or the World Cup help us to 'repudiate the global', and pay attention to the hegemony and heterogeneity of social relationships that are embedded in more fine-grained analyses of these events?

In many ways, the theoretical, methodological and epistemological issues and debates of globalization that I have engaged with reflect C. Wright Mills' belief that 'the sociological imagination enables us to grasp history and biography and the relations between the two in society' ([1959] 2000: 21). In attempting to bring the social into policy studies of globalization, I have shown that we are in a unique, historical position through which to gauge the impact of global change upon our individual and collective lives. Through the mixing and mingling of disciplines, through the travelling research imagination, through the reflexive critique of relationships of disjuncture, power and imbalance, we are able to develop a 'global consciousness' through which we can understand the historical and social contexts in which practices and experiences are located, and the impact of global events, processes and consequences on these.

Global sports policy is part of the biography of our time. It has emerged at this moment in time precisely because of the historical shifts in and expansion of both globalization and policy studies. The idea of an interconnected, inhabited world is by no means new; people and goods have travelled and communicated across borders for thousands of years. What is new, however, is the notion of global studies of policy or the development of a global policy that transcends borders and boundaries. The questions that can be both posed and answered by global studies of policy, in this case, as they relate to sport, provide a unique point of entry into our collective social and historical biography.

BIBLIOGRAPHY

Abaza, M. (2001) Shopping malls, consumer culture and the reshaping of public space in Egypt. *Theory, Culture & Society*, 18(5): 97–122.

Abraham, A., Sommerhalder, K. & Abel, T. (2010) Landscape and well-being: A scoping study on the health promoting impact of outdoor environments. *International Journal of Public Health*, 55(1): 55–69.

Adams, J. (2001) *Risk*. London: Routledge.

AFP (2011) Japan city to give radiation counters to children. http://hostednews/afp/article/ALeqM5hTcfz3z7V1EoAW09WHVP8ztRG6Zg [accessed 16 June 2011].

Agamben, G. (1998) *Homo sacer: Sovereign power and bare life*. Trans D. Heller-Roazen. Stanford, CA: Stanford University Press.

Agamben, G. (2005) *State of exception*. Trans K. Attell. Chicago, IL: University of Chicago Press.

Agamben, G. (2009) What is an apparatus? In *What is an apparatus? and other essays*. Trans D. Kishik & S. Pedatella. Stanford, CA: Stanford University Press.

Agustin, L. (2005) Migrants in the mistress's house: Other voices in the 'trafficking debate'. *Social Politics*, 12(1): 96–117.

Albanese, J. (2007) A criminal network approach to understanding and measuring trafficking human beings. In E.U. Savona & S. Stefanizzi (eds), *Measuring human trafficking. Complexities and pitfalls*. New York: Springer (pp. 55–71).

Al-e Ahmad, J. (1982) *Plagued by the West (Gharbzadegi)*. Trans. P. Sprachman. New York: Center for Iranian Studies, Columbia University.

Alegi, P. (2001) 'Feel the pull in your soul': Local agency and global trends in South Africa's 2006 World Cup bid. *Soccer & Society*, 2(3): 1–21.

Amara, M. (2008) The Muslim world in the global sporting arena. *The Brown Journal of World Affairs*, 14(2): 67–76.

Amara, M., Aquilina, D., Argent, E., Betzer-Tayar, M., Green, M., Henry, I., Coalter, F. & Taylor, J. (2005) *The role of sport and education in the social inclusion of asylum seekers and refugees: An evaluation of policy and practice in the UK*. Loughborough: Institute of Sport and Leisure Policy, Loughborough University and Stirling University.

Andersen, S. & Eliassen, K. (1993) *Making policy in Europe: The Europification of national policy making*. London: Sage.

Anderson, B. (1986) *The imagined community: Reflections on the origins and spread of nationalism*. London: Verso.

Anderson, B. & O'Connell Davidson, J. (2003) *Is trafficking in human beings demand driven? A multi-country pilot study*. Geneva: International Organization for Migration.

Andranovich, G. & Burbank, M. (2004) Regime politics and the 2012 Olympic Games. *California Politics and Policy*, 8: 1–18.

Andranovich, G., Burbank, M. & Heying, C. (2001) Olympic cities: Lessons learned from mega-event politics. *Journal of Urban Affairs*, 23(2): 113–31.

Andrèn, J. & Holm, J. (2008) *Swedish sport – international policy*. Stockholm: RiksidottsFörbundet.

Andrews, D. & Ritzer, G. (2007) The grobal in the sporting glocal. In R. Giulianotti & R. Robertson (eds), *Globalization and sport*. Oxford: Blackwell (pp. 28–47).

Appadurai, A. (1991) Global ethnoscapes: Notes and queries for a transnational anthropology. In Richard G. Fox (ed.), *Recapturing anthropology*. Santa Fe, NM: School of American Research Press (pp. 191–210).

Appadurai, A. (1996) *Modernity at large: Cultural dimensions of globalization*. Minneapolis, MN: University of Minnesota Press.

Appelbaum, R. & Robinson, W. (eds) (2005) *Critical globalization studies*. New York: Routledge.

Atencio, M., Beal, B. & Wilson, C. (2009) Distinction of risk: Urban skateboarding, street habitus, and the construction of hierarchical gender relations. *Qualitative Research in Sport and Exercise*, 1: 3–20.

Athanasiou, T. (1996) *Divided planet: The ecology of rich and poor*. Boston, MA: Little, Brown, Co.

Atkinson, G., Mourato, S., Szymanski, S. & Ozdemiroglu, E. (2008) Are we willing to pay enough to 'back the bid'? Valuing the intangible impacts of London's bid to host the 2012 Summer Olympic Games. *Urban Studies*, 45(2): 419–44.

Atkinson, M. (2009) *Parkour*, anarcho-environmentalism and poesis. *Journal of Sport and Social Issues*, 33(2): 169–94.

Atkinson, M. & Young, K. (2002) Terror games: Media treatment of security issues at the 2002 Winter Olympic Games. *Olympika: The International Journal of Olympic Studies*, 9: 54.

Australian Bureau of Statistic (2006) *Population characteristics, Aboriginal and Torres Strait Islanders*. www.abs.gov.au [accessed 20 April 2012].

Australian Football League (1995) *Anti-Racial and Religious Vilification Law*. http//afl.com.au [accessed 20 April 2012].

Australian Football League (2010) Current indigenous players in the AFL. www.afl.com.au [accessed 20 April 2012].

Auyero, J. (2001) *Poor people's politics: Peronist survival networks and the legacy of Evita*. Durham, NC: Duke University Press.

Babiak, K. & Wolfe, R. (2006) More than just a game? Corporate social responsibility and Super Bowl XL. *Sport Marketing Quarterly*, 15(4): 214.

Backett-Milburn, K. & Harden, J. (2004) How children and their families construct and negotiate risk, safety and danger. *Childhood*, 11(4): 429–49.

Bailey, R. (2005) Evaluating the relationship between physical education, sport and social inclusion. *Educational Review*, 57: 71–90.

Bairner, A. (2001) *Sport, nationalism and globalization – European and North American perspectives*. Albany, NY: State University of New York Press.

Bajc, V. (2007) Surveillance in public rituals: Security meta-ritual and the 2005 U.S. Presidential Inauguration. *American Behavioral Scientist*, 50(12): 1648–73.

Bale, J. & Maguire, J. (1994) *The global sports arena: Athletic talent migration in an interdependent world*. London: Frank Cass.

Bales, K. & Soodalter, R. (2009) *The slave next door: Human trafficking and slavery in America today*. Berkeley and Los Angeles, CA: University of California Press.

Ball, D.J. (2004) Policy issues and risk–benefit trade-offs of 'safer surfacing' for children's playgrounds. *Accident Analysis and Prevention*, 36: 661–70.

Ballinger, J. (2008) No Sweat: Corporate social responsibility and the dilemma of anti-sweatshop activism. *New Labour Forum*, 17(2): 91–8.

Banerjea, K. (2000) Sounds of whose underground? The fine-tuning of diaspora in an age of mechanical reproduction. *Theory, Culture and Society*, 17(3): 64–79.

Barber, B. (1995) *Jihad vs. McWorld*. New York: Times Books.

Baum, F. & Palmer, C. (2002) Opportunity structures: Urban landscape, social capital and health promotion in Australia. *Health Promotion International*, 17(40): 351–61.

Baum, M. (2008) New media and the polarization of American political discourse. *Political Communication*, 25(4): 345–65.

Bauman, Z. (1998) *Globalisation: The human consequences*. London: Polity Press.

BBC (2009) Pakistan cricket tour in doubt. *BBC News*. http://news.bbc.co.uk/sport2/low/cricket/7921384.stm/ [accessed 30 June 2010].

BBC (2011) Anti-cuts march: Tens of thousands at London protest. *BBC News*. www.bbc.co.uk/news/uk-12864353 [accessed 20 May 2011].

Beamish, R. & Ritchie, I. (2006) *Fastest, highest, strongest: A critique of high-performance sport*. London: Routledge.

Beck, U. (1992) *Risk society: Towards a new modernity*. London: Sage.

Beck, U. (1999) *World risk society*. Malden, MA: Polity Press.

Beck, U. (2002) The cosmopolitan perspective: Sociology in the second age of modernity. In S. Vertovec & R. Cohen (eds), *Conceiving cosmopolitanism: Theory, context and practice*. Oxford: Oxford University Press (pp. 180–90).

Beder, S. (2002) *Global spin: The corporate assault on environmentalism*. Glasgow: Green Books.

Beijing (2008) *One world one dream*. http://en.beijing2008.cn/spirit/beijing2008/graphic/ n214068253.shtml [accessed 5 March 2010].

Belanger, A. (2000) Sport venues and the spectacularization of urban spaces in North America: The case of the Molson Center in Montreal. *International Review for the Sociology of Sport*, 35(3): 378–97.

Ben-Porat, A. (2000) Overseas sweetheart: Israeli fans of English football. *Journal of Sport and Social Issues*, 24(4): 344–50.

Benn, T., Pfister, G. & Jawad, H. (eds) (2010) *Muslim women and sport*. London: Routledge.

Bennett, W.L. (2003) Communicating global activism. *Information, Communication & Society*, 6(2): 143–68.

Benyon, J. & Dunkerley, D. (2000) *Globalization: The reader*. London: Pluto Press.

Berglind, M. & Nakata, C. (2005) Cause-related marketing: More buck than bang? *Business Horizons*, 48(5): 443–53.

Bergsgard, N. (2000) National facilities for sport – 'yes please – All three'. Paper presented at Pre-Olympics Congress, Brisbane, 7–13 September.

Bergsgard, N., Houlihan, B., Mangset, P., Nødland, S. & Rommetveldt, H. (2007) *Sports policy: A comparative analysis of stability and change*. Oxford: Elsevier.

Bhaba, H. (2004) Statement for the critical inquiry symposium. *Critical Inquiry*, 30(2): 342–9.

Black, E. (2009) How sports fans can turn defeat into a victory for the economy. *London Evening Standard*, December, p. 40.

Bloodworth, A.J. & McNamee, M.J. (2010) Clean Olympians? Doping and anti-doping: The views of talented young British athletes. *International Journal of Drug Policy*, 21: 276–82.

Bloyce, D. & Smith, A. (2010) *Sport policy and development: An introduction*. London: Routledge.

Bond, D. (2010) Will the World Cup change South Africa? *BBC Blogs*, May. www.bbc.co.uk/blogs/davidbond/2010/05/will_the_world_cup_change_sout.html. [accessed 29 June 2010].

Book, K. & Carlsson, B. (2011) A diagnosis of environmental awareness in sport and sport policy. *International Journal of Sports Policy & Politics*, 3(3): 401–16.

Bourdieu, P. (1987) *Distinction*. London: Routledge & Kegan Paul.

Bourdieu, P. (1990) *In other words: Essays towards a reflexive sociology*. Stanford, CA: Stanford University Press.

Bourdieu, P. (1993) *Sociology in question*. London: Sage.

Boyle, P. & Haggerty, K. (2009) Spectacular security: Mega-events and the security complex. *Political Sociology*, 3: 257–74.

Brackenridge, C. (2001) *Spoilsports: Understanding and preventing sexual exploitation in sport*. London: Routledge.

Brackenridge, C. (2004) Women and children first? Child abuse and child protection in sport. *Sport in Society*, 7(3): 322–37.

Brackenridge, C. (2008) Child sexual abuse. In D. Malcolm (ed.), *The SAGE dictionary of sports studies*. London: Sage.

Brajer, V. & Mead, R. (2003) Blue skies in Beijing?: Looking at the Olympic effect. *Journal of Environment and Development*, 12(2): 239–63.

Bridgman, A. & Davis, P. (2004) *The Australian policy handbook*. Sydney: Allen & Unwin.

Brissonneau, C. & Ohl, F. (2010) The genesis and effect of French anti-doping policies in cycling. *International Journal of Sport Policy and Politics*, 2(2): 173–87.

Bruce, T. & Hallinan, C. (2001) Cathy Freeman: The quest for Australian identity. In D. Andrews & S. Jackson (eds), *Sport stars: The cultural politics of sporting celebrity*. London: Routledge (pp. 257–70).

Bryson, B. (2000) *In a sunburned country*. Toronto: Anchor Books.

Burawoy, M. (2005) For sociology. *American Sociological Review*, 70(1): 4–28.

Burawoy, M., Blum, J., George, S., et al. (2000) *Global ethnographies: Forces, connections and imaginations in a postmodern world*. Berkeley, CA: University of California Press.

Burdsey, D. (2011) The technicolor Olympics? Race, representation and the 2012 London Games. In J. Sugden & A. Tomlinson (eds), *Watching the Olympics: Politics, power and representation*. London: Routledge (pp. 69–81).

Butcher, J. (2003) *The moralization of tourism: Sun, sand … and saving the world*. London: Routledge.

Cabinet Office (1999) *Modernising government*. Cm. 4310. London: HMSO. Available at: www.archive-official-documents-co.uk/document/cm43/4310/4310-02.htm [accessed 9 June 2010].

Campbell, R. (2010) Staging globalization for national projects: Global sport markets and elite athletic transnational labor in Qatar. *International Review for the Sociology of Sport*, 46(1): 45–60.

Cantelon, H. & Letters, M. (2000) The making of the IOC environmental policy as the third dimension of the Olympic movement. *International Review for the Sociology of Sport*, 35(3): 294–308.

CARE for Europe (2006) Human trafficking. www.stoptraffik.org/default/aipx [accessed 17 April 2012].

Carter, T. (2006) Introduction: The sport of cities: Spectacle and the economy of appearances. *City & Society*, XVIII(2): 151–8.

Carter, T. (2011a) Interrogating athletic urbanism: On examining the politics of the city underpinning the production of the spectacle. *International Review for the Sociology of Sport*, 46(2): 131–9.

Carter, T. (2011b) The Olympics as sovereign subject maker. In J. Sugden & A. Tomlinson (eds), *Watching the Olympics: Politics, power and representation*. London: Routledge (pp. 55–68).

Cashman, R. (2004) Athens 2004: The no show game. *National Online Forum: Online Opinion*, www.onlineopinion.com.au [accessed 20 April 2012].

Castells, M. (1996) *The rise of the network society: The information age*. Oxford: Blackwell.

Castells, M. (2009) *Communication power*. New York and Oxford: Oxford University Press.

Castells, M. (2010) Globalization, networking, urbanization: Reflections on the spatial dynamics of the information age. *Urban Studies*, November: 2737–45.

Caudwell, J. (2011) Sex watch: Surveying women's sexed and gendered bodies at the Olympics. In J. Sugden & A. Tomlinson (eds), *Watching the Olympics: Politics, power and representation*. London: Routledge (pp. 151–64).

CBS (2008) Beijing remade for the Olympics. *CBS News*, 4 August. www.cbsnews.com/stories/2008/08/04/world/main4318385.shtml [accessed 5 October 2010].

Chalip, L. (1996) Critical policy analysis in sport: The illustrative case of New Zealand sports policy development. *Journal of Sports Management*, 10: 310–24.

Chan Kwok-bun, J., Walls, J. & Hayward, D. (eds) (2007) *East–West identities: Globalization, localization and hybridization*. Brill: Leiden.

Chappelet, J.-L. & Kübler-Mabbot, B. (2008) *The International Olympic Committee and the Olympic System: The governance of world sport*. London: Routledge.

Chapman, S. (2010) Influencing politicians to implement comprehensive tobacco control: The power of news media. In *Tobacco: Science, Policy, and Public Health*. New York: Oxford University Press (pp. 691–6).

Cheska, A. (1979) Sports spectacular: A ritual mode of power. *International Review for the Sociology of Sport*, 14(51): 51–72.

Chiba, N. (2004) Pacific professional baseball leagues and migratory patterns and trends: 1995–1999. *Journal of Sport and Social Issues*, 28(2): 193–211.

City of London (2011) http://city-of-london.com/london-olympics-2012.htm [accessed 23 January 2011].

Clark, J.D. & Themudo, N.S. (2006) Linking the web and the street: Internet-based 'dotcauses' and the 'anti-globalization' movement. *World Development*, 34(1): 50–74.

Cleland, J. (2011) The media and football supporters: A changing relationship. *Media, Culture & Society*, 32(2): 299–315.

Close, P., Askew, D. & Xin, X. (2007) *The Beijing Olympiad: A political economy of a sporting mega-event*. London: Routledge.

Coaffee, J. & Murakami Wood, D. (2006) Security is coming home: Rethinking scale and constructing resilience in the global urban response to terrorist risk. *International Relations*, 20(4): 503–17.

Coakley, J. (2004) *Sports in society: Issues and controversies*. New York: McGraw-Hill.

Coalter, F. (2007) *A wider role for sport: Who's keeping the score?* London: Routledge.

Coalter, F. & Allison, M. (2000) The role of sport in regenerating deprived areas. Scottish Central Research Unit. http://scotland.gov.uk/Resource/Doc/156589/0042061.pdf [accessed 20 April 2012].

Cohen, M., March, J. & Olsen, J. (1972) A garbage can model of organizational choice. *Administrative Science Quarterly*, 17: 1–25.

Cohen, R. & Kennedy, P. (2007) *Global sociology* (2nd edn). Basingstoke: Macmillan.

Colebatch, H. (2002) *Policy* (2nd edn). Buckingham: Open University Press.

Colebatch, H. (2006a) Policy, models and the construction of governing. In H.K. Colebatch (ed.), *The work of policy: An international survey*. Lanham, MD: Lexington Books (pp. 3–19).

Colebatch, H. (2006b) Mapping the work of policy. In H.K. Colebatch (ed.), *Beyond the policy cycle: The policy process in Australia*. Sydney: Allen and Unwin (pp. 1–19).

Coleman, J. (1990) *Foundations of social theory*. Cambridge, MA: Harvard University Press.

Coles, K. (2004) Election day: The cultural constructions of democracy through technique. *Cultural Anthropology*, 19(4): 551–80.

Collins, A. & Flynn, A. (2007) Engaging with the ecological footprint as a decision-making tool: Process and responses. *Local Environment*, 12(3): 295–312.

Collins, S. (2007) New Zealand. In B. Houlihan & M. Green (eds), *Comparative elite sport development: Systems, structures and public policy.* Oxford: Heinemann (pp. 218–41).

Collins, S. (2010) Finland. In M. Nicholson, R. Hoye & B. Houlihan (eds), *Participation in sport: International perspectives.* London: Routledge (pp. 109–25).

Connell, R. (2006) Northern theory: The political geography of general social theory. *Theory & Society,* 35: 237–64.

Connell, R. (2007) *Southern theory: The global dynamics of knowledge in social science.* Sydney: Allen & Unwin.

Connell, R. (2009) Peripheral visions – beyond the metropole. In J. Kenway & J. Fahey (eds), *Globalizing the research imagination.* London: Routledge (pp. 53–72).

Connell, R. (2011) Sociology for the whole world. *International Sociology,* 26(3): 288–91.

Connor, T. (2002) Rerouting the race to the bottom? Transnational corporations, labour practices and workers' rights to organize – the case of Nike, Inc. In B.E. Hernandez-Truyol (ed.), *Moral imperialism: A critical anthology.* New York: New York University Press (pp. 166–82).

Connor, T. & Dent, K. (2006) *Offside! Labour rights and sportswear production in Asia.* Melbourne: Oxfam International.

Cornelissen, S. (2004) Sport mega-events in Africa: Processes, impacts and prospects. *Tourism and Hospitality Planning & Development,* 1(1): 39–55.

Cornelissen, S. (2008) Scripting the nation: Sports, mega-events, foreign policy and state-building in post-apartheid South Africa. *Sport in Society,* 11(4): 481–93.

Cottrell, R. (2003) The legacy of Munich 1972: Terrorism, security and the Olympic Games. In M. de Moragas, C. Kennett and N. Puig (eds), *The legacy of the Olympics Games 1984–2000.* Lausanne: International Olympic Committee (pp. 309–13).

Council of Europe (1989) Anti-doping convention. http://conventions.coe.int/Treaty/EN/Treaties/Html/135.htm [accessed 1 May 2011].

Council of Europe (2006) *2006 World Cup: PACE asks FIFA to join the fight against trafficking in women.* Strasbourg: Council of Europe Parliamentary Assembly. http://assembly.coe.int/ASP/Press/StopPressView.asp?ID=1759 [accessed 20 June 2007].

Council on Foreign Relations (2003) National strategy on combating terrorism. www.cfr.org/terrorism/national-strategy-combating-terrorism-2003/p9071 [accessed 23 November 2011].

Crotty, M. (1998) *Foundations of social research: Meaning and perspective in the social sciences.* London: Sage.

Cunningham, J. & Beneforti, M. (2005) Investigating indicators for measuring the health and social impact of sport and recreation programs in Australian Indigenous communities. *International Review for the Sociology of Sport,* 40(1): 89–98.

Curi, M., Knijnik, J. & Mascarenhas, G. (2011) The Pan American Games in Rio de Janeiro 2007: Consequences of a sport mega-event on a BRIC country. *International Review for the Sociology of Sport,* 46(2): 140–56.

Cycling News (2011) Riders protest against radio ban at the Challenge Mallorca. *Cycling News,* February.www.cyclingnews.com/news/riders-protest-aganist-radio-ban-at-the-challenge-mallorca [accessed 21 May 2011].

Dahlgren, P. (2005) The internet, public spheres, and political communication: Dispersion and deliberation. *Political Communication,* 22(2): 147–62.

Darby, P. (2000a) Africa's place in FIFA's global order: a theoretical frame. *Soccer and Society,* 1(2): 36–61.

Darby, P. (2000b) The new scramble for Africa: African football labour migration to Europe. *The European Sports History Review,* 3(1): 217–44.

Darby, P. (2003) Africa, the FIFA presidency and the governance of world football: 1974, 1998, and 2002. *Africa Today,* 50: 3–24.

Darby, P., Akindes, G. & Kirwin, M. (2007) Football academies and the migration of African football labour to Europe. *Journal of Sport and Social Issues*, 31(2): 143–61.

Darnell, S. (2010) Power, politics and 'Sport for Development and Peace': Investigating the utility of sport for international development. *Sociology of Sport Journal*, 27(1): 54–75.

Darnell, S. & Hayhurst, L. (2011) Sport for decolonization: Exploring a new praxis of sport for development. *Progress in Development Studies*, 11(3): 183–96.

Davis, N. & Duncan, M.C. (2006) Sports knowledge is power: Reinforcing masculine privilege through fantasy sport league participation. *Journal of Sport and Social Issues*, 30: 244–64.

Davis-Delano, L. & Crosset, T. (2008) Using social movement theory to study outcomes in sport-related social movements. *International Review for the Sociology of Sport*, 43(2): 115–34.

Dayan, D. & Katz, E. (1992) *Media events: The live broadcasting of history*. Cambridge, MA: Harvard University Press.

DCMS (2007) *Our Promise for 2012: How the UK will benefit from the Olympic and Paralympic Games*. London: DCMS.

DCMS (2008) *Before, during and after: Making the most of the London 2012 Games*. London: DCMS.

Deacon, B. (1997) *Global social policy: International organisations and the future of welfare*. London: Sage.

Deacon, B. (2001) Welcome to global social policy. *Global Social Policy*, 1: 1–5.

Deacon, B. (2007) *Global social policy & governance*. London: Sage.

De Bois, M. (2008) Environmental ads: Greenwash or green communication? *Ad Map*, December: 500.

De Bosscher, V., Bingham, V., Shibli, S., et al. (2008) *The global sporting arms race: An international comparative study on sports policy factors leading to international sporting success*. Oxford: Meyer and Meyer.

De Bosscher, V., Shibli, S., van Bottenburg, M., De Knop, P. & Truyens, J. (2010) Developing a method for comparing the elite sport systems and policies of nations: A mixed research methods approach. *Journal of Sports Management*, 24: 567–600.

de Goede, M. (2008) Beyond risk: Premediation and the post-9/11 security imagination. *Security Dialogue*, 39(2–3): 155–76.

Debord, G. (1967) *Society of the spectacle*. London: Black and Red.

Di Tommaso, M.L., Shima, I., Strøm, S. & Bettio, F. (2009) As bad as it gets: Well-being deprivation of sexually exploited trafficked women. *European Journal of Political Economy*, 25(2): 143–62.

Diani, M. (2000) Social movement networks virtual and real. *Information, Communication & Society*, 3(3): 386–401.

Digel, H. (1992) Sports in a risk society. *International Review for the Sociology of Sport*, 27: 257–71.

Dirlik, A. (1996) The global in the local. In R. Wilson & W. Dissanayake (eds), *Global local: Cultural production and the transnational imaginary*. Durham, NC: Duke University Press (pp. 21–45).

Doezema, J. (2000) Loose women or lost women? The re-emergence of the myth of 'white slavery' in contemporary discourses of trafficking in women. *Gender Issues*, 18(1): 23–50.

Donnelly, P. (1996) The local and the global: Globalization in the sociology of sport. *Journal of Sport and Social Issues*, 20: 239–57.

Donnelly, P. (1997) Child labour, sport labour: Applying child labour laws to sport. *International Review for the Sociology of Sport*, 32(4): 389–406.

Donnelly, P. (2009) Sport and human rights. In S. Jackson and S. Haigh (eds), *Sport and foreign policy in a globalizing world*. London: Routledge (pp. 33–46).

Donnelly, P. & Petherick, L. (2006) Workers' playtime? Child labour at the extremes of the sporting spectrum. In D. McArdle & R. Giulianotti (eds), *Sport, civil liberties and human rights*. London: Routledge (pp. 9–29).

Dopson, S. & Waddington, I. (1996) Managing social change: A process-sociological approach to understanding change within the National Health Service. *Sociology of Health and Illness*, 18: 525–50.

Douglas, M. (1966) *Purity and danger: An analysis of concepts of pollution and taboo.* New York: Praeger.

Douglas, M. (1985) *Risk acceptability according to the social sciences.* New York: Russell Sage Foundation.

Douglas, M. (1992) *Risk and blame: Essays in cultural theory.* London and New York: Routledge.

Douglas, M. & Wildavsky, A. (1982) *Risk and culture: An essay on the selection of technical and environmental dangers.* Berkeley, CA: University of California Press.

Dubin, C.L. (1990) *Commission of inquiry into the use of drugs and banned practices intended to increase athletic performance.* Ottawa: Canadian Government Publishing Center.

Eckstein, S. (2002) Globalization and mobilization: Resistance to neo-liberalism in Latin America. In M. Guillen, R. Collins, P. England & M. Meyer (eds), *The new economic sociology*. New York: Russell Sage (pp. 330–68).

Elias, N. (1978) *What is sociology?* London: Hutchinson.

Ellaway, A., Macintyre, S., Mutrie, N. & Kirk, A. (2007) Nowhere to play? The relationship between the location of outdoor play areas and deprivation in Glasgow. *Health & Place*, 13: 557–61.

Erickson, B. (2011) Recreational activism: Politics, nature and the rise of neoliberalism. *Leisure Studies*, 30(4): 477–94.

Ericson, R. & Doyle, A. (eds) (2004) *Risk and morality*. Toronto: University of Toronto Press.

Ericson, R. & Haggerty, K. (1997) *Policing the risk society*. Toronto: University of Toronto Press.

Eriksen, T.H. (1995) The local, the global and the glocal. In T.H. Eriksen, *Small places, large issues*. London: Pluto Press (pp. 294–311).

Eriksen, T.H. (1997) Beyond platitudes: A review of Ulf Hannerz: *Transnational connections: Culture, people, places. Journal of the Royal Anthropological Institute*, Spring.

Eriksen, T.H. (2003) *Globalisation: Studies in anthropology*. London: Pluto Press.

Eriksen, T.H. (2007) *Globalisation*. Oxford: Berg.

Ewen, S. (1973) *Captains of Consciousness: Advertising and the social roots of consumer culture*. New York: McGraw-Hill.

Faligot, R. (2008) *The Chinese Secret Service: From Mao to the Olympic Games*. Paris: Nouveau Monde.

Falk, R. (1999) The monotheistic religions in the era of globalization. *Global Dialogue: The Globalization Phenomenon*, 11(1): 139–48.

Farrar, M. (2008) Analysing London's 'New East End': How can social science make a difference? *Sociological Research Online*, 13(5), www.socresonline.org.uk/13/5/7. html [accessed 2 December 2009].

Farred, G. (2002) Long distance love: Growing up a Liverpool football club fan. *Journal of Sport and Social Issues*, 26(1): 6–24.

Fasting, K., Brackenridge, C. & Walseth, K. (2002) Consequences of sexual harassment in sport for female athletes. *The Journal of Sexual Aggression*, 8: 37–48.

Fasting, K., Chroni, S., Hervik, S. & Knorre, N. (2011) Sexual harassment in sport towards females in three European countries. *International Review for the Sociology of Sport*, 46(1): 76–90.

Featherstone, M. (1990) Global culture: An introduction. *Theory, Culture & Society*, 7: 1–14.

Featherstone, M. (1995) *Undoing culture: Globalization, postmodernism and identity*. London: Sage.

Featherstone, M. & Venn, C. (2006) Problematizing global knowledge and the New Encyclopaedia Project: An introduction. *Theory, Culture & Society*, 23(2–3): 1–20.

Forrest, R. & Kearns, R. (1999) *Joined up places: Social cohesion and neighbourhood regeneration*. York: Joseph Rowntree Foundation.

Foster, K. (2005) Alternative models for the regulation of sport. In L. Allison (ed.), *The global politics of sport*. London: Routledge (pp. 63–86).

Foucault, M. (1977) *Discipline and punish: The Birth of the prison*. Trans A. Sheridan. New York: Vintage.

Foucault, M. (1991) Governmentality. In G. Burchell, C. Gordon & P. Miller (eds), *The Foucault effect*. Chicago, IL: University of Chicago Press (pp. 87–104).

Fox, J. (1991) Introduction: Working in the present. In R. Fox (ed.), *Recapturing anthropology: Working in the present*. Santa Fe, NM: School of American Research Press (pp. 1–16).

Francoli, M. & Ward, S. (2008) 21st century soapboxes? MPS and their blogs. *Information Polity*, 13(1–2): 21–39.

Frenkel, S. (2001) Globalization, athletic footwear commodity chains and employment relations in China. *Organization Studies*, 22(4): 531–62.

Friends of the Earth International (2006) 2008 Olympic plans to sacrifice rainforest should be aborted. www.foei.org/media/2006/0512.html [accessed 14 June 2009].

Furedi, F. (2002) *The culture of fear*. London and New York: Continuum.

Future Group (2007) *Faster, higher, stronger: Preventing human trafficking at the 2010 Olympics*. http://faculty.law.ubc.ca/perrin/pdf/Report%20on%202010%20Olympics%20and%20Human%20Trafficking.pdf [accessed 3 December 2010].

Gaffney, C. (2011) Rio's favela dwellers to be displaced in the rush to be ready. *The Independent*, 30 July. www.independent.co.uk/sport/football/international/rios-favela-dwellers-to-be-displaced-in-the-rush-to-be-ready-2328464.html [accessed 30 July 2011].

García Canclini, N. (1995) *Hybrid cultures: Strategies for entering and leaving modernity*. Minneapolis, MN: University of Minnesota Press.

Gardiner, G. (1997) Racial abuse and football: The Australian Football League's Vilification Rule in review. *Sporting Traditions*, 3: 87–90.

Garrett, R.K. (2006) Protest in an Information Society: A review of literature on social movements and new ICTs. *Information, Communication & Society*, 9(2): 202–24.

Germany Report to EU (2007) Experience report on human trafficking for the purpose of sexual exploitation and forced prostitution in connection with the 2006 Football World Cup in Germany. Brussels: Council of the European Union, German Delegation. 5006/1/07.

Gilberg, R., Breivik, G. & Loland, S. (2006) Anti-doping in sport: The Norwegian perspective. *Sport in Society*, 9(2): 334–53.

Gilchrist, P. (2005) Local heroes and global stars. In L. Allison (ed.), *The global politics of sport: The role of global institutions in sport*. London: Routledge (pp. 118–39).

Giulianotti, R. (2004a) Human rights, globalization and sentimental education: The case of sport. *Sport in Society*, 7(3): 355–69.

Giulianotti, R. (2004b) *Sport and modern social theorists*. London: Palgrave/Macmillan.

Giulianotti, R. (2005) Sport spectators and the social consequences of commodification: Critical perspectives from Scottish football. *Journal of Sport and Social Issues*, 29(4): 386–410.

Giulianotti, R. (2009) Risk and sport: An analysis of sociological theories and research agendas. *Sociology of Sport Journal*, 26: 540–56.

Giulianotti, R. & Klauser, F. (2010) Security governance and sports-mega-events: Towards an interdisciplinary research agenda. *Journal of Sport and Social Issues*, 34(1): 49–61.

Giulianotti, R. & Robertson, R. (2006) Glocalization, globalization and migration: The case of Scottish football supporters in North America. *International Sociology*, 21: 171–98.

Giulianotti, R. & Robertson, R. (2007a) Sport and globalization: Transnational dimensions. In R. Giulianotti & R. Robertson (eds), *Globalization and sport*. Oxford: Blackwell (pp. 1–6).

Giulianotti, R. & Robertson, R. (2007b) Forms of glocalization: Globalization and the migration strategies of Scottish football fans in North America. *Sociology*, 41: 133–42.

Goffman, E. (1959) *The presentation of self in everyday life*. New York: Anchor Books.

Gold, J. & Gold, M. (2009) Future indefinite? London 2012, the spectre of retrenchment and the challenge of Olympic sports legacy. *The London Journal*, 34(2): 179–96.

Goldfrank, W.L. (2000) Paradigm regained? The rules of Wallerstein's world-system method. *Journal of World-Systems Research*, 6(2): 150–95.

Graham, S. (ed.) (2004) *Cities, war and terrorism: Towards an urban geopolitics*. London: Blackwell.

Gratton, C. & Henry, I. (2001) *Sport and the city: The role of sport in economic and social generation*. London: Routledge.

Gratton, C. & Taylor, P. (2000) *Economics of sport and recreation*. New York: Spon.

Green, M. (2007) Policy transfer, lesson drawing and perspectives on elite sport systems. *International Journal of Sports Management and Marketing*, 2(4): 426–41.

Green, M. & Collins, S. (2008) Do policies determine politics?: Sport development in Australia and Finland. *Sport Management Review*, 11: 225–51.

Green, M. & Houlihan, B. (2004) Advocacy coalitions and elite sport policy change in Canada and the United Kingdom. *International Review for the Sociology of Sport*, 39(4): 387–403.

Green, M. & Houlihan, B. (2005) *Elite sport development: Policy learning and political priorities*. London: Routledge.

Green, M. & Houlihan, B. (2006) Governmentality, modernisation and the 'disciplining' of national sport policy organisations: Athletics in Australia and the United Kingdom. *Sociology of Sport Journal*, 23(1): 47–71.

Greener, I. (2002) Understanding NHS reform: The policy transfer, social learning and path dependency perspectives. *Governance: An International Journal of Policy, Administration and Institutions*, 15(2): 161–83.

Greenhalgh, P. (1998) *Ephemeral vistas: The expositions universelles: Great exhibitions and world fairs, 1851–1939*. Manchester: Manchester University Press.

Grossberg, L. (1997) Cultural studies, modern logics and theories of globalisation. In A. McRobbie (ed.), *Back to reality? Social experience and cultural studies*. Manchester: Manchester University Press (pp. 7–35).

The Guardian (2007) How Lisa Simpson got ahead at the Olympics, *The Guardian*, 5 June. www.guardian.co.uk/artanddesign/artblog/2007/jun/05/howlisasimpsontook-theolym [accessed 20 May 2011].

The Guardian (2011) Damon Hill urges Bernie Ecclestone not to reschedule Bahrain Grand Prix, *The Guardian*, 3 June. www.guardian.co.uk/sport/2011/jun/03/damon-hill-bahrain-grand-prix [accessed 7 November 2011].

Guillén, M. (2001) Is globalisation civilising, destructive or feeble? A critique of five key debates in the social science literature. *Annual Review of Sociology*, 27: 235–60.

Habermas, J. (1962/1989) *The structural transformation of the public sphere: An inquiry into a category of bourgeois society*. English trans. Thomas Burger, 1989. Cambridge, MA: MIT Press.

Habermas, J. (1991) The public sphere. In C. Mukerji & M. Schudson (eds), *Rethinking popular culture: Contemporary perspectives in Cultural Studies*. Berkeley, CA: University of Los Angeles Press (pp. 398–404).

Haggerty, K. (2003) From risk to precaution: The rationalities of personal crime prevention. In R. Ericson & A. Doyle (eds), *Risk and morality*. Toronto: University of Toronto Press (pp. 193–215).

Hajer, M. (1993) Discourse coalitions and the institutionalization of practice: The case of acid rain in Great Britain. In F. Fischer & J. Forester (eds), *The argumentative turn in policy analysis and planning*. Durham, NC: Duke University Press (pp. 42–76).

Hallinan, C., Bruce, T. & Burke, M. (2005) Fresh prince of Colonial Dome: Indigenous players in the AFL. *Football Studies*, 8(1): 68–78.

Hannerz, U. (1989) Notes on the global ecumene. *Public Culture*, 1: 66–75.

Hannerz, U. (1990) Cosmopolitans and locals in world culture. *Theory, Culture & Society*, 7: 237–51.

Hannerz, U. (1992) *Cultural complexity: Studies in the social organization of meaning*. New York: Columbia University Press.

Hannerz, U. (1996) *Transnational connections*. London: Routledge.

Hannerz, U. (2003) Being there... and there... and there!: Reflections on multi-site ethnography. *Ethnography*, 4(2): 201–16.

Hannerz, U. (2010) *Anthropology's world: Life in a twenty-first century discipline*. London: Pluto Press.

Hannerz, U. (n.d) Flows, boundaries and hybrids: Keywords in transnational anthropology. Working Paper (WPTC-2K-02), Department of Social Anthropology, Stockholm University.

Hansen Sandseter, E.B. (2009) Characteristics of risky play. *Journal of Adventure Education & Outdoor Learning*, 9(1): 3–21.

Hanstad, D.V. & Loland, S. (2009) Elite level athletes' duty to provide information on their whereabouts: Justifiable anti-doping work or an indefensible surveillance regime? *European Journal of Sport Sciences*, 9(1): 3–10.

Hanstad, D.V. & Skille, E. (2008) Politics, bureaucrats and a voluntary sports organization: The power play of Norwegian sports policy in the matter of anti-doping. *Sport in Society*, 11: 546–59.

Hanstad, D.V., Skille, E. & Loland, S. (2010) Harmonization of anti-doping work: Myth or reality? *Sport in Society*, 13(3): 418–30.

Hanstad, D.V. & Waddington, I. (2009) Sport, health and drugs: A critical re-examination of some key issues and problems. *Perspectives in Public Health*, 129 (4): 174–82.

Hardt, M. & Negri, A. (2001) *Empire*. Cambridge, MA: Harvard University Press.

Hargreaves, J. (2000) The Muslim sports heroic. In J. Hargreaves (ed.), *Heroines of sport: The politics of difference and identity*. London: Routledge.

Hargreaves, J. (2007) Sport, exercise and the female Muslim body: Negotiating Islam, politics and male power. In J. Hargreaves & P. Vertinsky (eds), *Physical culture, power and the body*. London: Routledge.

Harvey, J., Horne, J. & Safai, P. (2009) Alterglobalization, global social movements, and the possibility of transformation through sport. *Sociology of Sport Journal*, 26: 383–403.

Harvey, J. & Houle, F. (1994) Sport, world economy, global culture and new social movements. *Sociology of Sport Journal*, 11: 337–55.

Hay, C. & Marsh, D. (2000) *Demystifying globalization*. Basingstoke: Palgrave.

Hayward, P. (2009) The real deal? Hotels grapple with green washing. *Lodging Magazine*, February.

Held, D. & Kay, A. (eds) (2007) *Global inequality: Patterns and explanations*. Cambridge: Polity Press.

Held, D. & McGrew, A. (eds) (2007) *Globalisation theory: Approaches and controversies*. Cambridge: Cambridge University Press.

Hellenic Republic of Greece (2004) *Greek actions for the suppression of trafficking in human beings*. www.greekembassy.org/Embassy/Content/en/Article.aspx?office=1&folder=189&article=15996 [accessed 8 December 2010].

Hennig, J., Craggs, S., Larsson, F. & Laczko, F. (2006) *Trafficking in human beings and the 2006 World Cup in Germany*. Geneva: International Organization for Migration.

Henry, I. (2007) *Transnational and comparative research in sport: Globalisation, governance and sport policy*. London: Routledge.

Henry, I., Amara, M. & Aquilina, D. (2007) Multiculturalism, interculturalism, assimilation and sports policy in Europe. In I. Henry (ed.), *Transnational and comparative research in sport: Globalisation, governance and sport policy*. London: Routledge (pp. 115–43).

Henry, I. & Lee, P.C. (2004) Governance and ethics. In J. Beech & S. Chadwick (eds), *The business of sports management*. London: Pearson (pp. 25–41).

Henry, I., Amara, M., & Al-Tauqi, M. (2003) Sport, Arab nationalism and the Pan Arab Games. *International Review for the Sociology of Sport*. 38(3): 295–310.

Henry, I. & Uchiumi, K. (2001) Political ideology, modernity and sports policy: A comparative analysis of sports policy in Britain and Japan. *Hitosubashi Journal of Social Sciences*, 33: 161–85.

Heywood, L. & Montgomery, M. (2008) Ambassadors of the last wilderness? Surfers, environmental ethics and activism in America. In M. Atkinson & K. Young (eds), *Tribal play: Subcultural journeys through sport*. Bingley: Emerald (pp. 153–72).

Hoberman, J. & Møller, V. (eds) (2004) *Doping and public policy*. Odense: University of Southern Denmark.

Hoffman, B. (2002) Rethinking terrorism and counterterrorism since 9/11. *Studies in Conflict & Terrorism*. 25: 305–16.

Hoffman, L. (2006) Autonomous choices and patriotic professionalism: On governmentality in late-socialist China. *Economy & Society*, 35(4): 550–70.

Hogwood, B. & Gunn, L. (1984) *Policy analysis for the real world*. London: Oxford University Press.

Hong, F. (2004) Innocence lost: Child athletes in China. *Sport in Society*, 7(3): 338–54.

Hong, F. & Zhouxiang, L. (2008) *The rights to sport*. Beijing: Sichuan Science Press.

Hoppe, R. (2002) Cultures of public policy problems. *Journal of Comparative Policy Analysis*, 4: 305–26.

Horne, J. (2007) The four 'knowns' of sports mega-events. *Leisure Studies*, 26(1): 81–96.

Horne, J. (2011) Architects, stadia and sport spectacles: Notes on the role of architects in the building of sport stadia and making of world-class cities. *International Review for the Sociology of Sport*, 46(2): 205–27.

Horne, J. & Manzenreiter, W. (2002) Global governance in world sport and the 2002 World Cup in Korea/Japan. In J. Horne & W. Manzenreiter (eds), *Japan, Korea and the 2002 World Cup*. London: Routledge (pp. 1–25).

Horne, J. with Manzenreiter, W. (eds) (2006) Sports mega-events: Social scientific analyses of a global phenomenon. *Sociological Review Monograph Series*. Oxford: Blackwell.

Horton, D. (2006) Demonstrating environmental citizenship? A study of everyday life among green activists. In A. Dobson & D. Bell (eds), *Environmental citizenship*. Cambridge, MA: MIT Press (pp. 127–50).

Houlihan, B. (1990) The politics of sport policy in Britain: The examples of football hooliganism and drug abuse. *Leisure Studies*, 9: 55–69.

Houlihan, B. (1991) *The government and politics of sport.* London: Routledge.

Houlihan, B. (1994) Homogenisation, Americanization and creolization of sport: Varieties of globalization. *Sociology of Sport Journal*, 11: 356–75.

Houlihan, B. (1997) *Sport, policy and politics.* London: Routledge.

Houlihan, B. (1999) *Dying to win: Doping in sport and the development of Anti-Doping Policy 57.* Brussels: Council of Europe.

Houlihan, B. (2004) Civil rights, doping control and the World Anti-Doping Code. *Sport in Society*, 7(3): 420–37.

Houlihan, B. (2005) Public sector sport policy: Developing a framework for analysis. *International Review for the Sociology of Sport*, 40(2): 163–87.

Houlihan, B. (2011) Doping and the Olympics: Rights, responsibilities and accountabilities (watching the athletes). In J. Sugden & A. Tomlinson (eds), *Watching the Olympics: Politics, power and representation.* London: Routledge (pp. 94–104).

Houlihan, B., Bloyce, D. & Smith, A. (2009) Editorial: Developing the research agenda in sport policy. *International Journal of Sport Policy*, 1: 1–12.

Houlihan, B. & Green, M. (2008) *Comparative elite sport development: Systems, structures and public policy.* Oxford: Heinemann.

Houlihan, B. & White, A. (2002) *The politics of sports development: Development of sport or development through sport?* London: Routledge.

Howe, D. (ed.) (1996) *Cross-cultural consumption: Global markets, local realities.* London: Routledge.

Hudson, J. & Lowe, S. (2004) *Understanding the policy process: Analysing welfare policy and practice.* Bristol: Policy Press.

Hulme, D. (1990) *The political Olympics: Moscow, Afghanistan and the 1980 US boycott.* New York: Praeger.

Hulme, R. (2006) The role of policy transfer in assessing the impact of American ideas on British society. *Global Social Policy*, 6(2): 175–97.

Hulme, R. & Hulme, M. (2008) The international transfer of global social policy. In N. Yeates (ed.), *Understanding global social policy.* Bristol: Policy Press (pp. 49–72).

Hunt, L. (2007) *Inventing human rights.* New York: W.W. Norton.

Hutchins, B. (2008) Signs of meta-change in second modernity: The growth of e-commerce and the World Cyber Games. *New Media & Society*, 10: 851–69.

Hutchins, B., Rowe, D. & Ruddock, A. (2009) 'It's fantasy football made real': Networked media sport, the internet, and the hybrid reality of MyFootballClub. *Sociology of Sport*, 26(1): 89–107.

Hwang, Y. (2010) Olympiad, a place of linguistic struggle – the discursive constitution of 'human rights' in the 2008 Beijing Olympics. *Sport in Society*, 13(5): 855–75.

IAAF (2009) *Transfers of allegiance.* www.iaaf.org/athletes/transfer/index.html [accessed 15 March 2009].

Ignatow, G. (2011) What has globalization done to developing countries' public libraries? *International Sociology*, 26(6): 746–68.

International Labour Organization (1997) *ILO partnership to eliminate child labour in the soccer ball industry in Pakistan.* http://actrav.itcilo.org/actravenglish/telearn/global/ilo/guide/ilosoc.htm#Text%20of%20the%20agreement [accessed 26 September 2011].

International Labour Organization (2005) *A global alliance against forced labour.* www.ilo.org/public/english/standards/relm/ilc/ilc93/pdf/rep-i-b.pdf [accessed 3 January 2011].

IOC (1998) *Fact sheet: The Olympic Movement and the environment.* Lausanne: IOC.

IOC (2010) *Olympic charter*. Lausanne: IOC. Available at: www.olympic. org/Documents/ Olympic%20Charter/Charter_en_2010.pdf [accessed 23 May 2010].

IOM (2006) Germany's World Cup brothels: 40,000 women and children at risk of exploitation through trafficking. Statement of Ashley Garrett, IOM, Hearing before the House Committee on International Relations Subcommittee on Africa, Global Human Rights and International Operations, 4 May.

Jackson, S. (2004) Exorcising the ghost: Donovan Bailey, Ben Johnson and the politics of Canadian identity. *Media, Culture and Society*, 2(1): 121–41.

Jackson, S., Batty, R. & Scherer, J. (2001) Transnational sport marketing at the global/ local nexus: The adidasification of the New Zealand All Blacks. *International Journal of Sports Sponsorship and Marketing*, 3(2): 185–201.

Jackson, S. & Haigh, S. (eds) (2009) *Sport and foreign policy in a globalizing world*. London: Routledge.

Jackson, S. & Hokowhitu, B. (2002) Sport, tribes and technology: The New Zealand All Blacks *Haka* and the politics of identity. *Journal of Sport and Social Issues*, 26(1): 125–39.

Janssen, S., Kuipers, G. & Verboord, M. (2008) Cultural globalisation and arts journalism: The international orientation of arts and culture coverage in Dutch, French, German and US newspaper, 1995 to 2005. *American Sociological Review*, 73(5): 719–40.

Jarvie, G. (2007) Sport, social change and the public intellectual. *International Review for the Sociology of Sport*, 42(4): 411–24.

Jenkins-Smith, H. & Sabatier, P. (1994) Evaluating the Advocacy Coalition Framework. *Journal of Public Policy*, 14: 175–203.

Jennings, A. (1996) *The new Lords of the Rings: Olympic corruption and how to buy gold medals*. London: Pocket Books.

Jhally, S. & Lewis, J. (1992) *Enlightened racism: The Cosby Show, audiences and the myth of the American dream*. Boulder, CO: Westview Press.

Johnson, C. (2005) When are corporate environmental policies a form of greenwashing? *Business and Society*, 44(4): 377–14.

Jones, K. (2009) Terrorist attack targets international cricket match in Pakistan. http:// alethonewsa.wordpress.com/2009/03/04/terrorist-attack-targets-international-cricket-match-in-pakistan [accessed 6 June 2011].

Judd, B. (2010) Racism in football: White Australian Rules! *Indigenous Law Bulletin*, 7(20): 3–17.

Katwala, S. (2000) *Democratising global sport*. London: The Foreign Policy Centre.

Kay, T.A. (2007) Daughters of Islam: Family influences on Muslim young women's participation in sport. *International Review for the Sociology of Sport*, 41 (3–4): 357–75.

Kay, T.A. (2008) Daughters of Islam, sisters in sport. In M. Kwan, C. Aitchison & P. Hopkins (eds), *Geographies of Muslim identities: Diaspora, gender and belonging*. Aldershot: Ashgate.

Keech, M. (2003) England and Wales. In J. Riordan & A. Kruger (eds), *European cultures in sport: Examining the nations and regions*. Bristol: Intellect (pp. 5–22).

Keech, M. (2011) Youth sport and London's 2012 Olympic legacy. In J. Sugden & A. Tomlinson (eds), *Watching the Olympics: Politics, power and representation*. London: Routledge (pp. 82–96).

Kelly, L. (2002) *Journeys of jeopardy: A review of research on trafficking in women and children in Europe*. Child and Woman Abuse Studies Unit, University of North London.

Kempadoo, K. (2005) From moral panic to global justice: Changing perspectives on trafficking. In K. Kempadoo, J. Sanghera & B. Pattanaik (eds), *Trafficking and prostitution reconsidered: New perspectives on migration, sex work, and human rights*. London: Paradigm Publishers.

Kenway, J. & Fahey, J. (2009) Imagining research otherwise. In J. Kenway & J. Fahey (eds), *Globalizing the research imagination*. London: Routledge.

Keohane, R. (2002) *Power and governance in a partially globalized world*. London. Routledge.

Kidd, B. (2009) A new social movement: Sport for development and peace. In S. Jackson & S. Haigh (eds), *Sport and foreign policy in a globalizing world*. London: Routledge (pp. 22–32).

Kidd, B. (2010) Human rights and the Olympic Movement after Beijing. *Sport in Society*, 13(5): 901–10.

Kidd, B. & Donnelly, P. (2000) Human rights in sport. *International Review for the Sociology of Sport*, 35(2): 131–48.

Kingdom, J. (1984) *Agendas, alternatives and public policies*. Boston, MA: Little, Brown, Co.

Kingsley, J. & Townsend, M. (2006) Dig into social capital: Community gardens as mechanisms for growing urban social connectedness. *Urban Policy and Research*, 24(4): 525–37.

Kirby S., Greaves, L. & Hankivsky, O. (2000) *The dome of silence: Sexual abuse and harassment in sport*. London: Zed Books.

Klein, A. (2007) Towards a transnational sports studies. *Sport in Society*, 10(6): 885–95.

Konrad, G. (1984) *Antipolitics*. New York: Harcourt.

Kuper, S. (2006) *Soccer against the enemy: How the world's most popular sport starts and fuels revolutions and keeps dictators in power* (2nd edn). New York: Nation Books.

Laczko, F. & Gramegna, M.A. (2003) Developing better indicators of human trafficking. *Brown Journal of World Affairs*. Rhode Island: Brown University.

Lash, S. (2000) Risk culture. In B. Adams, U. Beck. & J. Van Loon (eds), *The risk society and beyond: Critical issues for social theory*. London: Sage (pp. 47–62).

Le Breton, D. (2000) Playing symbolically with death in extreme sports. *Body & Society*, 6(1): 1–11.

Le Tour (2010) Le Tour de France en chiffres. www.letour.fr/2012/TDF/HISTO/us/statistiques.html [accessed 13 July 2010].

Leite, J.C. (2005) *World Social Forum: Strategies of resistance*. Chicago, IL: Haymarket Press.

Lenskyj, H. (1998) Sport and corporate environmentalism: The case of the Sydney 2000 Olympics. *International Review for the Sociology of Sport*, 33(4): 341–54.

Lenskyj, H. (2000) *Inside the Olympic industry*. Albany, NY: State University of New York Press.

Lenskyj, H. (2002) *The best Olympics ever? Social impacts of Sydney 2000*. Albany, NY: State University of New York Press.

Lenskyj, H. (2008) *Olympic industry resistance: Challenging Olympic power and propaganda*. Stanford, CA: Stanford University Press.

Leonard, D. (2009) New media and global sporting cultures: Moving beyond the clichés and the binaries. *Sociology of Sport Journal*, 26: 1–16.

Lesjø, J. (2000) Lillehammer 1994: Planning, figurations and the 'green' Winter Games. *International Review for the Sociology of Sport*, 35(3): 282–93.

Leung, K., Bhagat, R., Buchan, M. & Gibson, C. (2005) Culture and international business: Recent advances and their implications for future research. *Journal of International Business Studies*, 36: 357–78.

Levermore, R. (2010) CSR for development through sport: Examining its potential and limitations. *Third World Quarterly*, 31(2): 223–41.

Levermore, R. (2011) The paucity of, and dilemma in, evaluating corporate social responsibility for development through sport. *Third World Quarterly*, 32(3): 551–69.

Levitt, T. (1983) The globalization of markets. *Harvard Business Review*, May–June: 92–102.

Lievrouw, L. (2001) *Alternative and activist new media*. Cambridge: Polity Press.

Lievrouw, L. (2006) Oppositional and activist new media: Remediation, reconfiguration, participation. *Proceedings of the Ninth Participatory Design Conference 2006*. New York: ACM Press (pp. 115–24).

Lipsky, M. (1980) Street-level bureaucracy: Dilemmas of the individuals in public services. London: Sage.

Little, H. (2006) Children's risk-taking behavior: Implications for early childhood policy and practice. *International Journal of Early Years Education*, 14(2): 141–54.

Little, P. (1995) Ritual, power and ethnography at the Rio Earth Summit. *Critique of Anthropology*, 15(3): 256–83.

Lloyd, R., Warren, S. & Hammer, M. (2008) *2008 global accountability report*. London: One World Trust.

LOCOG (London Organizing Committee of the Olympic Games and Paralympic Games) (2008) *The world in a city: Diversity and inclusion strategy*. London: LOCOG.

Lombardo, C., Zakus, D. & Skinner, H. (2002) Youth social action: Building a global latticework through information and communication technologies. *Health Promotion International*, 17(4): 363–72.

London 2012 (2011) *London 2012 sustainability policy*. www.london2012. com/documents/locog-publications/london-2012-sustainability-policy.pdf [accessed 10 September 2011].

London 2012 Olympic and Paralympic Games (2010) Diversity and inclusion. www. london2012.com/get-involved/jobs/working-for-locog/diversity-andinclusion.php [accessed 5 March 2010].

London Councils/GLE (2011) *The 2012 Games and human trafficking: Identifying possible risks and relevant good practice from other cities*. London: London Councils/GLE.

Lupton, D. (1999) *Risk*. London: Routledge.

Lupton, D. & Tulloch, J. (2002a) 'Life would be pretty dull without risk': Voluntary risk-taking and its pleasures. *Health, Risk & Society*, 4: 113–24.

Lupton, D. & Tulloch, J. (2002b) 'Risk is part of your life': Risk epistemologies among a group of Australians. *Sociology* 36(2): 317–34.

MacAloon, J. (2011) Scandal and governance: Inside and outside the IOC 2000 Commission. *Sport in Society*, 14(3): 292–308.

McCallister, T. (2009) Energy companies fight for green crown, *The Guardian*, 9 July [accessed 21 November 2009].

MacDonald, M. (1996) Unity in diversity: Some tensions in the construction of Europe. *Social Anthropology*, 4: 47–60.

McDermott, L. (2007) A governmental analysis of children 'at risk' in a world of physical inactivity and obesity epidemics. *Sociology of Sport*, 24(3): 283–301.

MacDougall, C., Wright, C. & Atkinson, R. (2002) Supportive environments for physical activity and the local government agenda: A South Australian example. *Australian Health Review*, 24: 178–84.

McGarry, K. (2010) Sport in transition: Emerging trends on culture change in the anthropology of sport. *Reviews in Anthropology*, 39: 151–72.

Macintyre, S. (2007) Deprivation amplification revisited: Or, is it always true that poorer places have poorer access to resources for healthy diets and physical activity? *International Journal of Behavioral Nutrition and Physical Activity*, 4: 32.

McLuhan, M. (1964) *Understanding media: The extension of Man*. London: Routledge & Kegan Paul.

MacNamara, L. (2000) Tackling racial hatred: Conciliation, reconciliation and football. *Australian Journal of Human Rights*, 6(2): 5–10.

MacNeil, M. (1996) Networks: Producing Olympic ice hockey for a national television audience. *Sociology of Sport Journal*, 13: 103–24.

Macrury, I. (2008) Re-thinking the legacy 2012: The Olympics as commodity and gift. *21st Century Society: Journal of the Academy of Social Sciences*, 3(3): 295–310.

Magee, J. & Sugden, J. (2002) The world at their feet: Professional football and international labour migration. *Journal of Sport and Social Issues*, 26(4): 421–37.

Maguire, J. (1994) Sport, identity politics, and globalization: Diminishing contrasts, increasing varieties. *Sociology of Sport Journal*, 11(4): 398–427.

Maguire, J. & Falcous, M. (2010) *Sport and migration: Borders, boundaries and crossings*. London: Routledge.

Maguire, J. & Pearton, R. (2000) Global sport and the migration patterns of France '98 World Cup finals players: Some preliminary observations. *Soccer & Society*, 1(1): 175–89.

Majundar, B. & Mehta, N. (2010) *Sellotape™ legacy: Delhi and the Commonwealth Games*. New Delhi: Harper Collins.

Malcolm, D. (2008) *Dictionary of sport studies*. London: Sage.

Mann, M. (2001) Globalization and September 11. *New Left Review*, 12: 51–72.

Mansfield, L. & Wheaton, B. (2011) *Leisure and the politics of the environment: Leisure studies. Special issue: Leisure and the politics of the environment*, 30(4): 383–6.

Manzenreiter, W. & Horne, J. (eds) (2004) *Football goes east: Business, culture and the people's game in China, Japan and South Korea*. London: Routledge.

Margetts, H. (2011) *Policy & internet*. www.psocommons.org/policyandinternet/ [accessed 13 May 2011].

Massey, D. (1991) A global sense of place. *Marxism Today*. 38: 24–9.

Massey, D. (2005) *For space*. London: Sage.

Mattelart, A. (2005) *Diversité culturelle et modialisation*. Paris: La Découverte.

Mazanov, J. (2009) Developing an agenda for social science research into drugs in sport. *Sport in Society*, 12(3): 273–5.

Merry, S.E. (2006) *Human rights and gender violence: Translating international law into local justice*. Chicago, IL: University of Chicago Press.

Miller, T., Lawrence, G., McKay, J. & Rowe, D. (2001) *Globalization and sport: Playing the world*. London: Sage.

Mills, C. Wright ([1959] 2000) *The sociological imagination*. Oxford: Oxford University Press.

Milovejevic, S. & Pickering, S. (2008) Football and sex: The 2006 FIFA World Cup and sex trafficking. *Termida*, 11(2): 21–48.

Mincyte, D., Casper, M. & Cole, C. (2009) Sports, environmentalism, land use, and urban development. *Journal of Sport & Social Issues*, 33(2): 103–10.

Morgan, G. (2003) Aboriginal protest and the Sydney Olympic Games. *Olympika: The International Journal of Olympic Studies*, 7: 23–38.

Morgan, M. (2008) London Olympics terror threat used to vastly increase surveillance powers. World Socialist Website, www.wsws.org/articles/2008/may2008/lond-m03s html [accessed 12 September 2009].

Morley, D. (1992) *Television, audiences and cultural studies*. London: Routledge.

Morley, D. & Robins, K. (1995) *Spaces of identity: Global media, electronic landscapes and cultural boundaries*. London: Routledge.

Mules, T.J. & Faulkner, B. (1996) An economic perspective on major events. *Tourism Economics*, 2(2): 107–17.

Munshi, D. & Kurian, P. (2005) Imperializing spin cycles: A postcolonial look at public relations, greenwashing, and the separation of publics. *Public Relations Review*, 31(4): 513–20.

Murphy, C.N. (2000) Global governance: Poorly done and poorly understood. *International Affairs*, 76(4): 789–803.

Murray, J. (2009) Legal action casts shadow over EDF's Green Britain Day. *Business Green*, 10 July.

Ndlovu, S. (2010) Sport as cultural diplomacy: The 2010 FIFA World Cup in South Africa's foreign policy. *Soccer & Society*, 11(1–2): 144–53.

Nederveen Pietese, J. (2004) *Globalization and culture: Global mélange*. Lanham, MD: Rowman & Littlefield.

Negrine, R. (2008) *The transformation of political communication: Continuities and changes in media and politics*. London: Palgrave.

Negus, K. (2002) The work of cultural intermediaries and the enduring distance between production and consumption. *Cultural Studies*, 16(4): 501–15.

Neuwirth, J. (2006) The World Cup and the johns, *International Herald Tribune*, 11 April. www.iht.com/articles/2006/04/10/opinion/edneuwirth.php [accessed 20 June 2007].

Newlands, M. (2010a) Green Britannia: Deconstructing 'Team Green Britain' and the London 2012 Olympic Games. In K. Gilbert & J. Savery (eds), *Sports and sustainability*. City, IL: Common Ground Publishing.

Newlands, M. (2010b) It may not wash off: Unforseen liabilities of claiming the 'Greenest Games'. *Rising East*, 2(1): 1–7.

Newman, P. (2007) 'Back the bid': The 2010 Summer Olympics and the governance of London. *Journal of Urban Affairs*, 29(3): 255–67.

Nicholls, S., Giles, A. & Sethna, C. (2011) Perpetuating the 'lack of evidence' discourse in sport for development: Privileged voices, unheard stories and subjugated knowledge. *International Review for the Sociology of Sport*, 46(3): 249–64.

Nixon, H. (1993) Social network analysis in sport: Emphasising social structure in sport. *Sociology of Sport Journal*, 10: 315–21.

Nixon, H. (1996) The relationship of friendship networks, sport experiences and gender to expressed pain thresholds. *Sociology of Sport Journal*, 13: 78–86.

Numerato, D. (2008) Czech sport governing bodies and social capital. *International Review for the Sociology of Sport*, 43(1): 21–34.

Nyong'o, T. (2010) The unforgivable transgression of being Caster Semenya. *Women and Performance: A Journal of Feminist Theory*, 20(1): 95–100.

O'Bonsawin, C.M. (2010) 'No Olympics on stolen native land': Contesting Olympic narratives and asserting Indigenous rights within the discourse of the 2010 Vancouver games. *Sport in Society*, 13(1): 143–56.

Ó Conchúir, D. (2011) New iPhone app sees ISC step up war on drugs. *Irish Examiner*, 6 May. www.irishexaminer.com/sport/other-sport/new-iphone-app-sees-isc-step-up-war-on-drugs-153740.html [accessed 13 May 2011].

O'Malley, P. (2001) Discontinuity, government and risk: A response to Rigakos and Hadden. *Theoretical Criminology*, 5: 85–92.

O'Malley, P. (2004) *Risk, uncertainty and government*. London: Glasshouse Press.

O'Malley, K. (2006) *Governing risks*. Aldershot: Ashgate.

OCIEP (2003) *Threats to Canada's critical infrastructure*. Ottawa: Office of Critical Infrastructure and Emergency Preparedness.

OECD (2001) *Knowledge management in the learning society*. Paris: OECD.

Office of Homeland Security (2002) *National strategy for homeland security*. www.dhs.gov/xlibrary/assets/nat_strat_hls.pdf [accessed 30 September 2010].

Ohmae, K. (1995) *The end of the nation state: The rise of regional economies*. New York: Free Press.

Olympic.org (2011) *Sport and the environment: Creating a lasting legacy*. www.olympic.org/content/olympism-in-action/environment/creating-a-lasting-legacy [accessed 30 November 2011].

Ong, A. (2009) On being human and ethical living. In J. Kenway & J. Fahey (eds), *Globalizing the research imagination*. London: Routledge (pp. 87–100).

OPSI (Office of Public Sector Information) (2006) London Olympic Games and Paralympic Games Act of 2006. www.opsi.gov.uk/acts/acts2006/ukpga20060012_en_1 [accessed 24 May 2010].

Ozga, J. & Jones, R. (2006) Travelling and embedded policy: The case of knowledge transfer. *Journal of Education Policy*, 21(1): 1–17.

Palmer, C. (1996) A life of its own: The social construction of the Tour de France. Unpublished PhD thesis. Department of Anthropology, University of Adelaide.

Palmer, C. (1998a) Le Tour du Monde: Towards an anthropology of the global mega-event. *The Australian Journal of Anthropology* (special edition 10): 'Anthropology and Cultural Studies: Ethnography and Culture in a Postmodern World', 9(3): 168–75.

Palmer, C. (1998b) Reflexivity in global popular culture: The case of the Tour de France. *Anthropological Forum*, VII(1–2): 29–48.

Palmer, C. (2000) Spindoctors and sports brokers: Researching elites in contemporary sport – a research note on the Tour de France. *International Review for the Sociology of Sport*, 35(3): 385–98.

Palmer, C. (2001) Outside the imagined community: Basque terrorism, political activism and the Tour de France. *Sociology of Sport Journal*, 18(2): 143–61.

Palmer, C. (2002a) Wheels of fortune: Nation, culture and the Tour de France. In H. Jenkins, T. McPherson & J. Shattuc (eds), *Hop on pop: The pleasure and politics of popular culture*. Durham, NC: Duke University Press (pp. 589–604).

Palmer, C. (2002b) Introduction to anthropology and sport (special edition). *The Australian Journal of Anthropology*, 13(3): 253–6.

Palmer, C. (2004) Death, danger and the selling of risk in adventure sports. In B. Wheaton (ed.), *Understanding lifestyle sport: Consumption, identity, difference*. London: Routledge (pp. 55–69).

Palmer, C. (2008) Policy from the pitch?: Soccer and young refugee women in a shifting policy climate. *Social Policy Review*, 20: 173–90.

Palmer, C. (2009) Soccer and the politics of identity for young refugee women in South Australia. *Soccer and Society*, 10(1): 27–38.

Palmer, C. (2010) 'We close towns for a living': Spatial transformation and the Tour de France. *Social & Cultural Geography*, 11(8): 865–81.

Palmer, C. (2011) *Violence against women and sport: A scoping review for Women's National Commission*. Women's National Commission. Violence against women and sport: A review. www.endviolenceagainstwomen.org.uk/data/files/evaw_violence_against_women_and_sport_ [accessed 20 April 2012].

Palmer, C. & Thompson, K. (2007) The paradoxes of football spectatorship: On field and on line expressions of social capital among the 'Grog Squad'. *Sociology of Sport Journal*, 24: 187–205.

Paquette, J., Stevens, J. & Mallen, C. (2011) The interpretation of environmental sustainability by the International Olympic Committee and Organizing Committee of the Olympic Games from 1994 to 2008. *Sport in Society*, 14(3): 355–69.

Parrish, R. (2003) The politics of sport regulation in the European Union. *Journal of European Public Policy*, 10(2): 246–62.

Payne, M. (2005) *Olympic turnaround: How the Olympic Games stepped back from the brink of extinction to become the world's best-known brand – and a multi-billion dollar global Franchise*. Twyford: London Business Press.

Peace, A. (1998) Anthropology in the postmodern landscape: The importance of cultural brokers and their trade. *The Australian Journal of Anthropology*, 9(3): 274–85.

Poli, R. (2010) Understanding globalization through football: The new international division of labour, migratory channels and transnational trade circuits. *International Review for the Sociology of Sport*, 45(4): 491–506.

Politico (2011) Full text of President Obama's announcement of Bin Laden's death. www.politico.com/news/stories/0511/54058.html [accessed 13 May 2011].

Polo, J.F. (2003) A côté du Tour: Ambushing the Tour for political and social causes. *International Journal of the History of Sport*, 20(2): 246–66.

Pound, R. (2004) *Inside the Olympics: A behind-the-scenes look at the politics, the scandals, and the glory of the Olympics*. London: Wiley-Blackwell.

Poynter, G. (2008) The 2012 Olympic Games and the reshaping of East London. In R. Imrie, L. Lees & M. Raco (eds), *Regenerating London: Governance, sustainability and community in a Global City*. Abingdon: Routledge (pp. 132–48).

Pujik, R. (2000) A global media event? Coverage of the 1994 Lillehammer Olympic Games. *International Review for the Sociology of Sport*, 35(3): 309–30.

Pucher, J. (2008) Making cycling irresistible: Lessons from the Netherlands, Denmark and Germany. *Transport Reviews*, 28(4): 495–528.

Pucher, J. & Bueler, R. (2007) At the frontiers of cycling: Policy innovations in the Netherlands, Denmark, and Germany. *World Transport Policy and Practice*, 13(3): 8–57.

Rand (2007) *Setting the agenda for an evidence-based Olympics*. Cambridge: The Rand Corporation Europe.

Rijpma, S. & Meiburg, H. (1989) Sports policy initiatives in Rotterdam: Targeting disadvantaged groups. Leisure and urban processes: Critical studies of leisure policy in Western European cities. In P. Bramahm et al. (eds), *Leisure and urban process: Critical studies of leisure policy in Western European cities*. London: Routledge.

Ritzer, G. (2000) *The McDonaldization of society*. Thousand Oaks, CA: Pine Forge Press.

Ritzer, G. (2004) *The globalisation of nothing*. Thousand Oaks, CA: Pine Forge Press.

Roberts, K. (2004) *The leisure industries*. London: Palgrave.

Robertson, R. (1992) *Globalization: Social theory and global culture*. London: Sage.

Robertson, R. (1995) Glocalization: Time–space and homogeneity–heterogeneity. In M. Featherstone, S. Lash & R. Robertson (eds), *Global modernities*. London: Sage (pp. 25–44).

Robertson, R. (2002) *Globalization*. London: Sage.

Robertson, R. & Scholte, J.A. (2007) *Encyclopedia of globalisation*. London: Routledge.

Robins, K. (1991) Tradition and translation: National culture in its global context. In J. Corner & S. Harvey (eds), *Enterprise and heritage*. London: Routledge (pp. 21–44).

Robinson, K. (2009) *The element*. New York: Penguin.

Robinson, V. (2008) *Everyday masculinities and extreme sport: Male identity and rock climbing*. Oxford: Berg.

Robinson, W. (2011) Globalization and the sociology of Immanuel Wallerstein: A critical appraisal. *International Sociology*, 26(6): 723–45.

Roche, M. (2000) *Mega-events and modernity: Olympics and expos in the growth of global culture*. London: Routledge.

Roche, M. (2003) Mega-events, time and modernity: On time structures in global society. *Time & Society*, 12(1): 99–126.

Roderick, M. (2006) *The work of professional football: A labour of love*. London: Routledge.

Rojek, C. (2010) Leisure and emotional intelligence. *World Leisure Journal*, 52(4): 240–52.

Rose, N. (1996) Governing advanced liberal democracies. In A. Barry, T. Osborne & N. Rose (eds), *Foucault and political reason*. London: UCL Press (pp. 37–64).

Rowe, D. (1999) *Sport, culture and the media: The unholy trinity*. Buckingham: Open University Press.

Rowe, D. (2003) Sport and the repudiation of the global. *International Review for the Sociology of Sport*, 38(3): 281–94.

Rowe, D. (2004) *Sport, culture and the media: The unruly trinity* (2nd edn). Maidenhead: Open University Press.

Rowe, D. & McKay, J. (2011) Torchlight temptations: Hosting the Olympics and the global gaze. In J. Sugden & A. Tomlinson (eds), *Watching the Olympics: Politics, power and representation*. London: Routledge.

Sabatier, P. (ed.) (2007) *Theories of the policy process* (2nd edn). Boulder, CO: Westview Press.

Sabatier, P. & Jenkins-Smith, H. (1988) Symposium Issue on 'Policy change and policy-oriented learning: Exploring an Advocacy Coalition Framework'. *Policy Sciences*, 21: 123–278.

Sabatier, P. & Jenkins-Smith, H. (eds) (1993) *Policy change and learning: An advocacy coalition approach*. Boulder, CO: Westview Press.

Sage, G. (1994) De-industrialization and the American sporting goods industry. In R.C. Wilcox (ed.), *Sport in the global village*. Morganstown, WV: Fitness Information Technology Press (pp. 38–51).

Sage, G. (1999) Justice do it! The Nike transnational advocacy network: Organization, collective actions, and outcomes. *Sociology of Sport Journal*, 16: 206–35.

Saguy, A. & Riley, K. (2005) Weighing both sides: Morality, mortality and framing contests over obesity. *Journal of Health Politics, Policy and Law*, 30: 869–921.

Samatas, M. (2007) Security and surveillance in the Athens 2004 Olympics: Some lessons from a troubled story. *International Criminal Justice Review*, 17(9): 220–38.

Sassen, S. (2002) *Global networks/linked cities*. New York and London: Routledge.

Sassen, S. (2007a) *A sociology of globalization*. New York: W.W. Norton.

Sassen, S. (2007b) *Deciphering the global: Its scales, spaces and subjects*. London: Routledge.

Sassen, S. (2009) Digging in the shadows. In J. Kenway & J. Fahey (eds), *Globalizing the research imagination*. London: Routledge (pp. 115–33).

Sassen, S. (2010) The global inside the national: A research agenda for sociology. *Sociopedia.isa*, pp. 1–10.

Satariano, W. & McAuley, E. (2003) Promoting physical health among older adults: From ecology to the individual. *American Journal of Preventative Medicine*, 25(3/2): 184–92.

Saunders, S. (2010) Greenest Games ever? Frontline voices confront Olympic Greenwash. Vancouver Media Co-op. http://vancouver.mediacoop.ca/story/2698 [accessed 29 November 2011].

Savage, M., Bagnall, G. & Longhurst, B. (2005) *Globalization and belonging*. London. Sage.

Savigny, H. (2002) Public opinion, political communication and the Internet. *Politics*, 22(1): 1–8.

Scherer, J. (2007) Globalization, promotional culture and the production/consumption of online games: Engaging Adidas's 'Beat Rugby' campaign. *New Media & Society*, 9: 475–96.

Scherer, J. & Davison, J. (2011) Promoting the 'arriviste' city: Producing neo-liberal urban identity and communities of consumption during the Edmonton Oilers' 2006 playoff campaign. *International Review for the Sociology of Sport*, 46(2): 181–204.

Scherer, J. & Jackson, S. (2010) *Globalization, sport and corporate nationalism: The new cultural economy of the New Zealand All Blacks*. Oxford: Peter Lang.

Schimmel, K. (2006) Deep play: Sports mega-events and urban social conditions in the USA. *Sociological Review*, 54: 160–74.

Schmidt, C. (2006) Putting the earth in play: Environmental awareness and sports. *Environmental Health Perspectives*, 114(5): 114–286.

Schneider, A. (2004) Privacy, confidentiality and human rights in sport. *Sport in Society*, 7(3): 438–56.

Schuerkens, U. (2003a) Social transformations between global forces and local life-worlds: Introduction. *Current Sociology*, 51:195–208.

Schuerkens, U. (2003b) The sociological and anthropological study of globalization and localization. *Current Sociology*, 51: 209–22.

Senn, A. (1999) *Power, politics, and the Olympic Games*. Champaign, IL: Human Kinetics.

Shamir, R. (2008) The age of responsibilization: On market-embedded morality. *Economy & Society*, 37(1): 1–19.

Shari'ati, A. (1986) *What is to be done? The enlightened thinkers and an Islamic renaissance*. Houston, TX: Institute for Research and Islamic Studies.

Shaw, C. (2008) *Five ring circus: Myths and realities of the Olympic Games*. Vancouver, BC: New Society Publishers.

Sherry, E. (2010) (Re)engaging marginalized groups through sport: The Homeless World Cup. *International Review for the Sociology of Sport*, 45: 59–71.

Shore, C. (2000) *Building Europe: The cultural politics of European integration*. London: Routledge.

Short, J. (2004) *Global metropolitan: Globalizing cities in a capitalist world*. London: Routledge.

Sinha, S. (2008) Seeking sanctuary: Exploring the changing postcolonial and racialised politics of belonging in East London. *Sociological Research Online* 13(5). http://socresonline.org.uk/13/5/7.html [accessed 2 December 2009].

Sklair, L. (2001) *The transnational capitalist class*. Oxford: Blackwell.

Solesbury, W. (2001) Evidence-based policy: Whence it came from and where it's going. London. ESRC UK Centre for Evidence Based Policy and Practice (pp. 1–11).

Spaaji, R. (2009) Sport as a vehicle for social mobility and regulation of disadvantaged urban groups: Lessons from Rotterdam. *International Review for the Sociology of Sport*, 44: 247–64.

Sparre, K. (2006) *Swedish ombudsman: Boycott World Cup in protest against prostitution*. www.playthegame.org [accessed 20 June 2010].

Sport England (2010) *Open space, sport and recreation*. www.sportengland.org/facilities_planning/planning_tools_and_guidance/planning_contributions/ppg17.aspx [accessed 15 October 2011].

Stafford, M., Sacker, A., Ellaway, A., Cummins, S., Wiggins, D. & Macintyre, S. (2008) Neighbourhood effects on health: A structural equation modelling approach. *Journal of Applied Social Science Studies*, 128: 109–20.

Stiglitz, J. (2003) Democratizing the International Monetary Fund and the World Bank: Governance and accountability. *Governance: An International Journal of Policy, Administration and Institutions*, 16(1): 111–39.

Stubbs, D. (2008) A sustainable agenda for London 2012. Paper presented at Changing the Way We Play ESRC Seminar Series, *Sustainable consumption and production: Forecasts and scenarios for more sustainable society*. The Brit Oval, London, 1 July.

Sudjic, D. (2005) *The edifice complex*. London: Allen Lane.

Sugden, J. (2011) Watched by the Games: Surveillance and security at the Olympics. In J. Sugden & A. Tomlinson (eds), *Watching the Olympics: Politics, power and representation*. London: Routledge (pp. 228–44).

Sugden, J. & Tomlinson, A. (1998) *FIFA and the contest for world football: Who rules the people's game?* Cambridge: Polity Press.

Sugden, J. & Tomlinson, A. (2005) Not for the good of the game. In L. Allison (ed.), *The global politics of sport: The role of global institutions in sport*. London: Routledge (pp. 26–45).

Sugden, J. & Tomlinson, A. (2011) Preface. In J. Sugden & A. Tomlinson (eds), *Watching the Olympics: Politics, power and representation*. London: Routledge.

Swynedouw, E. (2004) Globalisation or glocalisation? Networks, territories and rescaling. *Cambridge Review of International Affairs*, 17: 25–48.

Sze, J. (2009) Sport and environmental justice: 'Games' of race, place, nostalgia, and power in neoliberal New York City. *Journal of Sport and Social Issues*, 33(2): 111–29.

Taylor, T. & Toohey, K. (2006a) Impacts of terrorism-related safety and security measures at a major sport event. *Event Management*, 9(4): 119–209.

Taylor, T. & Toohey, K. (2006b) Security and spectator enjoyment at the Rugby World Cup 2003: Profiling visitor perceptions. *Tourism Review International*, 11(4): 257–67.

Taylor, T. & Toohey, K. (2007) Perceptions of terrorism threats at the 2004 Olympic Games: Implications for sport events. *Journal of Sport & Tourism*, 12(2): 99–114.

The Sunday Times (2008) Police warn over Games staffing. *The Sunday Times*. 1 June.

The Telegraph (2010) London 2012 Olympics: Government accused of 'devastating' legacy with school spending cuts. *The Daily Telegraph*, 20 October. www.telegraph.co.uk/sport/othersports/schoolsports/8076966/London-2012-Olympics-Government-accused-of-devastating-legacy-with-school-spending-cuts.html [accessed 20 May 2011].

Therborn, G. (2000) Globalizations: Dimensions, historical waves, regional effects, normative governance. *International Sociology*, 15(2): 151–79.

Thibault, T., Kihl, L. & Babiak, K. (2010) Democratization and governance in international sport: Addressing issues with athlete involvement in organizational policy. *International Journal of Sport Policy and Politics*, 2(3): 275–302.

Tomlinson, A. (1996) Olympic spectacle: opening ceremonies and some paradoxes of globalization. *Media, Culture and Society*, 18: 583–602.

Tomlinson, A. (2011) Lording it: London and the getting of the Games. In J. Sugden & A. Tomlinson (eds), *Watching the Olympics: Politics, power and representation*. London: Routledge (pp. 1–17).

Tomlinson, A. & Young, C. (2006) Culture, politics, and spectacle in the global sports event: An introduction. In A. Tomlinson & C. Young (eds), *National identity and global sports events: Culture, politics, and spectacle in the Olympics and the Football World Cup*. Albany, NY: State University of New York Press (pp. 1–14).

Tomlinson, J. (1991) *Cultural imperialism: A critical introduction*. London: Continuum.

Tomlinson, J. (1999) *Globalization and culture*. Chicago, IL: University of Chicago Press.

Tomlinson, J. (2002) Interests and identities in cosmopolitan politics. In S. Vertovek & R. Cohen (eds), *Conceiving cosmopolitanism*. Oxford: Oxford University Press (pp. 240–53).

Toohey, K. (2008) Terrorism, sport and public policy in the risk society. *Sport in Society*, 11(4): 429–42.

Toohey, K., Taylor, T. & Lee, C. (2002) The FIFA World Cup 2002: The effects of terrorism on sport tourists. *Journal of Sport Tourism*, 8(3): 167–85.

TOROC (2006a) *Projects: Climate protection — HECTOR*. www.torino2006.org/ENG/OlympicGames/spirito_olimpico/hector.html [accessed 7 April 2010].

TOROC (2006b) *Sustainability report. Torino, Italy: Organising Committee of the XX Torino 2006 Olympic Winter Games*. www.torino2006.org/ENG/OlympicGames/spirito_olimpico/rapporto_sostenibilita.html [accessed 7 April 2010].

Toynbee Hall (2009) *Olympics and prostitution fact sheet*. www.trustforlondon.org.
    uk/Prostitution%20and%20the%20Olympics%20Summit%20report.pdf [accessed
    5 June 2011].
Tranter, P.J. & Lowes, M. (2009) Life in the fast lane: Environment, economic and pub-
    lic health outcomes of motorsport spectacles in Australia. *Journal of Sport and Social
    Issues*, 33(2):150–68.
Tulloch, J. (2000) Terrorism, 'killing events' and their audience: Fear of crime at the 2000
    Olympics. In K. Schaffer & S. Sidone (eds), *The Olympics at the millennium: Power,
    politics and the games*. New Brunswick, NJ: Rutgers University Press (pp. 224–42).
UNESCO (2005) International Convention against Doping in Sport. http://unesco.org.
    en.ev.php [accessed 16 April 2012].
UNEP (United Nations Environment Programme) (2006) *Winter Olympics get green seal
    of approval*. New York: UNEP. www.unep.org/Documents.Multilingual/Default.asp?
    DocumentID=469&ArticleID=5141&l=en [accessed 29 November 2011].
UNEP (United Nations Environment Programme) (2008) *Beijing 2008 Olympic Games:
    An environmental review*. New York: United Nations. www.unep.org/publications/
    ebooks/beijing-report/Default.aspx?bid=ID0E1ZDI [accessed 28 November 2011].
van de Donk, W. & Foederer, B. (2001) E-movements or emotions? ICTs and social move-
    ments: Some preliminary results. In J. Prins (ed.), *Ambitions and limits on the cross-
    road of technological innovation and institutional change*. Cambridge, MA: Kluwer.
van de Donk, W., Loader, B.D., Nixon, P.G. & Rucht, D. (eds) (2004) *Cyberprotest: New
    media, citizens and social movements*. London: Routledge (p. 316).
Van Wynsberghe, R., Kwan, B. & Van Luijk, N. (2011) Community capacity and the
    2010 Olympic Games. *Sport in Society*, 14(3): 370–85.
Vancouver Organizing Committee for the 2010 Olympic and Paralympic Winter Games
    (2007) *Business plan and games budget*. Vancouver, BC: Author.
Verity, F.E. (2004) Building stronger communities: 'Risky' business in an environment of
    rising public liability insurance. *Just Policy*, 32: 21–7.
Verity, F.E. (2006) Line dancing… not lion dancing! *Australian Journal on Volunteering*,
    11(1): 50–8.
Vertovec, S. & Wessendorf, S. (2010) Introduction: Assessing the backlash against
    multiculturalism in Europe. In S. Vertovec & S. Wessendorf (eds), *The multicultur-
    alism backlash: European discourses, policies and practices*. Abingdon: Routledge
    (pp. 1–30).
Vinner, B. (2011) 2012 legacy will come a poor last after rush for gold. *The Independent*,
    21 May.
Voulgarakis, G. (2005) Securing the Olympic Games: A model of international coopera-
    tion to confront new threats. *Mediterranean Quarterly*, 16(4): 1–7.
WADA (2009) *World Anti-Doping Code*. Montreal: WADA.
Waddington, I. & Smith, A. (2009) *An introduction to drugs in sport: Addicted to win-
    ning?* London: Routledge.
Wagner, U. & Hanstad, D.V. (2011) Scandinavian perspectives on doping: A comparative
    policy analysis in relation to the international process of institutionalizing anti-doping.
    International Journal of Sport Policy and Politics, 3(3): 355–72.
Wall, M. (2007) Social movements and email: Expressions of online identity in the glo-
    balization protests. *New Media & Society*, 9(2): 258–77.
Wallerstein, I. (1974) *The modern world system: Capitalist agriculture and the origins of
    the European world-economy in the sixteenth century*. New York: Academic Press.
Wallerstein, I. (2000) *The essential Wallerstein*. New York: The New York Press.
Walseth, K. & Fasting, K. (2004) Sport as a means of integrating minority women. *Sport
    in Society*, 7: 109–29.

Ward, S. & Lusoli, W. (2005) 'From weird to wired': MPs, the internet and representative politics in the UK. *The Journal of Legislative Studies*, 11(1): 57–81.

Warren, I. & Tsaousis, S. (1997) Racism and the law in Australian Rules Football: A critical analysis. *Sporting Traditions*, 14(1): 27–53.

Wemyss, G. (2006) The power to tolerate: Contests over Britishness and belonging in East London. *Patterns of Prejudice*, 40(3): 215–36.

Wetzel, D. (2011) Sport mattered after 9/11 – not as a game, but as a gathering. http://news.yahoo.com/sports-mattered-after-9-11-not-as-a-game-but-as-a-gathering.html [accessed 20 September 2011].

Wheaton, B. (2007) Identity, politics and the beach: Environmental activism in Surfers Against Sewage. *Leisure Studies*, 26(3): 279–302.

Wheaton, B. (2008) From the pavement to the beach: Politics and identity in surfers against sewage. In M. Atkinson & K. Young (eds), *Tribal play: Subcultural journeys through sport: Research in the sociology of sport* (Vol. IV). Bingley: Emerald (pp. 113–34).

Wheeler, K. & Nauright, J. (2006) A global perspective on the environmental impact of golf. *Sport in Society*, 9(3): 427–43.

Whitson, D. & Macintosh, D. (1996) The global circus: International sport, tourism and the marketing of cities. *Journal of Sport and Social Issues*, 20(3): 278–95.

Wildavsky, A. (1979) *Speaking truth to power: The art and craft of policy analysis.* Boston, MA: Little Brown, Co.

Williams, Z. (2011) Radio free Benghazi – the war of words. *The Guardian*, 15 May. www.guardian.co.uk/world/2011/may/15/radio-free-benghazi-war-words [accessed 18 May 2011].

Wilson, B. (2007) New media, social movements, and global sport studies: A revolutionary movement and the sociology of sport. *Sociology of Sport Journal*, 24: 457–77.

Wilson, B. & Hayhurst, L. (2009) Digital activism, neoliberalism, the internet, and sport for youth development. *Sociology of Sport Journal*, 26: 155–81.

Wilson, D. (2004) Cricket's shame: The inside story. *New Statesman*, 17(836): 27–9.

Woods, N. (2002) Global governance and the role of institutions. In D. Held & A. McGrew (eds), *Governing globalization*. Cambridge: Polity Press (pp. 25–45).

Xu, X. (2006) Modernizing China in the Olympic spotlight: China's national identity and the 2008 Beijing Olympiad. *Sociological Review*, 54: 90–107.

Yeates, N. (2007) The global and supra-national dimensions of the welfare mix. In M. Powell (ed.), *Understanding the mixed economy of welfare*. Bristol: The Policy Press.

Yeates, N. & Holden, C. (eds) (2009) *The global social policy reader*. Bristol: The Policy Press.

Žižek, S. (2009) *First as tragedy, second as farce.* New York: Verso.

INDEX

Abel, T. 163
Aboriginal Australians 38n.7, 143n.6, 176
  'Black Magic' football stereotypes 29
  human rights abuses 144
  population clearance, Sydney 140
  misappropriation of imagery, Sydney
    Olympics 30–1, 149
  and racism in Australian Rules football
    27–8, 28–9
Abraham, A. 163
accountability 1, 63, 64
  and child protection 94
  environmental 162, 173,
    174, 180
ACORN 150
Adams, J. 96
'ad-busting' 73
Adidas 17, 73, 111, 146, 147
Advocacy Coalition Framework
  (ACF) 79–80, 84
Afghanistan 157, 186
Africa 39, 141
  depletion of athletes 147
  gap in research 115, 123n.7
African Cup of Nations 127
Agamben, G. 43
Agenda 21 171–2
Albertville Winter Olympics (1992) 170
Al-e Ahmad, J. 90
Al-Jazeera 64
al-Qaeda 124, 127, 142n.4
All Blacks 17
alterglobalization 145, 160n.2
Amara, M. 31
Amnesty International 16, 150
Andersen, S. 52
Anderson, B. 15, 71
Andrèn, J. 49–50
Andrews, D 24, 26, 28
Angola 127
anthropology 3, 11, 14,
  35, 188–9
Anti-Apartheid movement 73
anti-doping policy
  athletes' involvement 73
  capacity 50
  commitment 50–1
  comparative analysis 69–70
  complexity 49–50
  compliance 41, 51, 70

anti-doping policy *cont.*
  governance 15, 18, 24, 40–1, 47–52, 56,
    88, 163, 185
  testing protocols and athletes civil rights
    147–8, 159
  Tour de France as catalyst 112–13
  universality vs. particularity 48, 55
anti-globalization 2, 10, 26, 72–3, 145, 187
Anti-Racism and Religious Vilification Law,
  Australia 23, 27–8, 32, 73
apartheid 157, 158
Appadurai, A. 15, 16, 108, 110, 111, 120,
  121, 163
Aquilina, D. 31
architects, as cultural brokers 52–3
'arriviste cities' 109, 110, 147, 150, 162
Asian Games 16, 115
Asian World Cup (2011) 114
Askew, D. 54, 106, 111
Association International des Groups
  Cyclistes Professionels (AIGP) 113
asylum seekers 1, 16, 108, 186
Athens Olympics (2004) 116
  carbon dioxide emissions 168
  security issues 129, 132, 134
  sex trafficking 154
Athens Olympic Games Organizing
  Committee (ATHCOS) 134
athlete activists 73–4, 112–13, 157
athlete welfare 121, 186
  Tour de France 112–13
athletes' rights
  and drug testing protocols 50,
    147–8, 159
  and Olympic dehumanization 144
athletic migration and mobility 1, 12,
  16, 41, 153
  and anti-doping policy 14, 49
  and 'deskilling' of donor countries 147
  Tour de France 108–9
athletics 80
  doping in 46–7
Atkinson, G. 110–11
Atkinson, M. 125
Atlanta Agreement 147
Atlanta Olympics (1996) 80, 129
  bombing 127
  doping 47
Australia 49, 81, 123n.1, 158
  Anti-Terrorism Act (2005) 124–5